MURDER IN THE FAMILY

MURDER IN THE FAMILY

The Dr. King Story

Laura Haferkorn
PO Box 1456
Brighton ON K0K 1H0

DAN BUCHANAN

DUNDURN
TORONTO

Project Editor: Jennifer McKnight
Copy Editor: Britanie Wilson
Design: Courtney Horner
Printer: Webcom
Cover design by Laura Boyle
Cover images: Top: Daguerreotypes of Doctor and Sarah King produced by Hawley Sanford of Brighton. *Life and Trial of Dr. Wm. H. King, Reuben DeCourcey*
    Bottom: The Cobourg courthouse and jail. *Cobourg and District Images: http://images.ourontario. ca/Cobourg/18993/data?n=30*

Library and Archives Canada Cataloguing in Publication

Buchanan, Dan, 1951-, author
    Murder in the family : the Dr. King story / Dan Buchanan.

Includes bibliographical references and index.
Issued in print and electronic formats.
ISBN 978-1-4597-3076-2 (pbk.).--ISBN 978-1-4597-3077-9 (pdf).--
ISBN 978-1-4597-3078-6 (epub)

    1. King, William Henry, 1833-1859. 2. Murder--Ontario--Brighton.
3. Murderers--Ontario--Brighton--Biography. I. Title.

HV6535.C33B75 2015   364.152'30971357   C2015-900563-9
                                                 C2015-900564-7

2 3 4 5   22 21 20 19

  Canada

We acknowledge the support of the Canada Council for the Arts and the Ontario Arts Council for our publishing program. We also acknowledge the financial support of the Government of Canada through the Canada Book Fund and Livres Canada Books, and the Government of Ontario through the Ontario Book Publishing Tax Credit and the Ontario Media Development Corporation.

Care has been taken to trace the ownership of copyright material used in this book. The author and the publisher welcome any information enabling them to rectify any references or credits in subsequent editions.
                                                        —J. Kirk Howard, President

The publisher is not responsible for websites or their content unless they are owned by the publisher.

Printed and bound in Canada.

VISIT US AT
Dundurn.com | @dundurnpress | Facebook.com/dundurnpress | Pinterest.com/Dundurnpress

Dundurn
3 Church Street, Suite 500
Toronto, Ontario, Canada
M5E 1M2

In memory of my grandfather, Lloyd Ames, who loved to tell stories from the past. He hated the Dr. King story but, with prodding, eventually told me what he knew about it. Some of my interest in history comes from long visits with grandfather at Codrington, and from his passionate retelling of family lore. Today, I imagine he might have grumbled about the topic of my book, but I expect he also would have been one of the first at the library to check it out.

CONTENTS

FOREWORD

History has a way of catching up to the present, especially if it involves infidelity, the upper class in society, and murder. When closets are opened, graves revealed, and sins and betrayal confirmed, the stories begin to be told. When a noteworthy talent in researching genealogy and Eastern Ontario history happens to be a relative to the main character of some momentous crimes, the unravelling of these chronicles creates a masterpiece of analysis.

My first encounter with the author was through his online genealogy service "Trees by Dan." From my office in Toronto I was researching my heritage. My birthplace is Brighton, Ontario, but there was no indication on the "Trees" website that I was gathering worldwide information from a fellow native of the municipality of Brighton. Years later, when I returned to my hometown to retire and became involved in the local arts, culture, and history of the area, I met Dan Buchanan.

He was "Trees by Dan," and at the time lived mostly in Toronto. Fortunately for the Eastern Ontario community, Dan was about to establish himself more permanently back in Brighton. Along with cultivating his own roots, he readily became involved in preserving and sharing the cornucopia of history in the area. The Dr. King story turned out to be a lot of both. This book divulges numerous processes in the legal system of the era, the lifestyle of a small prosperous community with some recognizable names of influence from the past and an inside view of shifting relationships, one resulting in murder.

Dan obviously utilized his many skills and resources in research to uncover the accuracy of the information provided here. His ability to flush out unique connections and fit the theoretical puzzle into a presentable value is evident. I expect his direct connection to the gravestone of Dr. King and his family ties to the subject more than enhance the storytelling beauty of this detailed account you are about to enjoy.

As president of the Brighton Arts Council (BAC), I encouraged Dan to take to the stage his deep-rooted knowledge of local history. The BAC, in partnership with Brighton Public Library (BPL), produced a live presentation to relay historical facts and theories about a flood disaster in the Brighton area. The Breakaway, as it was known, changed the economy, roadways, and development of Brighton. Using the concept of a Human Book or Living Book, Dan provided a professional delivery of the occurrence and the outcome. With Dan's connection to the area where the disaster happened, the Living Book formula was appropriate. The BPL established a bar code for Dan in recognition of the success.

In 2014, the newly established History Open House weekend in Brighton invited Dan to deliver a comprehensive presentation of the Dr. King story, complete with artifacts and period costumes that were mostly supplied by Roger McMurray and the Proctor House Museum. Dan had been fine tuning and acquiring new detail on Dr. King and the results as they unfolded during the two-hour assembly proved to be enlightening and somewhat awe-inspiring. It is very likely that this opportunity to tell a more complete account of the families involved, the murder, intrigue, trial, and resulting interactions gave birth to the publication of this book.

Dan continues to present numerous deliveries of the Dr. King story, and several other history findings of varying lengths, throughout Eastern Ontario. With his ability to divulge detail and still add an influence of personality to his delivery, Dan achieves the art of relaying history in a form desirable by most readers and audiences — Dan Buchanan is known in Brighton, Ontario, as "The History Guy."

RONALD A. WADDLING
Brighton Arts Council (past President)
Brighton Public Library Trustee
Artist (visual, performing, literary)
GR&AT Productions Inc. Film and Stage (President — retired)
Producer of documentaries for Heritage Ontario

PREFACE

In 2010 I moved back home to Brighton, bringing my IT consulting practice with me. Under an arrangement with a consulting company in Toronto, I was able to continue to provide technical support to my client, a law firm in downtown Toronto, and at the same time become more engaged with history and heritage activities in and around Brighton. One important event that resulted was the Brighton History Open House (HOH) in February of 2013, which was such a success we had to do it again in 2014. It was during the planning for HOH 2014 that The Dr. King story came to the surface.

On the Sunday afternoon of the History Open House in 2013, Roger McMurray came up to me and introduced himself as the guy who had "The King Collection." I knew right away what he meant. We had spoken on the phone back in 2004 regarding the collection of items he had acquired that related to the King family. I was interested but very preoccupied with other things, so did not follow up. Now here he was, shaking hands with me.

Roger lives in Brighton, had heard of the History Open House, and felt it might be a vehicle by which he could present his collection and pursue his intent to donate it to Proctor House Museum. That day I thought my head would explode as I watched Roger pull out all the items and show them to the folks at the Proctor House display. Wow! What an amazing collection! Immediately my brain started churning.

Several times later in 2013 I discussed the possibility with Roger of using the History Open House as a platform for his donation of the collection to Proctor House. Both Roger and the people at Proctor House were amenable, so it was just a matter of working out details. The big problem for me was that I had to tell the Dr. King story in front of a crowd, and I had not done that before — much work was required to prepare for HOH 2014.

In September 2013 I sat down and started to create a PowerPoint presentation to tell the Dr. King story. After a week of little progress I finally realized I did not know enough about the details of the story to do this job, at least not in the way I wanted. So it was time to do some research. The Dr. King Story has been written many times, and I read all of them without being very satisfied. At this point I came to the conclusion that I must leave the PowerPoint presentation for now and write my own version of the story first, taking material from original sources; I could always pare the full story down to an effective PowerPoint presentation at a later time. It sounds obvious now but it was a revelation at the time.

After several visits to archives, museums, and libraries, I sat down to write the story. I found out very quickly that writing is hard work! I had to take genealogy breaks to stay sane. Oh, of course, I was still supporting the law firm in Toronto all this time — let's not forget that. It was an intense eight weeks or so until I finally came to the point where I didn't want to change another letter. After this, the PowerPoint presentation virtually created itself and I made ready for History Open House 2014.

However, I could not get the idea of publishing out of my head now that *the book* was there. It was burning a hole in my computer. A few years earlier I had met with Beth Bruder of Dundurn Press in Toronto and I felt Dundurn was the right publisher for this story. Beth has a cottage at Presqu'ile, so she appreciates the local history scene around Brighton, and Dundurn has published a lot of history books. I worked up my nerve and sent the story to Beth. After several months' consideration, Dundurn agreed to publish *Murder in the Family: The Dr. King Story*. And here we are.

Folks around Brighton know that my approach to history is to go back to original documents, add lots of practical context, and build an interesting and entertaining story. I have been studying history all my life and have a comprehensive knowledge of Ontario history, especially as it applies to the counties of Northumberland, Hastings, and Prince Edward. It is a rich history. The Dr. King story is populated by real people, who, like you and me, had to cope with the economy, the politics, and the technology of their time. We all make daily decisions based on our habits and our environment; so did the people in 1858, only they had to deal with the very rare crime of murder in their town.

The genre of true crime has never held any interest for me, as I have primarily concentrated on history. However, as I delved deeper into this story, I could not help being fascinated by the crime itself, as well as the character of the criminal. William Henry King was an exceptional child and, from the time he was old enough to listen, people commented on his intelligence. In their minds he was going to the top. True to form, King achieved a teacher's degree, medical degree, and a medical practice, all before he was twenty-six. But, as we often see, the hero has a dark side — as the investigators say, a pathology.

Dr. King was certainly flawed. Readers can judge for themselves, but it seems to me that Dr. King was so wrapped up in his own superior intelligence and major successes early in life that he failed to foster a most important thing — basic human empathy. The legal world is complex but morality often comes down to one thing: if we only think of ourselves and don't practise empathy for others, we are likely to veer off the straight and narrow. The Dr. King story is a lesson in empathy, or lack thereof.

Author's Note: Unless otherwise cited, quotations are taken from the materials reproduced in Appendix A: Transcription of Original Documents.

ACKNOWLEDGEMENTS

Staff at the archives, museums, and libraries I visited were a big help. I appreciate their patience and assistance. It was delightful to see that the Metropolitan Reference Library in Toronto had assembled all the Dr. King files into one section of microfilm, making it easy to retrieve electronic copies of the documents.

On another day, a pleasant drive to Peterborough was capped by the friendly assistance of Janice Millard, Curator of Archives, Special Collections, and Rare Books at the Trent University Archives. Then, Northumberland County Archivist, Emily Cartridge, provided the usual excellent support at the Northumberland County Archives in Cobourg. Library staff at Port Hope showed me exactly what I needed on microfilm as well. Research at the Brighton Public Library provided some wonderful surprises, including an interview done with my grandfather, Lloyd Ames, in the 1980s by a pervious writer who was pursuing the Dr. King story.

Special thanks to Roger McMurray for his generosity in donating the King Collection to Proctor House Museum, and for his permission to use some of the images in this book. Ann Rittwage at Proctor House Museum provided permission to use images of the collection, which is now housed at Proctor House, and also provided me with access to Dr. King's violin. Rose Ellery was gracious in allowing me access to the Dr. King book that has been in her family history collection for many years.

Encouragement is a good thing as well. My friend, Florence Chatten, a published author in her own right, has been unwavering in her support and enthusiasm for my history work in general, and this project in particular. Our intense discussions about local history are fun and enlightening.

Dot Connolly, who is the organizing force behind many of the history projects around Brighton, provided a mix of encouragement and constructive criticism while reviewing the manuscript and keeping the author and the book on the right track.

As a first-time author, the learning curve has been steep, but Dundurn Press provided me with lots of useful information and assistance, especially when slogging through the heavy work of editing. Beth Bruder has supported *Murder in the Family: The Dr. King Story* since our first discussions in 2013. I am happy to say that we share the conviction that this story deserves professional treatment and wide distribution.

In spite of all this wonderful help, there may be mistakes in the book. I take full responsibility for these and hope that readers will feel free to let me know about them. Telling history and the research involved is a process and not an event, and we should always be interested in improving on the information we have; it is a collaborative work that never ends.

CAST OF CHARACTERS

This book recounts a true story, which means that the story is populated by real people. Genealogy work has been done on many of the families mentioned in the book with details available on www.treesbydan.com. Here are the main characters in the book with a brief description of their context.

Name	Description
William Henry King	Murderer, son of George & Henrietta King, husband of Sarah Ann Lawson
Sarah Ann Lawson	Victim of murder, daughter of John M. and Elizabeth Lawson
George King	Father of William Henry King
Isaac Newton King	Next oldest brother to William Henry King
Mary Louisa King	Next oldest sister to William Henry King
Charles Wellington King	Brother of William Henry King
David Nelson King	Brother of William Henry King
Clinton M. Lawson	Older brother of Sarah Ann Lawson

George Henry King	Son of William Henry King & Sarah Ann Lawson, died age two months
Dorcas Garratt	Young woman Dr. King wrote letter to, summer 1858; daughter of Townsend Garratt
Hester Garratt	Aunt of Dorcas; wife of Thomas Garratt, brother of Townsend
Sarah Rachel Young	Cousin of Sarah King; wife of John B. Young
John B. Young	Husband of Sarah Rachel Lawson; merchant, south end of Murray Twp.
Margaret Augusta Nix	Cousin of Sarah King; widow of George Nix
Simon Davidson	Coroner for Northumberland Co.; conducted inquest, exhumation, for Sarah King
Melinda Vandervoort	Young woman Dr. King was infatuated with; daughter of John H. Vandervoort, Sidney Twp.
John H. Vandervoort	Father of Melinda; farmer in Sidney Twp., near Wall Bridge
Elizabeth Vandervoort	Mother of Melinda
Catherine Bate	Aunt of Melinda; lived south of Cape Vincent, New York State
Robert Barker	Druggist in Brighton; member of Coroner's Jury; transferred stomach to Kingston
Jared O. Clarke	Constable in Brighton; took Dr. King to Cobourg Jail
Joseph Ellison Lockwood	Postal clerk; interviewed during inquest
Professor Hempel	Doctor at Homeopathic Medical College, Philadelphia; testified for Dr. King

Professor Flanders	Doctor at Homeopathic Medical College, Philadelphia; testified for Dr. King
Mr. Justice Burns	Judge for Spring Assizes at Cobourg and Dr. King's trial
Hon. Thomas Galt	Crown Counsel
Hon. John Hillyard Cameron	Defence Counsel
Reuben DeCourcey	Old friend of Dr. King; published account of life and trial of Dr. King
Alexander Stewart	Constable assigned to live with Dr. King between sentencing and hanging
Dr. Pitkin Gross	Doctor in Brighton
Dr. Edward A. Fife	Doctor in Brighton
Professor Henry Holms Croft	Professor of chemistry at University College, Toronto; examined stomach
E. Moore	Agent with Grand Trunk Railway; took pickle bottle to Toronto
James Bonwell Fortune	Sheriff of Northumberland County during Dr. King incarceration
Glover Bennett	Jailer at Cobourg courthouse during Dr. King incarceration
Reverend Levi Vanderburg	Methodist minister in Cramahe, Percy; ministered to Dr. King; funeral service
Reverend William Bleasdell	Anglican minister in Trenton; baptized King children; visited Dr. King in jail
Mr. Ellis	Hangman
Dr. Norman Bethune	Testified at trial; Visited Dr. King during incarceration
Dr. Alexander Bethune	Archdeacon of York, presided at King hanging; uncle of Dr. Norman Bethune

MAP OF LOCATIONS

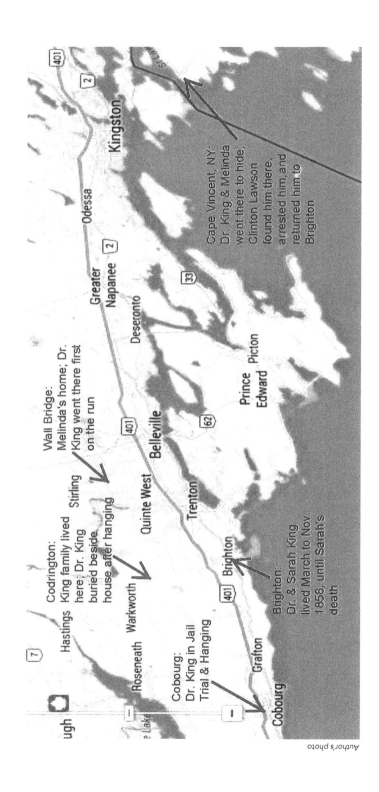

Wall Bridge: Melinda's home; Dr. King went there first on the run

Codrington: King family lived here; Dr. King buried beside house after hanging

Cobourg: Dr. King in Jail Trial & Hanging

Brighton: Dr. & Sarah King lived March to Nov. 1858, until Sarah's death

Cape Vincent, NY: Dr. King & Melinda went there to hide; Clinton Lawson found him there, arrested him, and returned him to Brighton

ONE

YOU CAN PICK YOUR FRIENDS, BUT NOT YOUR RELATIVES

Chestnut tree leaves crunched underfoot as I raked up another pile for my dog and myself to jump in. Skippy barked in anticipation and then submitted himself to another roll in the leaves. We wrestled as only a fourteen-year-old and his dog can do. What fun!

It was a sunny but cool Saturday morning in the fall of 1965 at my home in Codrington. The Buchanan farm straddled Highway 30, immediately north of the village of Codrington. The chestnut tree at the road was planted in the 1850s by George King, who had purchased the land after moving there from Northport, Sophiasburgh Township, in 1844. The large chestnut tree and the lilac bushes right beside the Codrington sign acted as a signpost and sentinel for the house that was occupied by successive King, Ames, and Buchanan families until 1973.

As usual, chores were underway on that pleasant autumn Saturday morning. The leaves did, in fact, need to be collected and disposed of sometime that day. Mother and the other kids were doing normal Saturday morning jobs in the house and my grandfather, Lloyd Ames, was in the shop working on machinery. The noisiest work that morning was the ploughing of the gardens, which was the responsibility of my father, Charles Buchanan. By this time Dad was in the small garden at the southeast corner of the house. He was driving the bigger of our two tractors, a Massey Ferguson 65 with a six-furrow plough on the three-point hitch.

This idyllic farm scene was suddenly shattered by a huge crash and the screech of metal on stone. In the next heartbeat, the tractor motor raced to a loud whine and then stalled. Dead silence. Skippy and I stopped rolling in the leaves, looked at each other, and then turned toward the garden. In a flash, our young legs carried us toward the source of the surprising sounds.

As we raced across the lawn to the garden, I took in a most unusual sight. The tractor was sitting in the middle of the garden, facing east. The large rear wheels of the tractor were dug down into the soft ground, giving the impression it was driving uphill. However, the most amazing part of the scene I approached was the plough, which was hiked up dizzyingly behind the tractor, with the rear end pointing to the tops of the pine trees at the west end of the garden. Something was very wrong here!

As Skippy and I approached the garden, the silence was broken by the voice of my dad. Charles Buchanan was a mild-mannered fellow. He had been pursuing the work of layman minister with the United Church — not just with the Codrington church, but increasingly doing work for other churches in the area. In fact, within a few short years, he would attend Queens University and obtain a degree in theology, which allowed him to achieve his dream of becoming a minister. However, these days, he was a farmer, and he could express himself explicitly, like most farmers under the right circumstances. This was such a time. His reaction did not last long, but I had the feeling the words that escaped him were effective, although not something I would repeat to my mother.

As my running shoes sank into the soft brown earth of the garden, Dad was climbing down from the tractor, having given up on starting it again. It was stuck! My contribution at this moment was the rather inane question, "What happened?"

Dad was not in a talking mood so I figured it was smarter to keep quiet.

Our attention focused on the plough. Dad walked around to the back of the plough, grasped it, and tried to shake it. Nothing moved; it was solid. Both of us were drawn to the real culprit — a piece of stone wedged tightly between plough points two and three. It was covered in dirt and Dad knelt down to scrape it clean. I could see that it was not a normal kind of rock since it had smooth surfaces and square corners. It was more like a piece of cement.

Soon I saw grandfather striding across the lawn, intent on finding out what all the racket was about. He did not approach the tractor right away but stood at the end of the garden, a few feet away from the plough. He was not pleased. Lloyd Ames never swore in front of me all the time we lived together. However, you could tell if he was unhappy. He stood with legs apart and fists firmly planted on hips, with an expression of stern annoyance.

In spite of my better judgement, I blurted out "What is it?" Grandfather stared straight at the stone under the plough and replied to my question with, "I know what it is." Dad spoke up as well, adding that he knew what it was too, but nobody said a word beyond that.

Well, what *was* it? The reader will have to indulge me here. As a young teenager, I knew little and cared less about family history. My main concern on that Saturday morning was which team the Leafs were playing that night and whether I would be allowed to stay up and watch the third period. As a result, I have to say that this is the last direct memory I have of that day. From here on, the story was assembled over several decades and many discussions with Lloyd Ames and Charles Buchanan. Both of them had foggy memories and personal preferences that did not fully match with my desire to know the story — but I persisted.

Eventually the story came together. The stone under the plough was the gravestone of the notorious William Henry King, the doctor who poisoned his wife in Brighton in 1858. He was the oldest child of George King and Henrietta Jenkins, and had lived on this farm from the time the family moved there in 1844, until he went off to Normal School in 1851. After he was hanged in Cobourg on June 9, 1859, his body was buried at the southeast corner of the house and a memorial was erected by his family.

On that Saturday morning in 1965, Dr. King's memorial was firmly wedged between two plough points. Dad and Grandfather managed to loosen the stone and pull it out from under the plough. The third plough point had caught the top end of the long granite memorial as it lay under the garden. The stone had been broken in half by the impact, with the top half wedged between the plough points. Once they had the stone free of the plough, they dragged the two halves to the area near the lilac bushes and left them there. Dad completed ploughing the garden and grandfather went back to the shop. I expect I eventually managed to finish raking up the chestnut leaves.

But that was not the end of it, for the episode continued the next day. On Sunday morning everyone went to church — except grandfather. He saw grandmother off on her short walk down the road to the Codrington United Church at the south end of the village. Then he waited until the rest of us had gone to church; he did not want any witnesses for what he was about to do. When the time was right, he put on his old coveralls, got into his Willy's Jeep, and drove up the road to the farm. When he arrived, he went directly to the shop and found his favourite sledgehammer. He had several, but this one was special. He had repaired it many decades before, after the original handle broke. The handle was now a solid piece of iron rod, which gave him the heft and feel he looked for in an effective sledgehammer. It would be perfect for the task at hand.

With the sledgehammer in the Jeep, he backed across the garden to the edge of the lilac bushes. He dragged the two pieces of stone onto the garden behind the Jeep. Then he took his favourite sledgehammer in hand and, with deliberate and energetic determination, proceeded to pulverize the two pieces of stone into hundreds of jagged pieces.

I recall the emotion that was evident in Grandfather's voice when he recounted the events of that day. He hated the Dr. King story. It annoyed him every time another newspaper or magazine article appeared on the topic, and that was often. These publications generated chatter in the community for a while and then it was forgotten until next time. While growing up, he had been acutely aware that the presence of the gravestone caused his mother a good deal of distress. The whole story was a huge blight on the honour of his family and he just wanted it to go away.

We can imagine then, the degree of satisfaction that Lloyd Ames derived from the direct, physical act of destroying the gravestone of that evil man who had caused his family such heartache. While he could not change the facts of history, he could rid his world of the one obvious, physical symbol of that history. It was the only thing he could do and now he had the chance. I don't doubt that he worked up a good sweat in the process.

The result was a pile of stone shards, which he gathered up and tossed into the back of the Jeep. Then he drove up on "The Hill." This was the simple name we used to identify the pastureland to the northwest of the main farm. In the old days they called it Cramahe Hill. We had two hundred acres of woodlot and pastureland, which was an excellent source of lumber; it was also where we pastured the beef cattle and let the cows roam during the day.

Access to The Hill was via the dirt road that goes west off Highway 30 at Goodfellow Road, north of Codrington. Grandfather came this way to feed the beef cattle each morning, so he was very familiar with the steep, washed-out road up to the gate. The Hill was made up of steep ravines, many large rocks, lots of sand, some trees, and, when not scorched by the July sun, some decent grass for grazing. A creek ran though the land at the north end.

The mission on this Sunday morning did not include cattle. Lloyd Ames unlocked the gate, drove through, and stopped to lock it behind him so the cattle wouldn't get out. He then drove the Jeep along the sandy trail across the plateau. He had only one thing in mind. I will let him tell you in his own words. When I asked him what he did next, he said, "I buried the stone pieces in a dozen places. Nobody will *ever* find them!"

So! It was done. That was the end of the Dr. King story — at least as far as Lloyd Ames was concerned.

TWO

HOW HAD IT COME TO THIS?

Doctor William Henry King stepped firmly up the wooden steps to the gallows. He held tightly to the arm of Reverend Levi Vanderburg, who took the prisoner to the prescribed spot near the front of the platform. The Reverend said goodbye to Dr. King and stepped back to join the others. Sheriff Fortune had preceded the pair onto the platform along with Archdeacon Bethune and Reverend William Bleasdell. There was going to be a hanging in Cobourg. It was just after 8:00 a.m. on Thursday, June 9, 1859.

Dr. King looked out over a crowd of ten thousand faces, all staring intently back in his direction. People had come from miles around to witness history. There had never been a hanging in Northumberland County and the next century would maintain that day's event as the only execution ever to take place at the Northumberland County jail in Cobourg. The crowd was quiet but electric with anticipation.

The subject of their interest was a twenty-six-year-old man, handsome by the standards of the day, with a full beard, neatly trimmed for the occasion. It would later be said that his countenance presented a heavenly radiance on that day, no doubt due to the hours of prayer and religious discussions of the previous days and weeks. But to those who knew him, William Henry King looked as he always did, calm and self-possessed, always extremely confident in his ability to control the situation.

But what a situation! How had this intelligent, well-grounded young man come to the gallows in Cobourg on this warm summer morning? It is a tale of human strengths exploited to serve the worst of human frailties. Dr. King had been convicted of poisoning his wife with arsenic. In the eyes of the law he was guilty of murder, but in the eyes of society he was also guilty of great betrayal; a husband who betrayed the trust of his wife and a doctor who betrayed the trust of his patient. There was great disgust across the province regarding what he had done and how he had done it. For most people, he could not swing too soon.

———

William Henry King was born November 20, 1833, in the small town of Northport, on the south shore of the Bay of Quinte in Sophiasburgh Township, Prince Edward County. In 1844, his parents, George and Henrietta King, moved their family of five children to Cramahe Township. Over the next few years, George King would purchase lots beside each other on the north side of the concession road that would run east and west through the middle of the future village of Codrington, which George King would name. This land was also on the east and west side of the road that ran north from Codrington, and would later become Highway 30. It was fertile land, particularly suited for growing wheat, which was a lucrative cash crop in those days.

After moving to Cramahe Township, the King family added another five children, for a total of ten. As the eldest of the family, William was responsible for the smaller kids, and his parents relied on him to do a lot of work on the farm. In fact, it is said that William showed an unusual aptitude for organizing and managing the farm work, and his father placed significant responsibility on his shoulders at a young age.

William King also showed an unusual aptitude for education from an early age. George and Henrietta King were a progressive couple, so they had many books; William devoured these, along with any newspapers that came his way. The interest and excitement William King showed for education may not have been rare in those days, but the ability of the family to afford to do something about it may have been. We can see evidence of this in 1851 when George and Henrietta King agreed to send their eldest son to Normal School in Toronto. The plan was that he would attend school in the fall and winter and come back home to help on the farm in the summer months.

William Henry King came to the Normal School in Toronto in the fall of 1851 when classes were still being held in the old parliament building. In 1852, William King and his classmates would move into a new and much larger structure built specifically to house the Normal School. This was one of many significant new schools that were built in this period, after the Reformers won the election in 1849 and Egerton Ryerson took charge of the public school system in Canada West. The intent was to produce many more teachers with much better credentials, and William King was well positioned to benefit from these changes. He would graduate in the spring of 1853 with a First Class Teacher's Certificate. He was well on his way.

THREE

MARRIAGE AND SEPARATION

During the early years that he attended Normal School in Toronto, William King took time to court Sarah Ann Lawson, a young lady who lived at Lawson Settlement, just south of Smithfield and east of Brighton. Sarah was born January 10, 1833, to John M. Lawson and Elizabeth Jane Lynderson, the middle child of seven. Her brothers, Clinton, George, and Monroe, would play active roles in the community around Smithfield and Brighton through the 1800s and well into the 1900s. We will meet her parents and her brother Clinton later in this story. In addition, Sarah had a lot of support from a large extended family, which included many cousins who lived nearby.

William Henry King and Sarah Ann Lawson were married on January 31, 1853. This union would have been viewed in the community as a very good match. Here were two young people from established farm families in the area and most folks would have talked about the happy and prosperous future that lay ahead for the young teacher and his wife. As for the two young newlyweds themselves, we can expect that Sarah was interested in gaining a safe and happy home life, which required an effective breadwinner and would potentially include several children. William, on the other hand, was keenly ambitious and would have seen Sarah as someone who could manage home and family while he concentrated on achieving prosperity and standing in the community.

After the wedding, William and Sarah King lived in Toronto until June 1853, when he graduated from Normal School. During the summer William taught school in the Brighton area as he had done in the previous years. Then, with his teaching certificate in hand, he secured a plum of a job at the new and progressive Central Public School at 75 Hunter Street West in Hamilton. The young couple moved to Hamilton for the beginning of the school year in September 1853 and William began to teach classes in physiology. A teaching position at this new school would have been a tremendous achievement for the young farm boy from Codrington.

Accounts of the story say that the Kings took in boarders both in Toronto and Hamilton to help make ends meet. That could be true, especially in Toronto when he was a student, but it was common in the 1850s for graduates from Toronto Normal School to earn a salary of seventy-five to one-hundred pounds* a year, which would have been considered a good middle-class income.

Unfortunately, marital bliss was fleeting. At some point late in the fall of 1853, Sarah left William in Hamilton and returned to Brighton to live with her parents. She explained at the time that she was pregnant and wanted to be under the care of her mother during her confinement. Sarah gave birth to a son, George Henry King, on January 12, 1854. Unfortunately, he was in trouble from the beginning and died just over two months later, on March 18, 1854. The child was initially buried near the Lawson home in Lawson Settlement but would eventually be moved with his mother to Mount Hope Cemetery in Brighton, where there is a fitting memorial for both mother and child.

As one might expect, the young couple was devastated by this tragedy. However, Sarah would have more to discuss with her parents than the death of their grandchild. She was very unhappy with the way William had been treating her, accusing him of acting like a tyrant. Testimony in the trial and evidence from Dr. King's writings would suggest that something very bad happened between the two young people during the late

---

* The Halifax pound, which is referenced here, was used during the mid-1850s and would have equalled about four U.S. dollars.

fall of 1853. We don't know what happened exactly, but Dr. King's attitude toward his wife changed dramatically.

Then, in a shocking development, Dr. King sent a nasty letter to Sarah, in which *he* accused *her* of infidelity. Sarah shared this letter with her parents and they were outraged. John and Elizabeth Lawson wrote a scathing letter back to their son-in-law, berating him for accusing his wife of such behaviour. On the contrary, they were quite sure it was Dr. King who was the guilty party. An exchange of heated letters ensued. Eventually, Dr. King wrote a letter of apology. However, at the bottom of his letter, he requested that all letters related to this episode be burned. On reading this, Sarah's father was said to have uttered some rich cuss words in the direction of his son-in-law. John Lawson was not the kind of man to give away such an obvious advantage, so the letters were kept in a safe place with a clear expectation that they might come in handy one day.

It was established at some point that Sarah would not go back to Hamilton. Good health had not been her friend as a general rule and the ordeal with the baby left her weak and craving the comfort of her mother's care. In addition, she felt uncomfortable with the situation in Hamilton and was happy to leave the next step up to her husband.

FOUR

DR. KING RETURNS TO BRIGHTON

During his time at Central Public School in Hamilton, William King was encouraged to study medicine by one of the senior teachers at the school, Dr. Greenlees. William pursued the idea, and in September 1856 enrolled at the Homeopathic Medical College in Philadelphia. The practice of homeopathic medicine had blossomed in the United States during the 1830s and 1840s, and this college was established in Philadelphia in 1848. Homeopathic medicine was based on the central dogma of "like cures like" and presented a major threat to orthodox medical thought and institutions of the time.

William Henry King attended the Homeopathic Medical College in Philadelphia for two years, returning home to Brighton during the summer months to help on the farm and teach in various schools in the area. His name appears in a list of teachers at Mount Olivet Public School near Codrington, although the exact year is not mentioned. By all reports he was a top student in Philadelphia. In 1857 he was elected as president of the Hahnemannian Medical Institute of the Homeopathic Medical College. In 1858 he graduated near the top of his class and could call himself Doctor King.

After graduation, Dr. King came back to Brighton. In his written confession he would provide his reason for locating in Brighton. He said, "My own parents as well as the parents of my wife would not consent to me to locate far away and the consequence was that on 17th March 1858 I commenced practice in Brighton, and alas! to my sorrow as it turned out." Be that as it may, Dr. William Henry King returned to Brighton with a medical degree and the expectation of earning a good living. Doctors were in great demand at that time and the community around Brighton had experienced two decades of growth and prosperity. As a graduate of Normal School and being in possession of a medical degree from a college in the United States, he would have been a celebrity of sorts.

When William came back to Brighton, he and Sarah reconciled. He promised to treat Sarah better, and Sarah, seeing the potential for prosperity and stability in the future, agreed to give him a second chance. They moved into a substantial house on Sanford Street in Brighton, on the northeast corner of Kingsley Avenue, in the area of today's Anglican church parking lot. A solid middle-class household was set up quickly and the front room made into a comfortable waiting room. As the doctor expected, the good matrons of Brighton filled his waiting room and brought their purses with them. Dr. King was said to be pleasant and gentlemanly, with manners that were easy and graceful. It is said he earned one-hundred to two-hundred pounds a year at this time, a very good income in those days. He could now indulge his desire to dress very well and project an image of prosperity.

The family situation appeared to improve as well. Dr. King behaved with more indulgence toward his wife and Sarah became engaged in managing the household of a doctor's home. Both families saw this as a positive step that provided a lot of potential for the future. We can expect that John and Elizabeth Lawson may have retained some scepticism considering the events of the past few years, but they were willing to give the young couple a chance.

FIVE

FLIRTATIONS

Things were good for a time, but not for long. Testimony at the trial would show that Dr. King started to flirt with attractive young women in the area as early as June, just a few months after reconciling with his wife and starting to practice medicine in Brighton. The first flirtation was with Dorcas Garratt, an attractive twenty-two-year-old woman who lived to the east of Brighton in Murray Township. She appears to have been a patient during the first months of his practice. Dr. King's self-serving testimony during the trial says that their communication began when the young lady sent him a letter asking rather provocatively if he felt she was healthy enough to be married. Apparently there was a fellow ready to marry her but she did not feel any passion for him and did not know what to do. Dorcas Garratt denied sending this letter to Dr. King.

What we do know is that Dr. King sent Dorcas Garratt a letter suggesting that he liked her very much, his wife was ill and would not live long, and, if she would avoid being married, he would certainly marry her when he was free. He even had the gall to tell her that she should educate herself in certain topics that would better prepare her for the roll of a doctor's wife.

Needless to say, Miss Dorcas Garratt rejected him out of hand. She rebuked him forcefully and even threatened to expose his misdeeds if he continued to pursue her. Dr. King wisely relented and wrote a letter of apology, a task for which he was gaining some experience. Miss Garratt kept the episode quiet, not wanting to experience the embarrassment of the inevitable public chattering such a story would create. Thus the episode was laid to rest.

During the summer of 1858 and into the fall, Dr. King pursued his medical practice. We can expect that he began to cultivate a social presence in the community as well, pressing Sarah to be more outgoing and entertaining when the local gentry came to call. Dr. King was naturally social and delighted in conversation and witty banter. He appreciated a good table with quality wine. Any respectable middle-class home in the 1850s would have a pianoforte and melodeon, and we know that Dr. King owned a violin, which now resides at Proctor House Museum. It was expected that the lady of the house would entertain the visitors, demonstrating her talents to the delight of all. Unfortunately, Sarah was not this way inclined. She had no musical talent and could not sing. She preferred to sit and knit, listening to the conversation and speaking with her women friends on occasion. Dr. King tried to "improve" her in his area but met with blank stares or a flat "no." It is clear from testimony at the trial that Dr. King was becoming increasingly annoyed with his wife in this regard.

Into this delicate situation came Miss Melinda Vandervoort. On September 23, 1858, Melinda was visiting with Sarah's parents in Lawson Settlement. Sarah and Melinda were old friends, so Sarah invited her to visit the new King home in Brighton. Melinda lived in Sidney Township, near the town of Wall Bridge, with her parents John and Elizabeth Vandervoort. She was twenty-one years old and extremely pretty, with many qualities that were well appreciated in those days. In particular, she had a sweet singing voice and liked to demonstrate her skill while playing musical instruments.

Melinda Vandervoort and William King had never met, but on this evening they sat in the parlour of the house on Sanford Street in Brighton and became very close very quickly. Melinda sang and played the pianoforte and the melodeon while William King watched, listened, and maybe joined in with his violin. He was smitten! One can only imagine what Sarah thought of this obvious flirtation. Of course, neither Sarah nor Melinda knew about his recent episode with Dorcas Garratt. In fact, there was a pattern of behaviour developing and it did not bode well for anyone.

Proctor House Museum, Brighton

Dr. King was most impressed with Melinda's musical talents and we can expect he accompanied her on his violin during their social evenings at the King house on Sanford street. After his demise, his violin was retained by the King family and passed down to Maud Davidson, a daughter of Isaac King, the Doctor's next younger brother. D'Arcy Davidson, a son of Maud's, assembled the King family history and kept the violin until his death in 1969 when his daughter, Jean Hammond, took possession. In 1995, Mrs. Hammond donated Dr. King's violin to Proctor House Museum in Brighton where it is on display today.

Dr. King was not the only one to be smitten. William and Sarah drove Melinda back to the Lawson home that night and, as they rode together in the back of the buggy, Melinda told Sarah that she had fallen in love with Dr. King's picture, which she had seen at the Lawson home a few days earlier. Sarah was rather startled at such a direct admission but did not take it seriously. She even told her husband about it on the way home! We are told that William laughed it off, saying it was just the meaningless prattling of a silly young girl.

Possibly, but the very next evening Melinda was in the King parlour again, singing and playing the pianoforte and melodeon. She entertained William and Sarah until late into the evening. The process of infatuation intensified through these hours of seemingly innocent social activity. For William, the contrast between Melinda and his wife must have been profound. The younger and very attractive Melinda expressed herself delightfully in music and speech and behaved in a manner that was measured but flirtatious. Sarah, on the other hand, could neither sing nor play musical instruments. She was more content as a spectator. If William expected to develop a position of leadership and respect in the community, which woman would be best to have as a wife? It's a hard thing to ask, but for him the answer was clear, and sitting right there in his parlour.

The affair continued when Melinda went home to Sidney Township. The first thing she did after returning home was to send a picture of herself to Dr. King. It would likely have been a daguerreotype, probably in an attractive frame. In those days it would have been called a "likeness." Melinda did not have to wait long for a response. Dr. King walked down to the post office in Brighton on Monday morning and "found the most precious thing (except the original) on earth." He was so overwhelmed by the gift that he went right home and wrote a letter to Melinda. The first words of that letter were, "Sweet little lump of good nature." Their letters back and forth would contain a lot of emotion expressed very eloquently. They could be very forward with each other in letters, although both hinted at the risk of being found out — yet it did not stop them.

The letters between William and Melinda in these heady days after they met also contain sinister hints that are chilling in hindsight. He asked Melinda, "Can you keep from sacrificing yourself upon the hymeneal altar for the next year?" This was more eloquent than his proposal to Dorcas Garratt, but amounted to the same thing. Then he would end his letter with, "Come and visit whenever you can. ---- is very sick — last night we thought she would die." In these letters, William would substitute dashes for Sarah's name in an attempt to avoid detection if someone else saw the letter. During the trial, this statement about Sarah being very sick was proven to be untrue. We can see that he was preparing the ground for his brutal plan.

SIX

WHITE POWDER

It was soon after this exchange of letters that Dr. King began to take action toward his ultimate objective. He began telling Sarah that she had a terrible condition, which he called cholera morbus, a very serious and infectious disease. The doctor made a point of telling family and friends that she was very ill and it was likely fatal. This was certainly alarming, but there was some discussion about the fact that Sarah did not feel sick at all. How could she have this kind of terrible condition and not feel the effects?

The answer came about two weeks later, around October 14. Sarah came down with abdominal pain and terrible cramps, along with bouts of vomiting and diarrhea. Her husband was her doctor and he would not permit another doctor to provide a second opinion. He insisted that he knew the condition of his wife better than anyone else. When pressed on the matter, Sarah voiced her confidence in him, even though she gradually became weaker from constant vomiting.

The trial would determine that since around October 14, the doctor had been administering medicine to Sarah in the form of a white powder that was mixed with water on a spoon. Several people mentioned that the powder would not dissolve in the water, and Sarah said it tasted like fire. It was white arsenic. The autopsy would show that Sarah had no serious condition but it was clear that she was four months pregnant. Dr. King knew about the pregnancy and used it to his advantage, telling Sarah and her parents that she also had a seriously ulcerated womb and would not likely survive her confinement, all the time feeding her the white powder. Sarah's condition deteriorated over the next two weeks, while Dr. King prayed loudly for her recovery.

When Sarah's condition became very serious and persistent, her parents came to the house on Sanford Street and stayed with their daughter. They sat up with her night and day and assisted in any way they could, fetching bedclothes and cold water. Clinton Lawson, Sarah's older brother, also came to visit. We can expect that he was there to comfort his sister but it may be that he was already concerned about the treatment Sarah was receiving from Dr. King.

The Lawsons grew more suspicious every day, and then, on the Saturday before Sarah died, an important discovery increased their suspicions even more. At the trial, Sarah's mother would testify that on that day, Dr. King had gone into town for a while, leaving his coat hanging on a chair in Sarah's room. Elizabeth Lawson then took matters into her own hands and rifled through the pockets of his coat. What did she find? Much to her amazement, she found the picture of Melinda — the "likeness" that Melinda had sent to him. Some of their letters were also found. However, rather than rave after Dr. King with the evidence, she left the items in his coat pockets and waited to see what would happen. Later that night she kidded him about rumours that he had a likeness of Miss Vandervoort. Of course, he denied it. This was filed away by the Lawson's for future reference. Clinton Lawson would testify regarding the likeness that "I have seen this portrait before. I saw it on the Saturday of the week preceding the Thursday on which my sister died; this, in connection with the finding other letters, excited my suspicion."[1]

These few days leading up to the death of Sarah Ann King were tense and very uncomfortable for everyone. Sarah was constantly vomiting and Dr. King insisted on continuing to administer the white powder. Sarah's parents were watching their daughter grow weaker every day and felt powerless to help her. Clinton Lawson was working up his suspicion to the point of taking action. The tension increased even more when John B. Young visited Sarah on the day before the likeness was found. He was the husband of Sarah Rachel Lawson, one of Sarah's cousins and a very good friend. His experience as a coroner came into play and he became very concerned when he learned of the way Dr. King was treating Sarah. He was especially worried about the doctor's reluctance to ask for another opinion. Then, a day after his visit, when he learned about the picture and letters being found, his suspicions became too great and he told Sarah's mother not to allow any more of the white powder to be given to Sarah. He also insisted that they call in another doctor. Mr. Young's deposition during the inquest made it clear that he suspected Dr. King of foul play several days before Sarah died.

With all of this pressure, the doctor relented and called Dr. A.E. Fife to the King home. Dr. Fife had seen Sarah several times before and knew she was pregnant. In his testimony at the trial, he would say that he felt "the symptoms Dr. King described in their general character, I did not consider inconsistent with a woman four or five months advanced in pregnancy."[2] He also said that he prescribed ipacacuanha and camphor to mitigate the effects of the vomiting. However, Dr. Fife was not given more than cursory access to Sarah and relied mostly on the advice of Dr. King. Professional courtesy may have come into play on this occasion. In any case, the visit of Dr. Fife changed nothing. Dr. King continued to administer the white powder and kept a tight rein on access to Sarah.

After Dr. Fife's visit, John Lawson, Sarah's father, was still extremely suspicious of Dr. King. On the day before Sarah died, he pressed Dr. King even harder, saying he would bring him before a jury if Sarah died. He insisted that they call for Dr. Pitkin Gross, a long-time friend and family doctor for the Lawsons. He was the longest-serving doctor in the Brighton area, having begun his career as a regimental surgeon during the War of 1812. Dr. King was animated in his refusal. He would not allow Dr. Gross to examine Sarah. He knew that Dr. Gross would not be nearly as easy to control as Dr. Fife and he argued that, in any case, they did not need to have Dr. Gross examine the patient because he knew that he would prescribe the same medicine that he prescribed for everyone: opium.

In a smart response, John Lawson asked the question, "Would it ease her?"[3] Dr. King was hard-pressed to say no to this and reluctantly agreed — not to call Dr. Gross, of course, but to give Sarah opium himself. He entered his office, where he always mixed his prescriptions, and produced a dose of opium, which he gave to Sarah. For a time, this seemed to improve her condition. In the end, Dr. Gross would see Sarah only a few hours before her death.

Now it was the evening of November 3, and Sarah seemed to respond well to the opium. She sat up and said she was feeling much better. In fact, she went so far as to tell her parents they should go to bed and get some rest. She insisted that she was feeling much better and that Dr. King would look after her that night. The parents reluctantly agreed and Sarah was sleeping when her mother finally went upstairs to bed.

SEVEN

DEATH AND BURIAL

The events of the next morning come to us from only one source — Dr. King himself. He would write in his confession that early on the morning of November 4 he found Sarah in a frantic state, crying out "Oh, Lord! Take me out of this world, I don't want to live. Can't you give me something?" His verbose and self-serving confession explains that this was more temptation than he could bear and he was drawn into a discussion with the Devil. The Devil made a very powerful pitch, telling Dr. King that he was respected in the community because he was a doctor and he could prescribe medicine as he saw fit. The Devil also hinted that if something did go wrong, he might end up with Melinda. This was the fateful moment when Dr. William Henry King stepped over that clear moral threshold that civilized society holds dear and decided to take decisive action to end the life of his wife. Of course, he had set himself on the path toward Sarah's death some time before and had taken action toward this goal, but now he was impatient with the incremental approach of the previous weeks. The arsenic had not produced the result he had hoped, and Sarah's family was closing in on him. He had to act now.

Again, Dr. King provides his own words in an exchange with the Devil: "I yielded to his suggestion, got a 1/2 oz. vial containing about 1 drachm of chloroform, which I gave her just at daylight." He would later insist that he did not feel this dosage would be fatal and was devastated when Sarah lost consciousness soon after he administered it.

Sarah's parents got up soon afterward and her mother found her in a partially unconscious state. She pulled Sarah onto a chair and tried to wash her and get her to eat something. Sarah went in and out of consciousness through the morning. Her mother testified that she tried to wake her by pinching her skin but she would not respond. Dr. King made various attempts to rouse her, including cold-water effusions and inhaling ammonia. Nothing worked. By the middle of the day, Sarah fell into a coma.

Testimony at the trial would say that Dr. Pitkin Gross was called to the King home only a few hours before Sarah died. It is unlikely that Dr. King would have called him, since he had such disdain for him, so it could be that a member of the Lawson family finally worked up enough anger to call for him. In any case, as he would testify, it was too late and he could do nothing for Sarah.

At one point in the afternoon, everyone was shocked when Sarah suddenly sat up and yelled something incoherent but then fell back into unconsciousness. She did not rouse again. Sarah Ann King died around seven o'clock in the evening of November 4, 1858. She was twenty-five years old.

On the death of his wife, Dr. King put on an extreme show of grief. It was said that he grieved violently, which some in attendance felt was a bit over the top. Another doctor came to the house and gave him a sedative and he slept through the night. Things had changed! There was finally another doctor in the house. The next morning he was recovered enough to deal with the funeral arrangements.

However, before planning for the funeral, the Lawson family had another matter to discuss with Dr. King. The next morning, they went to the King house and confronted him. They insisted that an inquest be called and that there be an autopsy to determine cause of death. This was not very common in the 1850s, but if there was enough evidence of potential wrong-doing, the local constable could order an inquest, which would include an autopsy. John and Elizabeth Lawson, along with other members of the family, had serious misgivings about the cause of death and wanted an autopsy to clear up any doubt. Dr. King, on the other hand, was dead set against it. He responded angrily, telling them that he would not allow an inquest. Then he pulled out the trump card by telling the grieving parents that Sarah had deliberately instructed him, as her husband and doctor, never to allow such desecration of her body. He was very convincing, as usual, so the parents relented — for a time.

The funeral was held on Sunday, November 7, and was very well attended. In the words of Reuben DeCourcey, in his account of the events, "On the following Sunday the remains of the mother and child were taken to Mr. Lawson's, and buried in a place selected by herself, near the dwelling."[1] Dr. King grieved loudly and some felt he might harm himself. He seemed genuinely distraught and many felt sympathy for him. Sarah's parents were not so inclined. They had seen too much and it made them suspicious. It was time to see that justice was done for their daughter.

Author's photo

Sarah Ann King was originally buried near her family home in Lawson Settlement, but later both Sarah and the infant son George Henry were buried in Mount Hope Cemetery with a proper memorial. This memorial can be seen today in the western section of Mount Hope Cemetery, just to the left of the road. The first lines of the inscription read: IN MEMORY OF THE UNFORTUNATE SARAH ANN KING, which describes Sarah's plight very well.

EIGHT

INQUEST AND FLIGHT

Soon after the funeral, events started to move fast. Only a few hours after Sarah was laid to rest, Clinton Lawson — her older brother — and a crew of helpers, drove up to the King residence on Sanford Street in Brighton with a large wagon, and proceeded to empty the King house of furniture. Later, Dr. King would say that this act was entirely unnecessary and would insist on retrieving some of his belongings. In fact, Sarah's family had provided most of the contents of the house earlier in the year. This act speaks volumes about the level of animosity that had developed between the Lawson family and Dr. King. It also shows us that Clinton Lawson was a man of action.

On Monday, the day after Sarah King's funeral, Dr. King left Brighton to attend to several medical appointments in the countryside. While he was away, John and Elizabeth Lawson sprang into action. They kicked the local grapevine into high gear by circulating information about Melinda's picture and letters, as well as the earlier letters regarding the Hamilton episode. This information rocketed around the community in a few hours. Very soon they had something in response. Miss Dorcas Garratt, who had rejected Dr. King's advances in the summer, caught wind of it and immediately told the Lawsons of her own experience. She brought in her letters and they were added to the growing pile of evidence. On another front, Robert Barker, the local druggist, let it be known that Dr. King had recently purchased large amounts of arsenic and morphine. Evidence was mounting.

At some point during that Monday, the eighth of November, John and Elizabeth Lawson made all of this information available to the constable at Brighton, and it was immediately decided that an inquest was required to determine the cause of Sarah King's death. A local coroner was assigned to the inquest and a coroner's jury was appointed. The coroner was Simon Davidson, of the Davidson family that lived north of Spring Valley. Inquest records for Northumberland County in the 1850s show his name on several inquests related to deaths in Brighton and Cramahe Townships, so he had good experience. Census records routinely listed him as a farmer, but he had other talents that would see him lead the most sensational inquest of his career.

The coroner's jury consisted of seventeen men from the local community. There were several farmers, as well as merchants and tradesmen of Brighton — a conscientious group that had the welfare of the community in mind. The coroner and the coroner's jury assembled at the Lawson home in Lawson Settlement on Monday evening, near Sarah Ann King's fresh grave. They exhumed the body, placed it on a door, and then carried the door to a local schoolhouse where they prepared for the autopsy. Three local doctors presided over the exhumation and autopsy. Dr. Pitkin Gross was there, along with Dr. A.E. Fife and Dr. Pellatiah R. Proctor. Doctor James Gilchrist of Cobourg also observed.

During the inquest, Dr. Proctor observed that:

> Dr. Gross made the incision and laid bare the stomach, liver and an impregnated womb…. The body presented a rather healthy appearance for one deceased. Body and organs were all in a healthy condition except lungs which presented a congested appearance but not sufficient to cause death. Womb contained a healthy foetus.[1]

They also reported that "a dark fluid was found inside the stomach."[2]

While the autopsy was under way at Lawson Settlement, Dr. King arrived back in Brighton and was met with a rude surprise. John Lawson

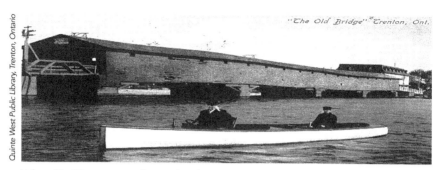

Quinte West Public Library, Trenton, Ontario

When Dr. King was confronted with an inquest in progress, he felt it was time to run. He drove his buggy down the York Road to Trenton and there he crossed the "Old Covered Bridge" that spanned the Trent River at that time. This bridge was designed by the same civil engineer who designed the Presqu'ile Lighthouse. It was built in 1833 and replaced in 1916. This image is a colourization of a Herington photo from a postcard dated around 1910.

confronted him at his home and made a point of telling him that an autopsy was being conducted on Sarah's body as they spoke. For Dr. King, this was really bad news. He recalled the argument with the Lawson family after Sarah died and realized that events were turning against him. Worse yet, it was suggested that a warrant might be issued for his arrest at any time.

Dr. King immediately began to panic. He yelled to John Lawson that he was rushing down to the schoolhouse to put a stop to this nonsense, but instead he steered his handsome carriage due east, down York Road toward Trenton. At the Trent River his horse clomped across the covered bridge and he turned north and raced out into Sidney Township. His destination was the home of his sweetheart, Melinda Vandervoort, who lived at the farm of her parents' near the town of Wall Bridge in the middle of Sidney Township.

Melinda's parents would testify at the trial that Dr. King knocked on the door of the Vandervoort home around ten o'clock that night, rousing John Vandervoort out of bed. Dr. King questioned in a loud voice whether this was the home of Melinda Vandervoort. His host confirmed that it was and the stranger stated that he had an urgent message to deliver to Melinda; he demanded to see her immediately. John Vandervoort had never seen Dr. King before and initially didn't know who he was, so we can expect there were some tense moments at the doorstep. When Melinda came downstairs she was astounded to see Dr. King at her home. She introduced him to her parents and then quickly manoeuvred him into the parlour where they could close the door and talk in private.

And talk they did, with great urgency. Dr. King told Melinda that his wife had died on Thursday and he was suspected of poisoning her. Melinda was very alarmed to hear that her picture and letter had become evidence in the hands of the constable. Dr. King insisted that both of them would be arrested in a matter of hours and the only course open to them was to flee across the border and wait for the dust to settle. Dr. King insisted that Melinda come with him to New York State to avoid being arrested.

After about an hour, John Vandervoort knocked on the parlour door and asked if the message had been delivered. A resounding "No!" came from inside the parlour and the anxious father joined his wife in the kitchen to wait until the two young people were finished talking. The discussion in the parlour lasted another half hour, as Melinda's parents waited anxiously. William and Melinda talked, and argued, and talked some more. It was a stressful time and they could not be sure of the best course of action. Through it all, Dr. King was adamant they must leave immediately for the border. In the end, Melinda agreed and suggested that they might go to the home of her aunt, Catherine Bate, who lived on a farm a few miles south of Cape Vincent, New York. It would be a safe place for them to stay for a while at least.

When the young couple finally emerged from the parlour, they laid out their plan to the alarm of Melinda's parents. Of course, they were reluctant to let their daughter go off in the middle of the night with a strange man who spread tales of death, poisoning, and arrest warrants. In the end, however, they agreed to allow Melinda to leave with Dr. King — on the condition that they go to the Bate home so they could be sure of a safe refuge. It must have been a fearful night for them, especially as they watched Dr. King's carriage speed out of their driveway and into the dark night in the wee hours of the morning with their precious daughter in tow. No doubt many prayers were said in the Vandervoort house that night.

NINE

THE AUTOPSY AND THE PICKLE BOTTLE

Back in Brighton, the work of the autopsy focused on Sarah Ann King's stomach. There was much certainty around the community that Dr. King had poisoned his wife with arsenic and it seemed obvious the stomach could provide evidence that could be used at trial. The doctors removed Sarah's stomach and placed it in a pickle bottle, the best vessel they could find to carry and protect the stomach. The problem was that when the stomach was placed in the pickle bottle, they could not find a cork or any proper seal for the top. When the coroner adjourned the coroner's jury late that night, he placed a piece of paper over the top of the bottle and wrapped a string around it — not ideal, but the best he could do at the time. Even though the pickle bottle had been washed thoroughly before being used in this way, the exact details of these proceedings would be of intense interest at the trial of Dr. King. One of the arguments put forward by the defence was that someone could have inserted a large quantity of arsenic into the stomach after it was removed from the body. The opening for this argument was the method used to secure the bottle that first night.

It's fair to say that the technology available to perform an autopsy on a body placed on a door in a schoolhouse in rural Canada West in 1858 was what we would call primitive, at best. On the other hand, there were procedures to protect evidence based on the tools at hand. While he was

Author's photo

Sarah Ann King's stomach and then her liver travelled in pickle bottles to be examined by Professor Henry Croft in Toronto. Resources were scarce in those days and the bottle did not have a cork or seal until the second day, when Robert Barker, the local chemist, found one and secured the bottle properly.

limited by his environment in many ways, Simon Davidson conducted the inquest with care and persistence. He would take twenty-two depositions from witnesses before he was finished.

The coroner had lots of work to do that night so he took the pickle bottle with him to Delong's Railroad Hotel, across from the Grand Trunk Railway Station in Brighton. There, in the dining room, he sat up all night transcribing depositions for the inquest. Beside him on the table was the pickle bottle containing Sarah King's stomach.

Early the next morning, Tuesday the ninth, the inquest resumed at the schoolhouse, with Simon Davidson leading the proceedings and the same doctors in attendance. Coroner Davidson would testify at the trial that the "next day the stomach was placed in a clean dish, in the presence of the jury, as Drs. Gross and Proctor wished again to see it, the post mortem examination having previously been conducted by candle light."[1] During the day, the examination was completed and the coroner secured the bottle containing the stomach, with the intent that it be sent to Kingston for further investigation at the laboratory at Queen's College.

The next day, Wednesday the tenth, the coroner handed the pickle bottle to Robert Barker, as had been arranged, giving him the task of taking it to Kingston. Robert Barker was a member of the coroner's jury and was well-known and respected in Brighton as a druggist and chemist. The first thing he did when he gained possession of the pickle bottle was install a cork from his chemist's shop. At least now the bottle was properly sealed. In his testimony at the trial, he tells us of his day:

> The bottle containing the stomach was delivered to me. The stomach was secured as described by the last witness. I received it on the morning of the 10th or 11th of November, and by the twelve o'clock train I went to Kingston. The package was in my carpet bag, which I kept in my hand all the time. In the evening I saw the Professor of Queen's College, who declined to give me a decisive answer until next morning. I left my bag in a closet of the laboratory, which I locked up. Next morning I called, took it away and returned to Brighton — the package being precisely in the same condition as when I received it.[2]

TEN

WARRANT AND ARREST

Friday, November 12 was a quiet day for Sarah King's stomach, but it was a very eventful day for Dr. King. He and Melinda had been at her aunt's farm south of Cape Vincent in New York State only a couple of days by this time. Melinda revealed in her testimony that Dr. King not only wanted to flee to the Unites States but had more elaborate ideas as well. She said, "At Belleville, Dr. King wished me to elope with him to the west. He drove as far as Shannonville and left his horse and took the cars about two o'clock in the afternoon … and stopped there over night."[1]

This fellow was always scheming. He thought he might be able to convince Melinda to escape to the west with him, thus leaving all of this mess behind and looking forward to starting over in a distant land where nobody knew them. This was a common idea in those days because there was so little communication between the settled east and the pioneering western parts of the continent. Everyone knew someone who had moved west to avoid trouble with the law or to remove the burden of an unwanted marriage or a heavy mortgage.

Then Melinda reveals, "When we arrived at the Cape, Dr. King proposed marriage to me and I objected. He also wished me to elope with him to New York and not go to my Aunt's, I also objected."[2] The young woman managed to withstand his persuasive words and insisted they proceed to her Aunt Catherine's home as she had promised her parents.

For Dr. King this must have been a frantic time, grasping at straws and watching over his shoulder every moment.

On the other hand, he was not so distracted that he did not remember to write a letter to his parents to tell them that he was safe and assure them of his innocence. George King, his father, provided a deposition to Simon Davidson, which says: "Received a letter from Dr. King on Thursday, expects mailed at Cape Vincent. Letter said he had left his home when he was made aware of charges against him; that he could not bear to be a prisoner and that he was not guilty of the charges."[3]

He had good reason to be worried. It was now that Sarah King's older brother, Clinton M. Lawson, stepped up and played a leading role in the story. Here we have it in his own words at the trial:

> … the coroner gave me a warrant to arrest Dr. King; I went to Kingston on Friday, and from that to Cape Vincent. From information I got at the post-office, I went six or eight miles up the country to the house of a man named Bate. Gordon, the United States Marshal, went into the house. I stopped before I got there, so that I might not be seen. He had not been in three minutes when Dr. King jumped out of the window. I ran after him. He was toward the woods, but as I was after him quick, he turned into a barn. We went in and found him under the straw in a hog's nest.[4]

Clinton Lawson was a man of few words but the ones he used were pointed. On cross-examination, he said, "I had a revolver; I said he must be shot if he ran; a lawyer told me that I had no right to shoot him, and told him so too."[5] Mr. Cameron, for the defence, asked if Dr. King then came with him, to which Clinton Lawson responded emphatically, "Well, I guess he did!"[6] Mr. Galt, for the prosecution, then asked Clinton Lawson whether Dr. King came *willingly* and the witness responded with even more force: "No, Sir; no Sir-ree!"[7]

It's clear that Clinton Lawson was intent on arresting Dr. King, so that he could face justice for the murder of his sister. We can speculate whether he would have shot the fugitive given the chance but the real point is that

The *Calendar of Prisoners* was a list of prisoners committed to Cobourg jail,
including Wm. H. King, prisoner number 5. His age is shown as twenty-five,
born in Canada, and his crime is murder. He was committed by the coroner, S.
Davidson, on November 14, 1858.

Dr. King thought he might, and that made all the difference. It is also
interesting that a Canadian who carried an arrest warrant and a pistol
could cross into New York State and solicit the support of a local United
States Marshal in apprehending a man suspected of a crime in Canada. It
seems there was a lot less concern about jurisdiction in those days and
certainly a lot less paperwork.

The two men came back to Brighton on the train the next day, and
Clinton Lawson delivered the suspect to Constable Jared O. Clarke in
Brighton. Constable Clarke did some preliminary investigating which
netted some useful evidence; he also interviewed Dr. King. He would
testify at trial that he found several letters in the prisoner's trunk, including those dealing with the episode the previous year, when Dr. King had
accused his wife of infidelity. He also said that the prisoner had insisted to
him that he had not given his wife arsenic, and that if she had any arsenic
in her system someone else had given it to her.

On the following day, Constable Clarke and Simon Davidson delivered
Dr. King to the Northumberland County Courthouse and Jail in Cobourg.
We can see a record in the "Calendar of Prisoners" for the Cobourg jail on
November 14, 1859, indicating the name Wm. H. King and the crime of
"Murder." The record also shows that he was "committed" by the coroner,
Simon Davidson. Justice could now take its course.

ELEVEN

SEARCHING FOR ARSENIC

The travels of the pickle bottle containing Sarah King's stomach were not over. The testimony of Simon Davidson says:

> I received the bottle from Mr. Barker, the same day he returned from Kingston. I placed it in a locked closet, and kept it until the morning of the 13th. I then started with it for Toronto. I got as far as Colborne, when, learning that King had been arrested, I determined to return. I gave the stomach to Mr. Keeble, the conductor, to take to Professor Croft.[1]

James Keeble testified:

> I am conductor on the Grand Trunk. On the 13th November last, I received a small box from Simon Davidson. He instructed me not to let it out of my custody until such time as I placed it in the hands of Professor Croft. This was about seven o'clock. I locked it in a cupboard of the baggage car used for bonded goods. Upon arriving in Toronto, I gave it to Professor Croft.[2]

The man who received Sarah King's stomach was Professor Henry Holmes Croft, professor of chemistry at University College, Toronto. At the trial, Professor Croft testified:

> The stomach was emptied into a glass with water. The liquid was allowed to settle; the upper part was poured off, and a sediment left. This sediment was found to contain arsenic. The fluid contents of the stomach was found to contain arsenic. I next examined the coats of the stomach, and found more arsenic in them. The quantity of arsenic I found in the stomach was eleven grains. I wrote to the Coroner to send me the liver and kidneys of the deceased.[3]

An examination of the stomach proved that it contained eleven grains of arsenic. However, Professor Croft could not determine whether the arsenic might have been added to the stomach after it was removed from the body. He knew that small amounts of arsenic would migrate into the liver and kidneys if arsenic had been present in the body before death. Therefore, he wanted to examine these other organs to see if they contained arsenic as well.

Professor Croft wrote a letter to Coroner Simon Davidson in Brighton, requesting that he exhume the body of Sarah King once more, remove the liver and kidneys, and send them to Toronto as he had done with the stomach. On November 19, Coroner Davidson convened the coroner's jury and proceeded to remove the liver from the body. It was placed in another pickle bottle, but this time a proper cork and seal were applied. We might note that the liver and kidneys were requested in Professor Croft's letter, but Coroner Davidson only mentions removal of the liver. Dr. Croft would later discuss his examination of the liver only, so it appears as if the kidneys were not removed.

Coroner Davidson took the pickle bottle containing the liver to the Grand Trunk Railway station, built just a year before, and handed it to Express Agent E.D. Moore. Mr. Moore testified at the trial, "On the 19th of November, I received a jar from the last witness, and kept it in my possession until I delivered it to Professor Croft."[4] On cross-examination, he added: "I placed the jar in an iron safe inside my car. It was locked up. Next day I delivered it to Professor Croft."[5] Here again was an opportunity for evidence to be tampered with and testimony was produced to satisfy the jury that the men who handled the evidence were trustworthy and had taken every possible care with the pickle bottles.

The liver was examined and Professor Croft explained that he found a small amount of arsenic. Then he added, with emphasis, "Arsenic cannot be put into the liver after death. It must have been taken in during life — that is the reason I wrote for the liver."[6] On cross-examination, Professor Croft seemed to cast doubt on the assumption that Dr. King had poisoned his wife with arsenic. He said that the eleven grains of arsenic in the stomach were not enough to cause death and that he found little of the kind of inflammation that one might expect to find in the inside lining of the stomach if large quantities of arsenic had been present in the stomach for some time.

He also raised the spectre of tampering with evidence when he said of the stomach, "It is possible to put arsenic in this portion of the body after death. I do not think the paper round the bottle was sealed. The box was sealed. I have no means of knowing whether arsenic was put into the stomach after death or not."[7] He then confused the issue by saying a little later, "I do not think the poison could have been taken into the stomach I examined long before death."[8]

While all this travelling of pickle bottles and examination of the organs of the unfortunate woman was taking place, the suspect in the case was being processed at the jail in Cobourg. A formal arrest warrant was issued for William Henry King on Friday, November 26, and we can expect that the event became a topic of conversation all around the province. An example of the widespread distribution of the story is provided by a death notice in *The Christian Guardian* on December 1. The notice read "King, Mrs. — Dr. King of Brighton was taken under coroner's warrant last Friday, and is being held on suspicion of murdering his wife who was buried 7 inst."

TWELVE

THE INQUEST:
DEPOSITIONS FROM WITNESSES

Simon Davidson took twenty-two depositions from witnesses during the inquest into Sarah King's death, mostly in the first few days from November 8 to 11. Only in the case of a couple of the doctors was there more than a single deposition from each witness. The most comprehensive testimony came from the doctors who had participated in the autopsy, but the most interesting information came from the testimony of a few people who were close friends and relatives of Sarah Ann King and visited her at the King house before she died.

Margaret Augusta Nix was a cousin of Sarah's who had visited her about a week before her death. She made note of the fact that Dr. King had told Sarah she had a fatal illness and was unlikely to survive her confinement. She also witnessed Dr. King giving Sarah a white powder as medicine, which would not easily dissolve in water. She was a bit surprised that one day Sarah was not very ill but the next was vomiting and in pain. Like others who visited Sarah at this time, Mrs. Nix was suspicious of the care Dr. King took to make sure Sarah was never alone with a visitor. He kept extremely close to his patient, especially when there were visitors present, and he always insisted on administering the medicine himself. Once, when he allowed her to give Sarah the medicine, she was uncomfortable with how closely he hovered over them.

Sarah Rachel Young, another of Sarah's cousins from Lawson Settlement, was a sister of Margaret Augusta Nix. She was a close friend to Sarah and visited her several times in the last few weeks of her life. Her testimony was very revealing as it described the frame of mind of both Sarah Ann King and her husband in those weeks before Sarah's death. Mrs. Young described how she had made remarks to Dr. King about the odd nature of Sarah's illness and pressed him on the idea of calling in another doctor. Dr. King had responded "indignantly" and told her that he knew about his wife's illness better than anyone else and that there would be no use calling another doctor. She said that Dr. King became very angry with her when she persisted with this line of questioning.

She also explained how, over the previous six months, Sarah King had "frequently made a confidant of me"[1] and had admitted how unhappy she was. It was in this discussion that Sarah said that her husband had been acting like a tyrant in Hamilton. Sarah Young described Sarah Ann King as being "frequently disheartened and low spirited."[2]

Sarah Young had another discussion with Dr. King in which he opened up and told her that he was dissatisfied with his wife, who he said, "was not a person to his mind."[3] His main complaint was that "she did not appreciate his attainments."[4] Sarah Rachel Young ended her testimony by saying: "The impression on my mind on hearing of her illness was that he would be glad she would die."[5]

Another witness was John B. Young, a merchant from Carrying Place who was also a coroner of Northumberland County, like Simon Davidson. He was also the husband of Sarah Rachel Lawson who had a close relationship with Sarah. Other than Clinton Lawson, who was Sarah's brother, John B. Young appears to have been the most suspicious of Dr. King, and certainly the most vocal in expressing his opinion. We can expect that he had discussed the problem with his wife and sister-in-law and was putting two and two together for himself.

John B. Young visited Sarah Ann King several times, starting October 14, when she became ill. His last visit was on Friday, October 26, six days before she died. On the next day, Elizabeth Lawson found the picture of Melinda Vandervoort in Dr. King's pocket and, although she put the items back in the coat, she made haste to tell the family about it. As soon as he heard this damning news, John B. Young decided to take action. He advised Sarah's parents to intervene and stop Dr. King from administering any more of the white powder. He was convinced that this white powder was poison and that Sarah would surely die if she continued to take it.

He also insisted that the parents call in Dr. Fife to provide a second opinion. The increased pressure from John B. Young and Clinton Lawson may be the reason John Lawson became more forceful with Dr. King about calling in another doctor. Now he felt he had support from others and it was not just his own fears that made him confront his son-in-law. In any case, Dr. King manipulated even the process of having another doctor involved, and the visit of Dr. Fife did not change the situation at all.

Another interesting piece of testimony came from the same John B. Young, who described his involvement a year earlier with Sarah Ann King and her father, John M. Lawson, regarding the notorious letters that Dr. King had written to his wife when she returned to Brighton to have her first child. Sarah had asked John B. Young to retrieve the letters from her father so she could send them to her husband. She said Dr. King had promised to treat her much better if she handed over the letters.

John Lawson refused to hand over the letters to Dr. King because he was very unhappy at his son-in-law's behaviour and wanted evidence at hand to use against him if there was to be further bad behaviour. John B. Young explains that he proposed to John Lawson that he copy the letters so that they could be sure to have a copy even though they would be sending the originals back to Dr. King.

This testimony also included the more technical point that the hand-writing in the letters was, in fact, that of Dr. King. John B. Young was one of several witnesses that testified to Dr. King's handwriting as part of the evidence gathered for the trial.

The most salacious testimony came from the two Garratt women. Dorcas Garratt was the young woman with whom Dr. King engaged in correspondence and Hester was her aunt. They described their experience earlier in the year when Dr. King sent a highly inappropriate letter to Dorcas. In this letter, he described how dissatisfied he was with his wife and mentioned that she was very ill and would likely die soon. He went on to suggest that Dorcas should not be in a hurry to be married, and that if he were single he would surely offer himself as a suitor.

Hester Garratt then testified that she had seen the letter, that it was most offensive, and that it was dated September 3. Hester uses stronger language than Dorcas, saying that in the letter to Dorcas, Dr. King had found it "almost intolerable"[6] since coming back from his medical studies and that she could "make a man of him."[7] Hester also goes a bit further, explaining that Dr. King had suggested to Dorcas that she might study certain subjects in order to better prepare herself for life as the wife of a doctor.

There were several individuals who testified for the inquest and provided confirmation of details that were already known. Joseph Ellison Lockwood testified that he had seen Dr. King pick up a package at the post office, which he said was "about the size of a likeness."[8] This refers to the daguerreotype that Melinda Vandervoort sent to Dr. King after their initial meeting at the end of September. Dr. King talked about going to the post office on a Monday morning, which was Monday, October 18, when Mr. Lockwood saw him pick up the package.

Robert Barker, the local druggist, testified that Dr. King had purchased a total of thirty-two grains of morphine from his shop in the few weeks before the death of Sarah Ann King. His wife, Mary Ann, said that she had sold Dr. King a half-ounce of arsenic on the 27th of September and five grains of morphine on the day before the death of Mrs. King. On cross-examination, she confirmed that it was in fact arsenic she had sold to Dr. King and she was sure because she remembered handing it to him herself.

A very interesting deposition came from George King, father of the prisoner. He started out by saying that he knew no more about the death of Sarah Ann King than the jurors. He told of receiving a letter from Dr. King, which he believed was sent from Cape Vincent. It explained that the fugitive had left home when he became aware of charges being pressed against him and that he "could not bear to be a prisoner."[9] He also wrote that his wife had many afflictions and it would be proven that he was not guilty of the charges.

The consternation of the father is evident as he describes how he and his wife were always on good terms with Sarah and that he never heard Dr. King say a harsh word to his wife. George King knew that there had been "some hardening of feeling"[10] between Dr. King and his in-laws after the death of the first child. However, he ends his testimony by saying that the last time Sarah had been in their home in Codrington she had departed with a friendly comment, assuring them that she would be back.

THIRTEEN

THE CORONER'S REPORT

The coroner, Simon Davidson, reconvened the coroner's jury on Saturday, November 27 at Richard Delong's Railroad House Hotel. The report that Simon Davidson produced begins by saying that it is "an inquisition undertaken for our Sovereign Lady the Queen," and then lists the names of the men in the coroner's jury — "Good and lawful men," who had been chosen to inquire as to the "when where how and after what manner the said Sarah Ann King came to her death."

He gets right to the point. The report says that William Henry King, physician, "not having the fear of God before his eyes but moved and seduced by the instigation of the devil" did poison Sarah Ann King "wilfully feloniously and of his malice aforethought to kill and murder" his wife.

The coroner was very clear in his report about the instrument of death. It says that "A large quantity of a certain deadly poison called white arsenic" was mixed and administered by Dr. King and that he "did cause her to take drink and swallow down" the mixture. The result of this was also clear, as the report says Sarah Ann King "became sick and greatly distempered in her body" and then languished over the night of November 3 and into the next day.

On that day the poison had its final effect, as Sarah Ann King, upon "the sickness and distemper occasioned thereby did die." According to the men of the coroner's jury, William Henry King "feloniously wilfully

The coroner's report was presented by Simon Davidson at Delong's Railroad Hotel on November 27, 1858. Along with the coroner, the seventeen members of the coroner's jury indicated their agreement by signing the second page of the report. This document, as well as the depositions taken during the inquest, are located in the Northumberland County Archives in Trent University, Peterborough.

and of his malice aforethought did kill and murder against the peace of our lady the Queen her Crown and dignity." The trial would not be held until April, but according to the coroner's report, the matter was settled.

At the top of the third page of the report, we see these words: "In witness whereof as well the said Coroner as the Jurors aforesaid have to this inquisition set their hands and seals on the day and year and at the place first above mentioned."[1] Below this, the coroner, Simon Davidson, affixed his signature and all seventeen jurors followed suit.

FOURTEEN

A DARK, DREARY, AND LONELY PLACE

Dr. King was a prisoner in Cobourg Jail from November 14, 1858, until he was hanged on June 9, 1859. The first five months spanned a long, cold winter, during which the fastidious Dr. King complained to everyone that he deplored the miserable conditions of his incarceration. He told Reuben DeCourcey that the place was "dirty, greasy and lousy; dark, dreary and lonely."[1] In spite of that, he maintained a very confident frame of mind, insisting to anyone who would listen that he was innocent. His feeling was that if he could speak in front of a jury of intelligent men that he would certainly go free.

During the long months leading up to the trial, Dr. King's friends worked hard on his behalf. Two medical men from Philadelphia, Professors Hempel and Flanders, were lined up as defence witnesses. Letters were exchanged with several eminent men in the United States and Canada resulting in letters of commendation, which would praise the character and good conduct of Dr. King during his medical studies in Philadelphia. Dr. King felt sure that all of these respected medical men would support the position that his wife had died of something other than arsenic poisoning.

Dr. King also kept busy writing letters to family and friends and anyone he felt might help him in his plight. Many letters were sent to addresses in New York State, which the authorities expected were family connections.

Cobourg and District Images: http://images.ourontario.ca/Cobourg/18993/data?n=30

TOP: The Cobourg courthouse and jail, where Dr. King was incarcerated and the trial and hanging took place, was on the northwest corner of Elgin and Burnham Streets in northwest Cobourg. The building had been built in 1832, but the courthouse and jail was moved to the new Victoria Hall in 1860, the year after the Dr. King episode. The building remained in place and was used well into the 1900s as the House of Refuge.

BOTTOM: Fire destroyed it in the 1930s and a new building was built in the same location with a different design.

RIGHT: In 1858, the Cobourg courthouse and jail was located at the northwest corner of Burnham and Elgin Streets in the northwest part of Cobourg. Here is a segment of the County Atlas Map for Cobourg (1878), which shows William Street, which today is Number 2 Highway going west out of downtown Cobourg. Number 2 Highway turns west at that intersection. The Golden Plough Lodge and the Northumberland County Offices are in that area today.

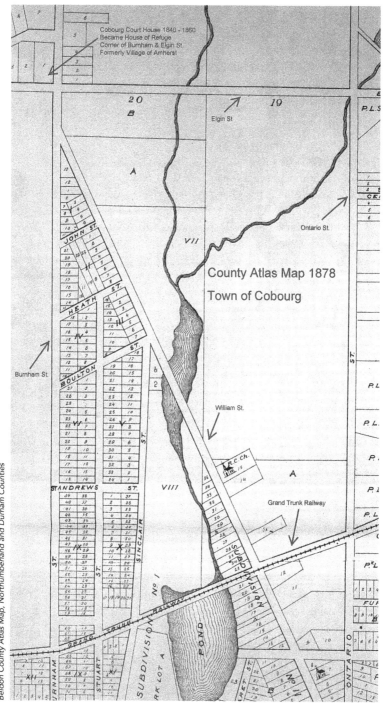

Cobourg Court House 1840 - 1860
Became House of Refuge
Corner of Burnham & Elgin St.
Formerly Village of Amherst

County Atlas Map 1878

Town of Cobourg

LETTER

FROM C. F. BUTLER, PRESIDENT OF THE HAHNEMANNIAN
MEDICAL INSTITUTE, PHILADELPHIA, TO DR.
KING, WHILE IN COBOURG GAOL.

Philadelphia, Pennsylvania, U. S. A.,
March 3d, 1859.

To whom it may concern:

At a regular meeting of the Hahnemannian Medical Institute of
the Homœopathy Medical College, of Pennsylvania, March 2d, 1859, Thos.
Geo. Edwards, M. D., of Texas, arose and laid before the Institute, the unfortunate position of our estimable acquaintance, and former President, William
Henry King, M. D., of Brighton, Canada West. Where it was unanimously
moved that this Institute do forward to the authorities concerned in the trial of
Wm. H. King, a concise statement, of the position, and unexceptional deportment of said King while a member of this Inst. Mr. King was elected President of this Institution at the commencement of the session of '57 and '58; and
retained the chair during the entire session. In this capacity Mr. King displayed eminent talent in conducting the affairs of of the Institution: winning
from all their respect and esteem for his decision of character and superiority
of intellect. As a student, Mr. King had no superiors in his class; as a man
he was universally beloved for his affable manners, and kind and gentle disposition. Mr. King we looked upon as a man of unexceptionable habits; his
seat in the College was never vacant, and his marked attention during lectures stamping him as a student in every sense of the word. Judging
from Mr. King's irreproachable conduct while a member of this institution, it
would seem that he is more the victim to the force of circumstances rather than
any intentional crime of his own. Hoping this testimonial of Mr. King's former unimpeachable character may receive some attention from your honorable
body, I am your obedient servant,

CHAS. F. BUTLER, Pres. Hahn. Med. Inst.
EDWARD RAWSON, Sec. Hahn. Med. Inst.

Dr. King corresponded with members of the Homeopathic Medical College in
Philadelphia in preparation for his trial. This letter indicates the high esteem
with which Dr. King was regarded following his successful two years at the
college. It was used as evidence for the defence.

There were so many of these letters that there was concern about what Dr. King was cooking up. Rumours of possible escape attempts started over the winter and escalated to a frenzy as the trial approached.

A great heartache for Dr. King was the fact that his next younger brother, Isaac Newton King, had left for California in the summer and was not at home to support him in his worst hour.

The two brothers were very close, having grown up together on the farm at Codrington, developing a great mutual respect. Unfortunately, we don't have any letters exchanged between the two brothers, but one related letter has amazingly survived. The King Collection, now residing at Proctor House Museum in Brighton and assembled by Roger McMurray of Brighton, includes a

New York Gallery, 25 Third St. S. F.

Isaac Newton King was Dr. King's next younger brother. He had gone to California to the gold rush in the summer of 1858, so was not present to support his older brother during his troubles. This picture is thought to be a portrait of Isaac King taken in San Francisco around 1859 before he came back to Canada.

small scrap of paper containing a touching note from Isaac to his parents. He does not mention the plight of his brother specifically, but comforts his parents by honouring them with the credit that he had reached the age of twenty-three "without one blemish or guilty stain to encounter."[2] We might expect that George and Henrietta King were much moved by this emotional note from a son so far away, especially in light of the horrible situation their eldest child was enduring at the time.

Eventually winter gave way and the long wait was over. Dr. King would have the chance to defend himself in a court of law. The first important step in this direction was the opening of the Spring Assizes in Cobourg on Monday, March 28, 1859. The Port Hope newspaper reported the next day that:

To My Parents

Dear Parents to you who has
been so kind, and who has
undergone so many troubles and
heardships for my own good
I feel it, my duty as I have
arived at the age of twenty
three to give you the credit and
Honour off my ariveing to this age.
without one blemished or guilty
Stain, to encounter
Cal, Michigan Box   Isaac A. King
Saturday February 1/59

Far from my native land I strow
Who has watched me through night and day
And to my Parents I will prove
To you my debts I never can pay
read the first and third together

While we don't have any letters that were exchanged between William and
Isaac King, we do have a touching letter that Isaac King sent to his parents on
the occasion of his twenty-third birthday. He does not mention the plight of his
brother, who was awaiting trial in Cobourg jail at the time, but credits his parents
with his accomplishment of reaching that age with no blemishes on his character.

> The Assizes Commenced yesterday. Mr. Justice Burns, pre-
> siding. The business before the Court is important. There are
> 90 civil and a good number of criminal cases on the docket.
> Dr. King of Brighton, will be tried this week, on the charge
> of poisoning his wife by the administration of arsenic.[3]

The assizes represented the traditional method of bringing the resources of the justice system of the province to the individual county courts. In the 1850s there were routine spring and fall assizes. Dockets were prepared leading up to each sitting of the court and in a few weeks of persistent courtroom proceedings, all cases would be disposed of. A judge and lawyers were assigned to each court and would travel to each county seat.

The next step was the arraignment. This took place three days later on Thursday, March 31 at the Cobourg courthouse. The Port Hope newspaper reported that on Thursday morning the grand jury had found a "true bill against Dr. King for the murder of his wife,"[4] and that he would be

The Assizes

Commenced yesterday. Mr. Justice Burns, presiding. The business before the Court is important. There are 90 civil, and a goodly number of criminal cases on the docket. Dr. King of Brighton, will be tried this week, on the charge of poisoning his wife by the administration of arsenic.

On March 29, 1859, the *Port Hope Weekly Guide* announced the opening of the Spring Assizes at Cobourg with Judge Robert Burns presiding. It would be a busy session with ninety civil cases on the docket and several criminal cases, highlighted by the sensational trial of Dr. King for the poisoning of his wife. *Port Hope Weekly Guide*, March 29, 1859.

Northumberland County Archives, Cobourg, Ontario

Dr. King.

On Thursday morning the Grand Jury found a true bill against Dr. King for the murder of his wife. It having been whispered about that he would be formally arraigned at the bar in the afternoon,—when the prisoner was brought up from the cells, the Court room was densely crowded. The prisoner is good looking and seemed to be rather amused than otherwise at the crowd of anxious onlookers. He turned round in the dock and calmly surveyed the mass of faces which were turned upon him by those in the body of the Court, and nodded to several of his acquaintances. To the indictment he pleaded "not guilty," in a quiet, clear voice. The Court asked him, if he was ready to take his trial. He did not reply, but merely looked at his Counsel, the Hon. J. Hillyard Cameron—who said that the prisoner was not ready for trial, but in all probability would be on Tuesday next, which day was then fixed upon by Mr. Galt, Crown prosecutor, to proceed to try the truth of Dr. King's plea.

"formally arraigned at the bar"[5] in the afternoon. There was pent up excitement to finally get a glimpse of the notorious murderer, so the courtroom was packed when Dr. King was led up from the cells.

The reporter felt that Dr. King was a good-looking man and commented that he appeared "rather amused"[6] at the crowd that followed his every step to the prisoner's dock. He "calmly surveyed the mass of faces"[7] and even nodded to some of his acquaintances. When asked to make a plea, he said "in a quiet, clear voice"[8] that he was not guilty. The Court asked him if he was ready to take his trial and he glanced to his defence counsel, Hon. J. Hillyard Cameron, who said they would be ready on Tuesday next. After this brief exchange, Dr. King was led back to his cell to await the start of the trial that would decide his fate.

Then, an event happened on April 1, the Saturday before the trial began, which set everyone on edge, especially the sheriff and constables at the jail. On this day, one of Dr. King's brothers, probably Charles Wellington King, who was eighteen at the time, made the trip to Cobourg to visit his brother. However, rumour had it that, before going to the jail, he paid a visit to the chemist shop in Cobourg, where he purchased some strychnine. One can imagine the alarm this supposedly innocent visit caused at the jail, just a few days before the trial of their most notorious inmate was to begin.

The jailer watched closely as Charles spoke through the peephole in the door to his brother, the prisoner. Nothing was exchanged between the two men. On being questioned regarding the strychnine, Charles King insisted he had purchased it for the purpose of poisoning foxes, which were common on the family farm at Codrington. In the account of the Dr. King story published by Wiman Publishing of Toronto, we find a rather dismissive comment about the professed use of the strychnine: "Excuses of this description are always at hand."[9] Finally, the young Mr. King left Cobourg, to the relief of those responsible for the security of the prisoners. We have no reason to believe that anything sinister was afoot during this episode, but it may come to mind later in our story as rumours surface of other possible scheming that may have been more real than imagined.

LEFT: The arraignment of Dr. King was reported under the headline, saying that the Grand Jury had found a *true bill* against Dr. King for the murder of his wife. *Port Hope Weekly Guide*, April 2, 1859.

FIFTEEN

THE TRIAL

The trial of Dr. King began on the next Monday morning, April 4. As crowds milled around the front of the Cobourg courthouse, *The Port Hope Weekly Guide* shouted the headline "Wife Poisoning Case," and provided several columns explaining the events of the story that were known at that time.

An account of the trial written by an old friend of Dr. King, Reuben DeCourcey, provides a picture of the scene outside the Cobourg courthouse:

> On the morning of the fourth every street, lane and avenue leading to the court house was filled with footmen and carriage men, hurrying to obtain admittance into the court room to hear the trial, and although at an early hour, when they assembled, it was one of the noisiest crowds I ever saw.[1]

The Cobourg jail and courthouse was on the northwest corner of Burnham and Elgin Streets, which was in the northwest part of Cobourg. The courtroom was in the east part of the building, on the main floor. It was said to accommodate four hundred persons but there were many more squeezed into it on this exciting day. Only a fraction of the many people who came to the courthouse with the hope of getting in actually made it inside.

DeCourcey goes on to say, "The excitement throughout the country as well as in the town was intense. Several ladies of the town came up in the morning but when they saw the crowd at the court house returned again, judging very wisely that that was not the place to wear hoops."[2] Indeed! He estimates that there were at least 1,500 people who came to the courthouse, including "a large number of medical men, besides the witnesses, and all the students from Victoria College."[3]

At 9:30, Dr. King was brought into the courtroom. DeCourcey says he entered "with a light, airy step, and very gentlemanly dressed, in a suit of black broadcloth, with a gold watch chain about his vest."[4] It seemed striking to those who saw him in the courtroom that such a gentlemanly fellow could be charged with such a crime. In the court he was the same old Dr. King, nodding pleasantly to those he recognized as friends, but then "he would cast a contemptuous glance"[5] in the direction of those who were not so favoured. It was thought by some that he exhibited amazing fortitude in difficult circumstances, but it is likely that others saw his behaviour as more evidence of his extreme self-confidence, bordering on arrogance.

While Dr. King was the centre of attention in the courtroom, others were to play a major role in determining his fate. Judge Robert Burns had been appointed to the Spring Assizes in Cobourg and brought a

Northumberland County Archives, Cobourg, Ontario

COBOURG ASSIZES!!
WIFE POISONING CASE!
TRIAL OF Dr. KING.
BEFORE JUDGE BURNS.

As the trial commenced at the Cobourg courthouse, the *Port Hope Weekly Guide* shouted the headline "Wife Poisoning Case" and provided several columns explaining the events of Dr. King's case. *Port Hope Weekly Guide*, April 4, 1859.

good reputation for fairness and thoroughness to the job. He had been appointed to the Court of Queen's Bench in 1850 and was also appointed as chancellor of the University of Toronto in 1857, succeeding William Hume Blake. Judge Burns was expected to conduct a no-nonsense trial. His reputation as a quiet but efficient adjudicator of the law was welcome in the courtroom in Cobourg, in view of the highly excited public involvement in the case of Dr. King.

The Crown prosecutor was the Honorable Thomas Galt, who had been created Queen's Counsel in 1858 and was well-known as a very successful solicitor with wide knowledge of criminal law. He was one of three brothers who had come to Upper Canada at the behest of his father, John Galt, who was instrumental in the creation and early management of the Upper Canada Company. His brother, Alexander Galt, became prominent in the political life of Upper Canada and would play an important role in the struggle for Confederation.

Counsel for the defence of Dr. King was John Hillyard Cameron, who had been appointed Queen's Counsel in 1846. He had also been elected to the Legislative Assembly several times. At the time of Dr. King's trial he was involved in serious financial difficulties due to an economic panic, which had caused severe losses in his holdings. Nonetheless, Mr. Cameron was considered an excellent choice to defend Dr. King, and he worked hard to meet his obligations.

Of course, Dr. King's fate was also in the hands of the jury. DeCourcey lists the jury members as Joseph Rosevear, William Hoskins, William Humphries, Richard Barrett, William Smith, Jonathan Porter, Levi Dudley, Daniel Rightman, William Robinson, William Clarke, Samuel Haggart, and Henry Alger. There had been seven challenges by the defence but none by the Crown. Joseph Rosevear was a thirty-nine-year-old farmer who was born in Cornwall, England, but now had a growing family and a prosperous farm near Cold Springs, north of Cobourg. Daniel Ryckman was a successful farmer near Hilton, in Brighton Township, and could have been familiar with both the King family of Codrington and the Lawsons of Lawson Settlement. William Humphries was a merchant and leading citizen of Warkworth. Levi Dudley was a farmer near the village of Dundonald in Cramahe Township. Henry

Alger was a thirty-one-year-old farmer who lived north of Colborne. Dr. King would certainly be judged by his peers.

The case was opened by Crown counsel, Mr. Galt. He insisted that the jurors must eliminate all prejudice from their minds regarding the accused — that at this moment he was as innocent as each of them in the eyes of the law, until proven to be guilty by the court. He explained that the accused was charged with the murder of his wife and that he was accused of using his particular knowledge as a doctor to prepare "certain appliances within his reach"[6] to accomplish the act of poisoning his wife. Mr. Galt stressed that Dr. King was a physician by profession and therefore had the opportunity to poison the deceased because he was not only her husband, but was acting as "her medical attendant."[7]

There followed a description of the events leading up to the death of Sarah Ann King. Mr. Galt asked the jury to establish that Dr. King "was in a position to accomplish the deed,"[8] and said that it was important to determine that "those means by which the deceased had come by her death were within his reach."[9] He then told the jury that he would prove that the deceased was in good health up until October 14, when she began to experience "violent pains, accompanied with retching and finally died on 3d November."[10] The doctors who were to testify would confirm that there was no cause of death other than poison, and that eleven grains of arsenic were found in the stomach of the deceased.

Crown Counsel then addressed the issue of motive. He said, "this motive would be found in the prisoner's affections and illicit intercourse with another woman."[11] He would prove that Dr. King had murdered his wife in order to more freely express his feelings for this other woman. He had the opportunity, the technical knowledge, and the desire to be rid of his wife.

Even more "repugnant to human feeling"[12] was the fact that the accused told the family and friends of the deceased that she could not be delivered of the child she was carrying, but that "she must cease to breathe before she gave birth."[13] The accused had persisted in telling everyone that the deceased had a serious disease of the womb that would cause her early death. However, testimony of the doctors would show that no such disease existed in the body of the deceased.

The Crown would also prove that Dr. King had administered a white powder to the deceased, which floated in water and was difficult to mix. Witnesses would testify that after the deceased took this substance, she experienced severe vomiting and a burning thirst, which Professor Croft would describe as common symptoms of arsenic poisoning.

Mr. Galt lastly raised an issue that he felt the defence would press. Dr. King practiced homeopathic medicine, which included the administering of arsenic as a treatment in some cases. In this light, it could be suggested that he had made a mistake in administering arsenic to his wife in the manner he had done it, and therefore it would be difficult to prove intent. Counsel for the Crown "entreated the jury to weigh well the evidence which would be given on that point."[14]

SIXTEEN

THE CORONER AND THE DOCTORS

The first witness called by Mr. Galt was Simon Davidson, the coroner. We have a record of the testimony of the witnesses but not of the words used by counsel to ask the questions, so we must imagine the questions based on the responses of the witnesses. Simon Davidson explained how the inquest was held with special attention to the autopsy of Sarah King's body. Most of his testimony dealt with the handling of the stomach and the pickle bottle that was used to transport it to Professor Croft in Toronto.

The security of the pickle bottle would be cast in doubt by the defence, and the Crown was intent on demonstrating clearly to the jury that there had been little or no chance of contamination or tampering. The defence would voice the idea that someone might have put arsenic into the stomach after it was removed from the body. There was such animosity between Dr. King and certain members of the Lawson family that it was thought someone might attempt to inject incriminating evidence into the situation, in an attempt to ensure his conviction. The Crown, on the other hand, would prove that the arsenic had been inside the stomach of the deceased before she died.

Mr. Davidson would say, "I did not leave the room from the time the stomach was taken from the deceased until I placed it in a bottle. The bottle was a pickle bottle. I washed it out with cold water."[1] He took the pickle bottle with him that night of November 8, after the initial late-evening session of the coroner's jury, and went straight to Mr. Delong's

Hotel in Brighton to spend the night. The next morning he returned to the schoolhouse with the pickle bottle and the autopsy continued.

The security of the pickle bottle was not explained adequately until Robert Barker gave his testimony as the next witness. He had been a member of the coroner's jury and had been present throughout the inquest. He said:

> The mouth of the bottle was not corked on the day the stomach was taken from the body, it was merely covered with paper and tied down with strings. Next day I procured a cork, and when the jury re-assembled the Coroner produced the bottle in the same state as it had been the day previous.[2]

Mr. Barker then explained how he had taken the bottle to Kingston in order to have it examined by a professor of Queen's College, but his request was declined and he returned to Brighton the next day, when he returned the bottle to Mr. Davidson. It is unclear why Robert Barker's visit to Kingston was unsuccessful, but it delayed the very critical process of testing the contents of the stomach by at least two days, which we might expect annoyed Mr. Davidson a good deal.

Simon Davidson was recalled to testify after Mr. Barker, and he explained to the court that he had resolved to take the stomach to Professor Croft himself on November 13, but was only at Colborne when he heard that Dr. King had been captured and would be coming back to Brighton very soon. He resolved to return to Brighton immediately to meet and take responsibility for the prisoner. In order to ensure the safe delivery of the stomach, he found James Keeble, the conductor of the Grand Trunk Railway train, handed him the pickle bottle, and charged him with delivery of it to Professor Croft in Toronto. Mr. Keeble testified next and confirmed that he had received the bottle from Mr. Davidson and had immediately secured it in a cupboard in the baggage car. Upon arrival of the train in Toronto he personally handed the bottle to Professor Croft.

The testimony of Professor Henry Croft was much anticipated. The Crown expected him to confirm what everyone believed — that it was arsenic that caused the death of Sarah Ann King. At the same time, it was felt he would determine one way or another whether arsenic could have been inserted into the stomach after death. The nasty rumours about tampering with the stomach during the travels of the pickle bottle were fodder for public discussions, but had the potential to muddy the waters for the Crown. They wanted a definitive answer from the professor.

The testimony of Professor Croft was detailed and professional but annoyingly indefinite on the big questions. He confirmed that he had found eleven grains of arsenic in the stomach but that the lining of the stomach was relatively healthy, "except for a slight blush at the extremes."[3] He said that the paper around the bottle was not sealed but the box it came in was. He continued, "I have no means of knowing whether the arsenic was put into the stomach after death or not."[4]

But this was not the end of it. After examining the stomach he was dissatisfied with the evidence he had seen and requested that the coroner exhume the body again and this time extract the liver. On examining the liver, Professor Croft found small amounts of arsenic. At the trial, he could say definitely, "arsenic cannot be put into the liver after death. It must have been taken in during life,"[5] which proved beyond any doubt that Sarah Ann King had consumed significant quantities of arsenic before she died, enough to allow small amounts of the substance to migrate into her liver.

The last part of Professor Croft's testimony is technical and a bit confusing for the man on the street. He talked about experiences he recalled in his career with arsenic poisoning, musing that sometimes it can lead to death rather quickly and sometimes it can take long periods of time. He repeated that he felt there should be more inflammation of the stomach tissues if arsenic had been present for several weeks. He also speculated that "some poisons have a cumulative effect,"[6] which might seem sensible to us but left him open to ridicule by Crown Counsel and some of the medical men involved in the trial.

In the end, Professor Croft would not come out and say that Sarah Ann King had died of arsenic poisoning, as the Crown had hoped. Pressed by Mr. Galt on cross-examination, he would say that "the absence of the usual indications by no means excludes the possibility of the presence of arsenic in the stomach."[7] In spite of the confident words of the coroner's report, the exact cause of death was still uncertain.

The next witness was Dr. Pellatiah Russell Proctor, who had participated in the inquest and provided testimony about the general condition of the body, as well as the stomach. He made clear that he had not used the word "inflammation," but preferred "congestion" for the effect he found in the stomach lining and in a few other places. He also admitted that he had never examined anyone who had died of arsenic poisoning. The most interesting part of Dr. Proctor's testimony was information about the condition of the womb, which he said contained a healthy fetus that was between three and four months old.

Another doctor who took part in the inquest was Dr. A.E. Fife and he followed Dr. Proctor on the witness stand. Dr. Fife told of seeing Sarah Ann King several times in the weeks before her death and of discussing her illness with Dr. King. He was inclined to accept that her symptoms were due to pregnancy and was satisfied to treat her for the vomiting. On cross-examination he indicated that his direct contact with the deceased had been very limited as Dr. King was always present and providing the bulk of the diagnosis and treatment. He made a point of telling the court that he had prescribed substances for Mrs. King that would have been grey or yellow in appearance, in contrast with the distinctive white powder that Dr. King was giving his wife. It is from this witness that the court also heard of the fall from the buggy Mrs. King had experienced some months before her death, saying, "she complained to me of a pain in the head — that was all."[8]

The last of the medical men to testify was Dr. Pitkin Gross, who had also taken part in the inquest. He made it clear that he had not been asked to visit Mrs. King until a few hours before her death, and we can see from his testimony that he had little regard for Dr. King. During the autopsy he had noticed that the liver was hardened and he was sure this was due to a large amount of arsenic in the body. He emphasized that Dr. King had been giving his wife a white powder that would not dissolve in water, which made it clear to everyone that it was arsenic. He also made a point of saying that he found no evidence of ulcerations of the womb, a condition in his wife that Dr. King had been reporting for some time. On the other hand, he also said that he found no obvious cause of death when he examined the body.

SEVENTEEN

FAMILY AND FRIENDS

The court adjourned for fifteen minutes after the testimony related to the post mortem was complete. The jury and the guests had sat through some long and tedious testimony about medicine, the autopsy, and white powder, and were anxious to hear more interesting information from the family of the deceased. When the court reconvened after the break, they would have their wish. The first witness was Elizabeth Jane Lawson, mother of the deceased.

Mrs. Lawson spoke softly and clearly, in short sentences, and with firm knowledge of what she had experienced. The Crown felt that it was critical to the case that they presented to the jury the specific recollections of the mother and primary nursemaid of the deceased, and the one who had spent the most time with her during those weeks before her death. She knew Sarah Ann King better than anyone else and had stuck by her side as she slowly slipped into illness and despair. The court was after facts, of course, but empathy for this witness would go a long way toward a conviction.

Elizabeth Lawson began from the very first indication of illness on October 14, when she found Sarah to be suddenly very ill. She told how Dr. King met her at the door and began to explain how sick her daughter was. She participated that day and many times afterward in giving her daughter the white powder mixed with water on a spoon. She was one of the few who would be allowed by the doctor to perform this important task. The white powder always made Sarah vomit soon after taking it, and the vomiting would continue for some time. After taking the medicine, Sarah routinely complained of being extremely thirsty and of a burning sensation in her mouth and throat. Mrs. Lawson felt it was one of her primary duties to keep a tumbler of cold water by her daughter's bedside in order to make her more comfortable. She stated simply, "from that day to the day of her death, I was not absent from the house more than one hour."[1]

On cross-examination, Mrs. Lawson provided a telling piece of testimony about her daughter. She explained:

> About three weeks before she was taken ill, she was alone at my house, and told me that her husband had said to her that her womb was ulcerated and in such a state that she might drop off in the night, and he being alone with her it might be considered strange; he had told her to tell me this; I recollected some conversation taking place about Dr. Fife examining her; she asked what was the use; she did not positively decline; she did not decline; she said. "William Henry, you know what is the matter with me, — why send for Dr. Fife?"[2]

Mrs. Lawson then told the court of her discovery of the likeness of Melinda Vandervoort, as well as the letters. She had seen his coat hanging in her daughter's room and had deliberately looked into the pockets. We might surmise that this act was the result of some kind of suspicion about the motives of Dr. King. Whatever the intent, she was amazed to find a picture of the pretty young Miss Vandervoort, who she knew had visited the King home a few weeks before. It may have been a shock, but the dedicated mother took the opportunity to use it as a test of Dr. King. She testified that, "I did not tell him that it had been found, I said it has been so rumoured, but he denied having such a likeness,"[3] providing, as she had hoped, more evidence that might be used against him later.

The most difficult part of the testimony of Elizabeth Lawson came as she described the events of the last day of her daughter's life and her subsequent death. She and her husband had kept vigil in Sarah's room the day before she died and in the evening they were encouraged when Sarah sat up and said she was feeling better. Her parents waited about an hour after she went to sleep and, on that positive note, went to bed themselves, with assurances from Dr. King that he would watch over her during the night. In the morning, when they went into Sarah's room, Dr. King commented that she had never slept better. Mr. Lawson tried to say goodbye to his daughter, as he had to go to work; however, she did not answer. He was afraid she would not awake.

Her mother took a different approach. She immediately set to work bathing her daughter with cold water and talking to her to make her wake up. She realized, however, that Sarah was not able to hear her. She was only partially conscious and totally unable to respond. Her mother testified, "I tried to wake her, and called her name; — she tried to open her eyes, but could not!"[4]

The effect of this testimony on the jury and the gallery was dramatic. The account we have from Reuben DeCourcey explains it very well, as he says, "the way in which the mother of the deceased gave her testimony was very affecting; the prisoner leaned over the side of the box with his eyes firmly upon her, all the time she was giving her evidence."[5]

The next witness to testify at the trial was Dr. Norman Bethune, a very respected doctor and professor of surgery at the Toronto School of Medicine. He began his comments by saying that he had been in the courtroom for the whole trial and the evidence he heard suggested that the symptoms of the deceased "are such as are caused by an irritant poison."[6] He also stated that "arsenic does not always produce redness of the stomach,"[7] citing a case he had been involved with in Yorkville in the past year. Dr. Bethune was accustomed to speaking directly and ended his testimony by saying, "I have heard the way in which deceased died described; a large dose of arsenic would produce such effects."[8]

Dr. E.M. Hodder was another highly regarded doctor who taught at the Toronto School of Medicine. He testified that he agreed with Dr. Bethune about the symptoms of the deceased being consistent with arsenic poison but he then said something that was controversial. He said, of arsenic, "I consider it to be a safe medicine,"[9] which seemed to leave the door open for the idea that Dr. King, in practicing homeopathic medicine, might have been justified in using arsenic.

Testimony was then provided by Margaret A. Nix, who was a cousin of Sarah Ann King. DeCourcey says she was an aunt but, in fact, the two women had paternal grandfathers who were brothers. Mrs. Nix confirmed much of the detail of Mrs. Lawson's earlier testimony, describing in detail how the white powder was administered to the patient, telling the court how on one occasion Dr. King had her take the medicine from his hand and give it to Sarah.

Next in line was John M. Lawson, father of the deceased. For the most part, Mr. Lawson recounted the events leading up to the death of his daughter much the same as his wife had done earlier. However, he was much more animated and specific with his words when he described the confrontation he had with his son-in-law. DeCourcey gives us Mr. Lawson's words and we can't improve on them. He said:

> I visited my daughter when I heard she was ill; I asked her husband what was the matter with her; he said that she was cankered right through and that her womb was nearly closed up; he said before her face that her case was incurable — that she must and would die. I urged upon him to get other doctors several times; he at last said he would have Dr. Fife; I did not consider that he [Dr. Fife] did any good, and I wanted other doctors; Dr. King on these occasions would get quite angry with me. The night before my daughter died I said, "William Henry, if God spares my life, I will have a jury of doctors in the morning"; he asked me who I should have; I said Dr. Gross for one; he said Dr. Gross was the greatest enemy he had, and that he knew what he would give my wife; I asked what Dr. Gross would give, and he said calomel or opium.[10]

On cross-examination he confirmed that the last medicine he saw Dr. King give Sarah was opium, about 1:00 p.m. on November 3, the day before she died.

The anger and frustration of the grieving father comes out in his testimony. One can imagine this large, forceful man speaking before the court that day. He would have been holding back his tears at the loss of this beloved daughter and, at the same time, trying to control his white-hot anger at the man a few feet away in the prisoner's box. His words, more clearly than any, demonstrated the conceit of Dr. King and showed everyone the utter lack of empathy he felt for his poor wife, telling her directly that she must die from a horrible condition in her body.

After that dramatic testimony Sarah Rachel Young came to the witness stand. She was a sister of Margaret Augusta Nix and therefore a cousin of Sarah Ann King. Her testimony was similar to that of Margaret Nix and she added some interesting information about conversations she had with Dr. King in the weeks leading up to Sarah King's death. She said, "In conversation with him about her, he told me that she was not to his mind — a very good wife to get money, but he would like her improved in many respects."[11] This testimony supported the motive put forward by the Crown that Dr. King had murdered his wife so he could consort with another woman.

EIGHTEEN

SWEET LITTLE LUMP OF GOOD NATURE

The next witness generated a lot of curiosity in the jury and gallery. Melinda Vandervoort stepped up to the witness stand, skirt swishing and a very attractive bonnet perched delicately on her lovely head. Mr. Galt asked Miss Vandervoort why she had sent her likeness to Dr. King. She responded by saying that Mrs. King had asked her to send the likeness and that she "never had any improper intercourse with Dr. King." On further questioning by Mr. Galt in reference to the likeness and the letters, Melinda said "I directed the likeness to Dr. King; I thought that when I got the letter it was written for amusement; I sent him this letter in answer, for amusement!"

Mr. Galt was clearly not happy with Miss Vandervoort's testimony and responded sarcastically, "Go down; I must read these letters, but do not wish to do so in your presence! (severely)." DeCourcey included the word "severely" for emphasis. Then Mr. Galt began to read the letter, dated October 10, which Dr. King had sent to Melinda after she sent him her picture. The first words of the letter were, "Sweet little lump of good nature." One can imagine the tone of voice used by Mr. Galt in uttering these bizarre words. It gets better: "I walked to the P.O. this morning (Monday) and found the most precious thing (except the original) on earth; better to me than all California."

If the Crown wished to demonstrate the motive they had established for the murder of Sarah Ann King, they need not go further than this letter. Dr. King writes to Melinda " … but could I indulge in the hope that those winning and genial smiles would ever be found in my possession, all troubles would then cease." He was just getting warmed up. He then made the same suggestion to Melinda he had made to Dorcas Garratt only a few weeks before, "Can you keep from sacrificing yourself upon the hymeneal altar for the next year?"

In the midst of their lovers' banter, both Melinda and Dr. King were concerned about being found out. He said in his letter to her, "… if you correspond with me I will guarantee upon my word and house that detection shall never happen; you are, therefore, perfectly safe." In spite of those comforting words, closer to the end of the letter he said: "You will observe that this letter is anonymous for fear somebody might get your keys, and read it; as it is, if they should they would not be wiser but my name shall be -----. You know whom it is from just as well as if my name was appended."

The last sentence of the letter provides another example of using dashes in place of a name. He writes, "Come and visit whenever you can. ----- is very sick — last night we thought she would die." The men of the jury would remember this last sentence and combine it with other testimony to show very clearly that Dr. King was spinning a web of lies in pursuit of his objective. He lied to his wife by telling her she had an incurable disease and would not survive her confinement. He constantly lied to Sarah's parents and other visitors, telling them he knew how to treat the patient better than any other doctor. Now it was obvious he was also lying to Melinda, telling her that his wife had been so ill they thought she might die, when it was clear Sarah had not become ill until several days later.

The second letter was dated October 18, and was written by Melinda in response to Dr. King's letter of the tenth. She begins, "Yours of the 10th instant came to hand in good repair, and exceedingly pleased was I while perusing its contents." Melinda tries hard to be discrete but is also intent on sending the right message to her ardent admirer, "… as circumstances are with you, it appears almost in vain for me to think of you only as a friend. Yet something seems to whisper, 'still hope.'" Would the ladies in the gallery have gasped at that last phrase? It has a chilling effect in light of subsequent events.

Near the end of the letter, Melinda teases her beau, "Well now, Dr., don't you think it very wrong for me to correspond with you? I'm afraid if known it would destroy 'Annie's' happiness." She closes the letter, signing herself "Your unwavering, L----, VAN." Mr. Galt ended with a flourish and the gallery was disappointed that the performance was over. DeCourcey describes the scene from the point of view of the prisoner: "While the letters were being read, the prisoner showed no sense of shame; but rather seemed to share the amusement which could not be repressed." Unfortunately, the entertainment was at an end — back to serious business.

NINETEEN

THE VANDERVOORTS AND CLINTON LAWSON

The next witness to step onto the stand was John H. Vandervoort, Melinda's father. One can imagine his dismay and embarrassment at the prospect of following so close upon such testimony. However, he gathered his nerve and did his duty. "The prisoner came to my house in Sidney, about ten o'clock that night, on the 8th November. I had never seen him before,"[1] he said. He then went on to explain that Dr. King insisted on delivering a message to Melinda in private and that the two young people had gone into another room, where they remained for an hour. "I went and asked if that message was delivered yet," he said. "They said no. By and by they came out."[2]

At that point, Mr. Vandervoort told the court how Dr. King had explained to the anxious parents about the death of his wife, the inquest, and the matter of a likeness of Melinda being found. He said that "a warrant was issued for his apprehension and for that of Melinda also,"[3] and that flight was the only solution. "He urged me to allow him to take her to her aunt's on the other side. I consented to this."[4] It's hard to understate the inadequacy of the sentence "I consented to this." Why would Melinda's parents let their daughter go out of the country with a man who was a total stranger to them? This may speak to the persuasiveness of Dr. King; he certainly had a talent for talking others into his way of thinking.

On cross-examination, Mr. Vandervoort gave the answer, "King did not say anything to him about the Lawson's threatening to shoot my daughter."[5] We have to imagine the question that might have solicited this kind of response. Threats to shoot Melinda are not mentioned in any other part of the trial documents or reports but the idea must have been present in the public in order to end up in the courtroom, whether it represented truth or rumour. Following Mr. Vandervoort, his wife, Elizabeth, came to the witness stand. She did not add anything to the testimony, other than to say that Dr. King had insisted he was innocent.

The next witness was much anticipated. Everyone had heard many times about Clinton Lawson's expedition to Cape Vincent to apprehend the fleeing Dr. King. He came to the stand with his earthy simplicity, trying hard to mask the seething anger he felt for the prisoner. He explained how the coroner had given him the warrant for Dr. King's arrest, then said, "I went to Kingston on Friday, and from that to Cape Vincent. From information I got at the post-office, I went six or eight miles up the country to the house of a man named Bate."[6]

He told of how he had arrived at the Bate farmhouse with U.S. Marshal Gordon, who had gone to the front door while he hung back. "He had not been there three minutes when Dr. King jumped out of the window. I ran after him. He was towards the woods, but as I was after him quick, he turned into a barn. We went in and found him under the straw in a hog's nest."[7]

Mr. Cameron, for the defence, enquired of the witness whether he had been armed. Clinton Lawson responded, "I had a revolver. I said he must be shot if he ran; a lawyer told me that I had no right to shoot him, and told him so too."[8] Mr. Cameron then tried to make it look better for his client by asking the witness to confirm that Dr. King had actually come with him at this point. The witness shot back defiantly, "Well, I guess he did!"[9] Mr. Galt then jumped in to make a point, asking Clinton Lawson if Dr. King had come with him *willingly*. To this the witness answered with even greater force, "No, Sir; no Sir-reee!"[10] The judge may have had hush the courtroom after this amusing episode, possibly grinning along with the rest, subtly.

The last witness to testify for the Crown was Jared O. Clarke, the constable who had taken charge of Dr. King after Clinton Lawson delivered him back to Brighton. During his investigation, he found the letters in Dr. King's trunk. Mr. Clarke had also escorted the prisoner to Cobourg, along with the coroner, Simon Davidson. He testified about a conversation he had with Dr. King on the fourteenth of November. He said, "The prisoner told me that he had given his wife poison, but that he had not given her arsenic … if it was given to her at all, someone else must have given it to her."[11] These words would have surprised the court. They all knew that Dr. King had insisted on his innocence since his arrest. Besides, it was clear to everyone that he had poisoned his wife with arsenic.

After Constable Clarke's testimony, Mr. Galt bowed to the judge and said, "This is the case for the Crown, my Lord."[12] Now it was time for the defence to present their case. Mr. Cameron worried that he could not finish examining all eight witnesses that afternoon and asked the judge if the court could be adjourned until the next morning. The judge flatly refused. This trial was going to be completed *today*!

TWENTY

THE DEFENCE

The first witness for the defence was Dr. Charles J. Hempel. There was a fuss when several of the jurymen declared that he had not kissed the Bible properly during the administering of the oath. He was made to do it a second time — and then a third time, just to make certain. DeCourcey said, "The episode created quite a commotion in the jury box."[1]

Dr. Hempel introduced himself by saying, "I am Professor of Materia Medica and Therapeutics in the Homeopathic College of Pennsylvania."[2] The defence was relying on Dr. Hempel to be the lead expert regarding the type of medicine Dr. King had learned at the college in Pennsylvania. He went on to say, "I know the prisoner. He studied under me two sessions,"[3] which established the relationship between Dr. Hempel and Dr. King.

The doctor then proceeded to provide a lesson in homeopathic medicine. It was an attempt to educate the jury in the theory and practice of this new and often misunderstood method of treating disease. He began, "The gist of homeopathic practice is this — for the cure of disease we administer medicines which, if taken by a healthy person, would produce a like disease."[4] The defence wanted to remind the jury that Dr. King was treating his wife for cholera morbus, so Dr. Hempel spoke immediately about this dreaded disease:

We might be called upon to prescribe for a disease which has exactly the very same symptoms as those produced by arsenic, and might be considered by persons who did not know it to be a disease, to be a case of arsenical poisoning. Thus, in cholera morbus the symptoms occur, for which a physician would prescribe arsenic; and the symptoms of arsenic if prescribed in a large dose would be exactly like the symptoms of cholera morbus.[5]

For the layman, this probably seems all too convenient. The doctor was trying to convince the jury that Dr. King had been perfectly right in administering arsenic to his wife because she was suffering from cholera morbus, a disease that would cause vomiting and nausea, just the same as arsenic.

Then he moved on to deal with the vomiting and nausea as symptoms of pregnancy. "These symptoms are generally found to exist five or six weeks after conception; they may exist during the whole term, or the first five or six months of pregnancy."[6] We hear an echo of Dr. Fife's diagnosis here, even though neither doctor examined the deceased to any great degree when she was ill. It is a theory that tries to explain symptoms in a context other than arsenic poisoning.

Hitting all the available topics, he addressed the issue of inflammation in the stomach. "In my judgement, I do not think that deceased could have taken so large a dose of arsenic as Professor Croft found without leaving more marks of inflammation."[7] After recounting some of his own experiences with arsenic poisoning, he gave his opinion about the amount of arsenic that would be required to cause death: "To produce such a result, I should think not less than ninety or one hundred grains would have to be administered."[8] Then he added that if that much arsenic had been administered, he would expect to find about sixty grains of the substance in the stomach after death. Dr. Hempel also left the court with some suggestions about what he felt had caused the death of Sarah Ann King. The list included, "in consequence of her nervous system having been exhausted ... disease of the neck of the womb ... local irritation."[9]

On cross-examination, Dr. Hempel responded to a question from Mr. Galt about the competency of Dr. King as a doctor. He explained that the prisoner had received his degree at the medical college in Philadelphia in March of 1858 and that "Dr. King was in our college two sessions; he was one of our best students…. I consider Dr. King competent for practice after studying for two sessions in our college."[10]

Dr. Hempel then took aim at the doctors who conducted the autopsy. "I am not satisfied with the post mortem. From the examination they made, the physicians could not tell whether ulcers existed or not."[11] He felt that ulceration could have been in the interior of the womb and the doctors did not look closely enough to find it. He also said that arsenic could cause death in small or large doses, depending on the state of the system. There was more rambling technical jargon about the use of arsenic, but in the end, he said, "Deceased must have taken arsenic."[12]

Mr. Cameron then re-examined Dr. Hempel on the particular point of the fall Sarah Ann King was said to have experienced some weeks before she became ill. He said, "The fall of deceased would likely aggravate the malady. The accident might not have any serious results till several weeks have elapsed and then have induced vomiting, sinking, enervation and coma resulting in death."[13]

The defence then brought up a second medical man from Philadelphia to the witness stand. This was Dr. A.H. Flanders, who said, "I hold the chair of Chemistry and Toxicology in the same College as Dr. Hempel."[14] He had only recently begun studying homeopathic medicine, having practised conventional medicine for eleven years. Mr. Flanders had not known Dr. King when he was at the college in Philadelphia, and he had never treated a case of arsenic poisoning, but he explained that he had done experiments on dogs and cats which he held to be similar to humans in terms of symptoms of arsenic poisoning.

When asked by Mr. Galt about the cause of death in this case, he attributed it to the fall from the buggy, calling it "a very obscure case."[15] Even more controversial, he said that he believed the arsenic had been put into the stomach after death. DeCourcey adds in brackets at this point, "hissing in the court which was suppressed."[16] Mr. Galt was not going to let this go unchallenged. "Do you set your opinion against that of Dr. Croft, a man who is well known in your own country, and has had cases in your side of the water as well as this?"[17]

Professional courtesy fell away as Dr. Flanders replied emphatically, "Professor Croft is *not a physician*, sir! I graduated in Philadelphia in 1850."[18] Mr. Galt took the challenge and pursued the witness by asking him to confirm his previous testimony that he had not been involved in any cases of arsenic poisoning in humans, but had studied the effect of arsenic on cats and dogs. Dr. Flanders agreed and this caused some snickering in the court; the judge may have had to silence the gallery.

Mr. Galt was not finished. "And you think it more likely that the fall from the buggy caused the death of the deceased, than the arsenic found in her stomach?"[19] A strong positive response from the witness resulted in murmurs from the court. At this point, Mr. Galt lost all patience and said, "Then I have nothing more to say to you — you may go!"[20]

The last witness of the day was another doctor, this one from closer to home. Dr. Thomas Nichol of Simcoe County stepped to the witness box, saying that he had known Dr. King in college in Philadelphia and had boarded with him during one of the sessions he attended. Dr. Nichols described how he had experimented on himself to learn the effects of arsenic in the body. He had conducted several experiments, which included taking small doses of arsenic over several weeks and recording the development of symptoms, paying particular attention to the cumulative effect.

As to the case at hand, he agreed with the previous witness that the amount of arsenic present in the deceased body was not adequate to cause death. He felt, as Dr. Flanders had said, that the fall from the buggy may have contributed to the death but had not caused it outright. His final conclusion was that "in a stomach where eleven grains of arsenic were found and there was no inflammation, I should look for other causes of death."[21]

When Dr. Nichol had finished his testimony the clock was approaching half past six, so the court was adjourned for the day.

On the second day of the trial, the court convened at 9:30. The courtroom was again filled to capacity and expectations were high. There were only three witnesses for the defence remaining. The first to take the stand was Henry Belford, who was reeve of Brighton Township and a resident of the Orser neighbourhood, later called Mount Olivet, not far from Codrington. Mr. Belford testified that he had known the prisoner since about 1845, when the King family had moved to the area. He recalled that William King had taught at the schoolhouse across the road from his farm for four months before going to Normal School in Toronto. The witness then added, "I have formed a very high opinion of the prisoner's character. I have had frequent intercourse with him. He has always been an advocate of temperance and morality."[22]

Richard Delong was the next witness. He was the owner and operator of the Delong Railroad Hotel in Brighton, near the train station. Mr. Delong told the court that he had known Dr. King from the spring of 1858, when he began attending to his family as part of his medical practice. He and his family were very satisfied with Dr. King's treatments and considered him to be a competent doctor.

The third witness that was scheduled for the defence did not appear in court, so the evidence for the defence was closed.

TWENTY-ONE

CHARGE TO THE JURY

Judge Burns then took the floor. DeCourcey records that, "His Lordship in charging the jury remarked that the questions had been so fully laid before them by the learned counsel, that there remained but little for him to say, beyond reading the evidence, and making such few remarks as seemed necessary."[1] Then, quite to the contrary, he proceeded to say a good deal, quickly covering many disparate points.

He made note of Barker's testimony that the cork was not in the bottle until the second morning, when he took the pickle bottle to Kingston. He mentioned the fact that Professor Croft said there was little inflammation in the stomach, which might be positive for the prisoner, but that another medical witness suggested that inflammation might vary in different circumstances.

The judge commented on the testimony of Mrs. Lawson that, because she was the mother of the deceased, we might expect to be against the prisoner. It was the duty of the jury to see the facts confirmed by the testimony of other witnesses. Next, he addressed the suggestion that Sarah Ann King's death might have in any way been caused by the fall from the buggy. He said, "according to the mother, it affected her daughter very little, and she drove to Consecon the same day."[2] Judge Burns made a point of saying that it was important to "note the exact position of affairs"[3] regarding this issue because the defence had placed much stress on it.

He then took up the question of how Dr. King had pronounced so early in his wife's illness that she was in grave danger and would not likely survive her confinement. He said, "This was a strange remark for a husband to make to his wife."[4] Certainly, as her physician, he had a duty to his patient to apprise her of a dangerous condition. However, we also see that Dr. King told Sarah Rachel Young that his wife did not suit him in many respects and then he told Melinda Vandervoort in a letter that his wife had been so ill they thought she would die — several days before Sarah King's illness began.

Judge Burns then commented on a topic that many of us may be compelled to ask about. He said:

> The jury would remember King went to Vandervoort's, and remained, late at night, closeted with the girl. What passed on that occasion we know not. Neither party examined Melinda Vandervoort, or put any questions with respect to what had taken place, but the interview occurred.[5]

We may recall that Mr. Galt had provided some entertainment for the court when he dismissed Miss Vandervoort and read the letters aloud. It seems odd that he did not then examine her further regarding her discussions with Dr. King and the events of the flight to the Bate farm. Melinda got off rather light at the trial, it seems, and the judge made a point of this to the jury.

The next issue he addressed was the confusion around the arsenic and conflicting testimony given by the medical witnesses. After giving the different sides of the argument, Judge Burns said, "Reducing the whole question to as few points as possible, they would stand in this way. First, what was the primary cause of death?"[6] The trick was to consider whether the arsenic had been administered as a poison, with intent to harm the patient, or if it had been used as a medicine, under the theories of homeopathic practice. Arsenic was certainly found in the stomach of the deceased, so it was the duty of the jury to determine Dr. King's intent in administering the arsenic to his wife.

Then, the judge spoke about the attempts of the defence to suggest that the stomach Professor Croft received was not the stomach of the deceased, and that the arsenic had been inserted into it after death. There was the problem with inflammation not being as great as one expected, but he called this a minor issue. He found it interesting that the defence presented several scenarios regarding the cause of death, including the fall from the buggy and complications related to her pregnancy. Then, the jury must take into account the testimony of Constable Clarke, who told the court that Dr. King had said to him on the day of his arrest that he had poisoned his wife, but not with arsenic. It was up to the jury to sort through all of this.

On a completely different topic, Judge Burns noted, "The two attempts of the prisoner to escape must also be taken into account; but the jury must be careful not to take that as an absolute proof of guilt."[7] The judge was referring to Dr. King's flight to Cape Vincent as one attempt to escape and was likely including the rumours of a plot to break him out of jail, which would have been fresh in the minds of the members of the jury during the trial.

Judge Burns concluded his remarks by reminding the jury of their responsibilities to the prisoner and to society. They had to make sure the prisoner was not convicted "on mere suspicion … if they were convinced of his guilt, they must not raise any fanciful doubt in their own minds for the purpose of rendering a verdict of acquittal."[8] At the same time, he emphasized that "… society could not exist without a proper administration of the law."[9] If guilt was determined, they must enforce the law, and if not, they must acquit. His last words were, "might God assist them to come to a right conclusion."[10]

TWENTY-TWO

THE VERDICT AND THE SENTENCE

It was three o'clock in the afternoon before the jury retired to consider a verdict. They could not come to an agreement at that time so the jury was sequestered for the night. At ten o'clock the next morning, April 7, the jury returned to the court. They had reached a verdict.

The clerk of the court put the usual question to the jury: "How say you, gentlemen; is the prisoner guilty or not guilty?"[1]

DeCourcey describes the scene he witnessed. "The foreman, amidst most profound silence, returned a verdict of guilty, with a strong recommendation to mercy."[2]

The prisoner was the only person in the room who was shocked by the verdict. Dr. King lost his composure for the first time in all these days and months of incarceration and trial. Everyone could see that he struggled to keep himself under control as he was led away from the court, back to his cold, lonely cell.

At this time, the newspaper industry kicked into high gear. On April 9, *Port Hope Tri-Weekly Guide* published a huge block of columns containing all the details from the trial. On the front page, the editors explained the approach they had taken under very unusual circumstances.

> We did not issue a paper yesterday, as we were anxious to give the full account of the exciting trial, recently concluded, in one number. To day we publish a sheet and a half, which contains

the evidence, the speeches of the Counsel, and Judges charge complete. We are indebted to the *Globe* for the speeches and charge of the Judge. We took full notes of the evidence during the trial; but our Compositors availed themselves of the *Globe's* printed report of the evidence on the part of the prosecution, as it could be more rapidly set up than manuscript. The evidence on the part of the defence is as we took it down; and in some respects is slightly different from the *Globe's* report.[3]

The Guide then provides a generous paragraph in praise of Sheriff James Fortune for his efforts in managing the event of the trial at Cobourg courthouse.

The *Port Hope Weekly Guide* newspaper declined to print its normal paper on April 8, while the Dr. King trial was still ongoing, but on April 9 a blockbuster issue contained all the news. On the front page there was an article explaining how this issue of the paper came together in collaboration with the *Globe*. The article also praised the handling of the trial by Sherriff James Fortune, under extremely unusual circumstances. It is the page and a half of columns about the Dr. King Trial that are found in the newspapers on that day, and the same material made its way into the two accounts that were published after the hanging. *Port Hope Weekly Guide*, April 9, 1859.

The Weekly Guide

PORT HOPE, APRIL 9, 1859.

Dr. King's Trial.

We did not issue a paper yesterday, as we were anxious to give the full account of the exciting trial, recently concluded, in one number. To day we publish a sheet and a half, which contains the evidene, the speeches of the Counsel, and Judges charge complete. We are indebted to the *Globe* for the speeches and charge of the Judge. We took full notes of the evidence during the trial ; but our Compositors availed themselves of the *Globe's* printed report of the evidence on the part of the prosecution, as it could be more rapidly set up than manuscript. The evidence on the part of the defence is as we took it down ; and in some respects is slightly different from the *Globe's* report.

Too much praise cannot be given to Mr SHERIFF FORTUNE for the efficient manner in which he performed the difficult task of keeping the great crowd who could not gain access to the Court Room, in order and good nature. His arrangements were well and timely made, and thoroughly carried out by the staff of officers under him. It seemed perhaps hard to many who had travelled miles to be present at the trial to be shut out ; but as the multitude would have filled a room five times as large as the one in which the Court was held, it is obvious that no blame can be attached to Mr. Sheriff Fortune.

Northumberland County Archives, Cobourg, Ontario

Too much praise cannot be given to Mr. Sheriff Fortune for the efficient manner in which he performed the difficult task of keeping the great crowd who could not gain access to the Court Room, in order and good nature. His arrangements were well and timely made, and thoroughly carried out by the staff of officers under him. It seemed perhaps hard to many who had travelled miles to be present at the trial to be shut out; but as the multitude would have filled a room five times as large as the one in which the Court was held, it is obvious that no blame can be attached to Mr. Sheriff Fortune.[4]

Dr. King was back in the courtroom on the afternoon of Saturday, April 9 for sentencing. DeCourcey tells us that there was great anticipation in the packed courtroom due to the rumours going around that the prisoner was planning to speak before sentence was passed. He was brought up from his cell at about three o'clock and placed in the dock. "He was of an ashy paleness. The healthy color that ringed his cheeks during the trial was fled, and it seemed that the shadow of death had since his conviction prematurely settled upon his face."[5]

We must remember that Reuben DeCourcey, who was recording these events, had been a close friend of William King since the two were teenagers, so he knew the man well. His impressions of Dr. King at that moment were charged with emotion: "The confidence, almost superciliousness of manner which characterized him whilst listening to the witnesses for the prosecution and defence — had given way, and he seemed to fully realise the awful position in which he stood."[6]

Dr. King scanned the bar for his defence counsel, Mr. Cameron, but found that he was not present. This seemed to deflate him, and onlookers would later say that the absence of Mr. Cameron had a very negative impact on the prisoner.

After two other prisoners were sentenced to thirty days in jail for stealing wheat, Mr. Galt rose and addressed Judge Burns, "I move, my Lord that sentence be passed on William Henry King."[7]

Judge Burns addressed the prisoner, "William Henry King, you have been convicted of the crime of murder; what have you to say that sentence of death be not now passed upon you?"[8]

A profound hush fell over the courtroom. Dr. King, in a clear, firm voice, said, "I have this much to say, that upon my most solemn oath, I am not guilty of the charge laid against me. I have no doubt of this; my conscience is perfectly clear upon this point."[9]

After Dr. King had spoken, His Lordship was again the centre of attention for everyone in the courtroom. In a grave but even voice he performed his most solemn duty as judge of the Spring Assizes for Northumberland County. He spoke directly to the prisoner, not with sympathy but with concern for the journey this man was to take in the next weeks. The courtroom was silent in anticipation of his words.

He began by stating that the prisoner had been afforded the benefit of "a fair and impartial trial by an intelligent jury,"[10] and had been assisted by able counsel.

Close of the Assizes.

SENTENCE OF DEATH PASSED ON DR. KING.

On Saturday afternoon, the Cobourg Spring Assizes terminated. It being understood that Dr. King was to receive his sentence, and a rumour having obtained extensive circulation that the prisoner intended to speak before sentence was passed upon him, the Court Room was crowded in every part. About 3 o'clock he was brought up from the cell in which he has been so long confined, and placed in the Dock. He was of an ashy paleness. The healthy color that tinged his cheeks during the trial was fled; and it seemed that the shadow of death had since his conviction by the Jury prematurely settled upon his face. The confidence, almost superciliousness of manner which characterized him whilst listening to the witnesses for the prosecution and defense—had given way, and he seemed to fully realize the awful po-
  in which   ood. He walked into the

Northumberland County Archives, Cobourg, Ontario

The heading was "Close of the Assizes," but the attention of the public was focused on the sentencing of Dr. King. The article in the *Port Hope Weekly Guide* on April 12, 1859, described for its readers the much-altered manner and appearance of the man who had been so confident and even arrogant. *Port Hope Weekly Guide*, April 12, 1859.

After all that, and in spite of the benefit of the doubt always being in favour of the prisoner, the jury had brought down a verdict of guilty. The judge made clear that he agreed wholeheartedly with the verdict and felt that, in light of all the information, "they could not conscientiously do otherwise."[11]

Judge Burns then said:

The finding of the jury was accompanied by a recommendation to mercy. It is not in my power to avert from you the punishment which the law inflicts upon those who are convicted of the crime laid to your charge. I will not fail, however, to forward the recommendation to mercy to the proper quarter; but I must say plainly that I cannot add the weight of my position to it.[12]

The judge was not only unwilling to consider any mercy in the case of Dr. King, but he tried very hard to dissuade the prisoner from having any allusions that a higher power might step in to lessen his punishment. He added with emphasis, "I am thus plain that you may know your exact position, and how little reason there is to hope for the influence of the Executive in your behalf."[13]

The judge then turned to the spiritual well-being of the prisoner: "You are, as I said before, a man of education; and it is not necessary for me to advise you to make an early application at the Throne of God for the forgiveness of your sins, as a preparation to meet your God."[14]

Judge Burns had one final duty to perform. He looked directly at the prisoner and said:

> It now only remains for me to pass the sentence of the court upon you, that you be confined in the Common Jail until Thursday, the 9th day of June next, on which day you are to be taken to the place of execution, and there hanged by the neck until you are dead. And may the Lord have mercy on your soul.[15]

Dr. King had maintained a high degree of composure during the remarks of the judge and the reading of the sentence. However, "in a few seconds after His Lordship ceased speaking, the condemned man's lip quivered, and burying his face in his handkerchief he wept convulsively."[16]

The account that comes down to us from that moment is eloquent:

> One by one, props on which he had relied were knocked from under him, the Judge had extinguished the last ray of hope. An ignominious death stared him in the face; from it there

was no escape. He had assumed a calmness and a confidence that he did not feel. But nothing now was to be gained by deception. Human nature resumes its sway; and the man of strong will wept. Better so than that he went to his dungeon unmoved. It gives grounds for the belief that his heart is not so seared that repentance is impossible or improbable.[17]

TWENTY-THREE

UNFORTUNATE MAN

William Henry King was sentenced to hang on June 9, 1859. Immediately after the sentence was passed down, the authorities in Cobourg began to make arrangements to deal with the prisoner during the two months leading up to the hanging. They had never executed a man in Northumberland County so there was little in the way of precedent for them to follow, at least locally. We can expect that they took instruction from the appropriate experts in Toronto who knew what to do. Of course, everyone wanted a *good* hanging.

We can see from their actions that there were two priorities established right away. One was to make sure the prisoner did not escape. This may seem like a given for us, but in the 1850s prisoners escaped from jail more than occasionally. The high degree of public interest generated by the crime, then the trial, and now the prospect of a hanging was not lost on the authorities.

As the account says, "Mr. Bennett, the Jailer, took Dr. King from amongst the other prisoners and put him in an apartment alone, south side of the jail, underground." The "Mr. Bennett" mentioned here was Glover Bennett, who had been the "Gaoler" at Cobourg for many years and would hold that post until his death in 1875. He and his family lived in an apartment in the jail, which included the services of three servants. The jailer lived on the premises so he could keep a very close watch on all the inmates. He would watch Dr. King more closely than any other prisoner for the next two months.

The isolated location of the prisoner was a good start, but another important step was taken. A constable was assigned to the prisoner. His name was Alexander Stewart and he was to be a constant companion for Dr. King until the hanging. He would sleep in the cell beside him, get up when he got up, and go to bed when he went to bed. He would act as the gatekeeper for the prisoner, in cooperation with Glover Bennett, the jailer, and James Fortune, who was the sheriff of Northumberland County.

As it turned out, besides filling his role as Dr. King's companion and gatekeeper, Alexander Stewart took it upon himself to keep a daily journal of his time with Dr. King. At first it was a brief record of who visited and how Dr. King was feeling. However, as the days past, the two men bonded in the manner of captor and captive. They talked every day and shared prayer sessions and discussions with clergymen. As the weeks passed, Stewart's entries became longer and more expressive, punctuated by interesting insights into Dr. King's frame of mind and struggle of conscience. It makes for fascinating reading.

The other condition that needed to be met in order to have a *good* hanging was to have a prisoner who behaved himself on the scaffold. You could not have a prisoner come onto the scaffold and blubber about how innocent he was. That just wouldn't do. For Dr. King this would be a tall order. In the first weeks after sentencing the prisoner was very depressed, constantly moaning to nobody in particular, "O what an unfortunate man I have been!"

There was an important job to do with the prisoner, which was both spiritual and institutional. There was a very strong sense in the world of the 1850s that even a criminal such as Dr. King was capable of repentance and absolution. The religious men of the community looked at this situation as an opportunity to apply their considerable resources to make sure Dr. King confessed his sins before he went to the gallows. It would be a glorious victory for the established churches to have him fall into line with their wishes and do so publicly. On the first day of his job as Dr. King's cellmate, Alexander Stewart ends his journal entry by saying, "I sleep in a cell next to Dr., thought it was a dreary place." Indeed. And there would be many more dreary days in this place before June 9.

TWENTY-FOUR

VISITORS AND STRUGGLES OF CONSCIENCE

On the second day, Friday, April 15, Stewart tells us that Dr. King rose around six and said that he had rested badly that night. He asked if he could see his mother, adding, "If I am executed, it will bring my mother to her grave." Later in the morning, Sheriff Fortune came to Dr. King's cell to tell him two things. First, he granted the request that Dr. King could see his mother. Second, he made it very clear that "there was no hope of a commutation of his sentence." This last point was made forcefully and repeatedly. The prisoner needed to understand that this was the endgame and he had to prepare himself for it. For the time being, the prisoner was not convinced.

Around eleven o'clock, Reverend Levi Vanderburg came to see Dr. King, the first of many visits from clergymen and ministers that Alexander Stewart would record over the next two months. Reverend Vanderburg was beginning a difficult journey that would take both he and Dr. King through weeks of emotional and spiritual turmoil. Reverend Vanderburg appears to have been the King family minister at Codrington, and he took charge of the spiritual life of the prisoner, making it his priority to see him through, including the unhappy tasks of accompanying the prisoner to the gallows and conducting the funeral service.

Reverend Vanderburg would visit Dr. King almost every day until the hanging. Alexander Stewart was thorough in listing everyone who visited each day; the records show that Reverend Vanderburg missed visiting Dr. King only five days out of the whole two months until the hanging. When he came, he would spend extended periods of time with Dr. King, talking and praying, and reading the bible. Stewart tells us on this first day that "Mr. Vanderburg, Wesleyan Minister, came in to see him, stayed with him three or four hours, talking faithfully with him, and prayed with him." After he was gone, Reverend Bredin came in for a short visit. The pattern of prayer and reflection was set for the daily routine of the following months, which would work diligently to develop Dr. King's mind to the point where he was comfortable with admitting his guilt and was satisfied he would attain salvation.

On Saturday the sixteenth Dr. King again asked for his mother after rising, this time saying "could she stay with me all the time how I would like it." On this morning, Dr. King received one of the most distinguished men who would grace his dreary cell. Dr. Norman Bethune was a professor of medicine in Toronto, who would later be known as the grandfather of Dr. Norman Bethune, the famous Canadian missionary and doctor in Spain and China in the early 1900s. Dr. Bethune had testified at the trial and he would play a significant role in Dr. King's spiritual development.

Dr. Beatty also came in that day, followed by Reverend Vanderburg, who spent the entire afternoon with Dr. King. Alexander Stewart recorded that "Mr. Vanderburg prayed before leaving, an excellent prayer, after prayer Dr. King wept profusely.... I talked with him in the evening on the promises of the Gospels. Dr. believed all I said but complained of a want of genuine faith, read and prayed with him." Even this early in the process, Alexander Stewart was starting to participate by assisting the prisoner when he found him in distress.

Sundays were marked with particular reverence and prayer during the next weeks. Stewart recorded that on this first Sunday of his own journey with Dr. King, after morning prayers, the prisoner "seemed very penitent ... paid great attention" while Stewart read from the gospel of Ezekiel, both men agreed that it was an excellent book. Reverend Vanderburg again spent most of the afternoon with the prisoner, Stewart recording that Dr. King was "... fond of Vanderburg, speaks highly of him."

On the eighteenth we see the normal visits from men of the cloth, along with a tantalizing entry that says, "After dinner a schoolmaster, a relative to Dr. called to see him about 4 o'clock." It is not clear who this relative might have been, but he does not appear to be mentioned again as a visitor. Dr. King also received a letter from J.R. Clarke on this day, probably related to the attempts by his defence team to obtain a commutation of the death sentence. Stewart does not comment further.

TWENTY-FIVE

MUST LOOK TO GOD

The next day Stewart noticed that Dr. King "prayed earnestly and penitently for mercy and forgiveness," and that later in the day, after the regular visits from Reverend Vanderburg and others, he seemed "more composed and confident in God's mercy, a fine day."

Outside the jail, people were talking about Dr. King. An article in the *Port Hope Weekly Guide* on April 19 denied the rumours that Dr. King had attempted to escape and went on to hope that the ongoing visits by clergymen would convince Dr. King to give up his insistence that executive clemency was possible. In these early days after the conviction and sentencing, he was still persisting in his innocence, telling anyone who would listen about all the flattering letters he had received from important people in the U.S. as well as Canada.

On the twentieth, Alexander Stewart took two hours to go home, but was back in time to see "Dr.'s uncle and cousin in to see him told him of bad success of his petition in Percy and Seymour." There is no other mention of this petition, but it appears from this that some relatives had distributed a petition he made up to see if they could gather enough signatures to persuade the powers that be to commute his death sentence. This must have been disheartening, to be rejected by his neighbours.

Who were this uncle and cousin? It is very tantalizing to speculate from a family history standpoint, since we do not know for sure who George

King's parents were. An uncle of Dr. King would be a brother of his father. There is strong evidence that George King's surname had been Leroy before he came to Upper Canada in the 1820s. This uncle and cousin could have been some of Dr. King's Leroy relatives from the U.S. We should keep this in mind for later.

The rejection of his petitions seemed to hit home more forcefully the next morning when Stewart records that Dr. King "seemed to feel bad that all the world was against him … seems nothing for me but execution." Later in the day, the two men discussed the case and Dr. King insisted that his wife had not died of arsenic poisoning. Then, after spending another couple of hours with Rev. Vanderburg, Dr. King said "he must look to God, as he expected little from man."

April 22 was Good Friday, and Alexander Stewart began his journal by recording that the jailer opened their cell doors at six o'clock "and brought in our usual quota of bread, being a 4 lb loaf each day." Dr. King seemed initially hopeful as he sent another petition out of the jail with a prisoner whose time had run out. However, he soon became morose, saying "This is Good Friday, it will be the last I'll ever see," sighed deeply, said he felt worse last night than he had ever felt: "O, that it could be undone, I believe that I did wrong, I have ruined my father for life."

Dr. King.

A rumour that King had attempted to escape from the Jail has been current in Town for some days. The report has no foundation in fact. He is visited daily by clergymen of various denominations who take an interest in his spiritual welfare. Archdeacon Bethune was with him last week, and we understand that his attempts to awaken the better feelings of his nature were not altogether fruitless. He still persists in his declarations of innocence ; and shows those who call upon him the flattering letters he has received since his incarceration, from men of position in Canada and the United States. There is not the slightest reason to believe that the Executive clemency will be exercised in his case, and this fact the clergymen impress upon his mind.

The *Port Hope Weekly Guide* of April 19, 1859, contained a small article with Dr. King's name as the title, which was sure to draw immediate attention only ten days after the sentencing. The article puts an end to rumours of escape that were about town and expressed the hope that all the visits from clergymen might cause him to face his guilt, but it was early yet.

In the afternoon, J.R. Clarke called to follow up on his letter and confirmed to Dr. King that there was no chance of commutation of the death penalty. Two other ministers, Reverend Earl and Murpee visited this day, along with the faithful Vanderburg, who read and prayed with Dr. King and Alexander Stewart until dusk.

The routine developed that the prisoner would bathe on Saturday mornings, shortly after breakfast and prayers. Dr. King expected to see his mother on Saturday the twenty-third, but was disappointed when she did not appear. The prisoner was feeling very low now, lamenting that the white blanket of snow he could see from his cell window was the last he would ever see. He was in and out of his cell several times during the day, praying for extended periods of time, and more than once wept profusely. Stewart records that he said, "O that my life could be spared, must be hanged, what disgrace it will bring on my parents, O will God hear my prayers, how awful if my soul be lost."

Another Lord's Day dawned with snow and frost on the ground, with Dr. King continuing to lament its presence as a reminder of the short time he had left. He spoke of hearing, during prayers that night, someone telling him that he might be reprieved. Stewart sees that "Dr. seemed cheerful for a time." However, later in the day, "Dr. very sad, still clinging to hopes of a reprieve." Reverend Vanderburg was there for one of his regular visits and, seeing this frame of mind, he used some very strong, plain language with Dr. King, followed by more prayer.

The next day was more of the same. Stewart walked and prayed with the prisoner for a time in the morning; then, Reverend Vanderberg was there again, staying while Stewart went home for three or four hours. Even the jailer, Glover Bennett, joined in the job of moving Dr. King along — when he came to lock up that day, he talked with Dr. King and Stewart for a while, then he told the doctor. "to make up his peace with God and prepare for the worst and if he had peace with God he would have no fear of death. Dr. said that was his daily prayer." Everybody was getting into the act.

On Tuesday the twenty-sixth, Dr. King had a visit from another distinguished churchman, Bishop Smith, who "talked very kindly and plain to him for about an hour; he told him that all manner of sin and blasphemy should be forgiven unto men … urging Dr. King to seek salvation as it was attainable even to him." Dr. Beatty and Dr. Powell visited and gave him a book about "Bishop Taylor's holy living and dying."

The mood on the following day was improved for a time, as Dr. King received three letters from the United States and then spent some time answering them. Stewart went home for three hours and when back in the jail seems to have felt philosophical. He writes about his subject: "He never looks at a newspaper or talks about the world, but seems deeply serious and concerned for his soul's salvation, but truly it is a bitter cup to drink, the cup of true penitence."

TWENTY-SIX

HE CAN PRAY LIKE A MINISTER

Thursday the twenty-eighth began with a loud commotion in the cells opposite Dr. King, where another prisoner was causing a disturbance. Stewart comments that this sort of prisoner should have been taken to an asylum instead of the common jail. He notes that on this day "The Dr. read and prayed, he can pray like a minister, I followed and enjoyed sweet peace, praise God." It seems that Alexander Stewart was becoming more personally engaged in his duties with his neighbour cellmate. Dr. King had expected to see his mother this day but was disappointed when she did not appear. He ended the day by writing a letter to his father.

Stewart also records an event that happened outside the jail. Dr. King and much of North America had been following the trial of Daniel Sickles, a U.S. senator who had murdered a man for indiscretions with his wife. Extensive columns appeared in the *Globe*, providing a hungry public with all the salacious details. One of these columns included the sentencing of Dr. King in Cobourg, just below the Sickles article. On this day, April 28, Mr. Sickles was found not guilty of murder due to the circumstances related to his wife. Stewart records, "We heard that Sickles was acquitted, the Dr. felt bad, and said why can't I be freed also, bemoaning his sad condition greatly." All night the commotion continued in the cell nearby.

The next morning Dr. King complained that he had not slept well, fretting over the news of the Sickles trial, which he could not help comparing to his own. Reverend Vanderburg was back again, and Stewart went out for a short time, returning to find the prisoner in fairly good spirits. He explains that "Rev. Mr. Vanderburg takes great pains to instruct and comfort the Dr.'s mind, almost every day the Lord rewards him in these endeavours to save a soul from death, and thus hide a multitude of sins."

Saturday meant another welcome bath day for the prisoner. On this day, Alexander Stewart would comment randomly about some of the foibles and habits of Dr. King that he had learned after living in close quarters with him for several weeks. He had learned that Dr. King slept more soundly during the wee hours of the morning. It also appeared that the prisoner relished prayers after breakfast because his language was more earnest and penitent. Dr. Bethune visited again and "talked very faithfully and affectionately to him, gave him good sound advice then prayed with him, left him a programme of daily exercises and prayers to be used by him." Reverend Vanderburg was in again as well. Activity in the jail was worth recording this day: "Three prisoners put in today — one for peddling obscene books, one for stealing flour, and one named John Farreli, from Chicago, for robbery."

The first day of May was another Lords Day, but the spirits of Alexander Stewart were not buoyed by the change in calendar. He begins his journal entry with some mournful thoughts:

> Now summer returns after a long and tedious Canadian winter; but summer and winter are alike here — no vegetation here — no buds or blossoms — no balmy zephyrs or odoriferous breezes, but on the contrary, gloomy walls — barred and grated windows, iron doors, and arched stone canopy over our head — surely this place is not made to entertain beings but demons or the worst malefactor, then we must lie in iron beds and tho' lying alone are not alone; as bad as we are, we are not allowed on this hallowed day to get out to hear God's word preached nor enjoy the softening and civilizing influence of female society, no! the law sternly demands justice to be executed on the offender, but no mercy.

The gloom was accentuated by the arrival of two letters from Dr. King's brother, Isaac, who was in California. The prisoner said, "My poor Isaac, how it will wound your heart, you need to feel so proud of me, now how fallen." Stewart records that "after tea, Mr. V., the Dr. and myself all engaged alternatively in prayer trusting God was with us."

Monday, May 2 was one of the very few days there were no visitors for Dr. King. He had expected his father to come but he did not arrive. More prayer and Alexander Stewart found Dr. King to be feeling sad. He also mentions that a prisoner named John Farreli had escaped from the jail that day. This was the robbery suspect who was arrested on April 30, an episode that provides a backdrop for the Dr. King story. It clearly demonstrates that escape from the Cobourg jail was not unknown and was likely a serious concern of the authorities at the time Dr. King was incarcerated there.

Tuesday was more active. The English curate, Reverend James, came in and "talked with him, he told him he need not build himself up on any false hope of commutation of his sentence as he believed there would be no change." Instead, he urged the prisoner "earnestly to prepare for death as time is on the wing, and the 9th of June was daily getting nearer." After this encounter, "the Doctor felt very bad, and wept bitterly, he was very sad and sorrowful a long time." Reverend Vanderburg came in, as well as Mr. Hughes and Glover Bennett, the jailer, which seemed to cause the Doctor to cheer up a little.

On the morning of the fourth, Dr. King was still very sad, but this day would be monumental for the prisoner. At long last, his mother was to visit! She came in the afternoon, driven from Codrington by Charles King, William's brother, next oldest after Isaac. Stewart records that Henrietta King was "in with him alone about two hours, she gave him some very good advice." He also spoke with his brother through the iron door, "told him to be a good boy, obey his parents, keep the Sabbath, and never do anything wrong." After his mother went away "Dr. wept and sobbed violently; said he would never see his mother but once again."

The gloom lifted a bit on Thursday, the fifth, as the warmth of spring was enjoyed by the other prisoners who were let out for the first time to enjoy the fresh air. Reverend T. Alexander came from Percy Township to speak with Dr. King. Reverend Alexander stayed for a time and "explained to us the 51st Psalm; a favourite Psalm here with us; it seemed as if the Psalmist had just penned it to meet our case." Dr. King wrote a letter to his brother Isaac in California — a difficult task under the circumstances.

May 6 is the only day that Alexander Stewart specifically records in his journal that nothing happened that was worth reporting, even though Dr. King sent a letter to his brother Isaac and Dr. Bethune visited. On this uneventful day, Stewart feels compelled to record that the prisoner is constantly seeking Christ.

TWENTY-SEVEN

NO MERCY FROM MEN

Saturday brought the weekly bathing after breakfast. Alexander Stewart witnessed a very emotional outburst by Dr. King:

> … he engaged with much feeling and earnestness, felt very sad forenoon evidently deep conviction of sin. Said the way of transgressors is hard said I am a great sinner, the chief of sinners, was almost despairing of God's mercy, said he was willing to give him to Christ, but could not feel that God had accepted him.

Reverend Vanderburg had gone to Toronto the day before and came back with some very sobering news. He had seen the governor and had exhausted all possibility of hope for the prisoner. The journal says that Reverend Vanderburg was "out of all hope of Dr. being reprieved," and on hearing this news, Dr. King "cried and wept sore. Said, I must see mercy from God, I see will get no mercy from men." This was an intense, all-day session, and Stewart tells us that "towards evening, Dr. more composed, me home two hours." On lockup at seven o'clock, Dr. King was heard to lament about the fact that Sickles was acquitted but he was going to hang. It just didn't seem fair!

Another Lord's Day arrived. Dr. King confided to his cellmate that he had a bad night and was feeling sad and dejected. Later, "Dr. said he had but few more Sabbath's to live, very melancholy today."

Now we can see that Alexander Stewart takes his job as custodian of the prisoner to another level. He is distressed at the plight of the prisoner and tries to explain it, as much to himself as to anyone else. He writes: "He still looked upon God as an angry judge, did not yet see him as a God reconciled in Christ. Told him I thought any sinner who sincerely repented of sin and earnestly sought forgiveness could not be lost." Dr. King replied that he "wanted to make sure his sins forgiven before he went to the scaffold."

After evening prayers and some Psalm reading, "We then both engaged earnestly in prayer. I trust God heard us and will answer our prayers in his own good time. Lord grant that this the time of our extremity may be the time of thy opportunity. Lord save us for thy name and for his mercies sake. Lord increase our faith." The way Stewart records these intensive prayer sessions suggests that he is walking the path with the prisoner, struggling to find salvation and to gain peace of mind in this dire situation. We might imagine how much of a life-changing event this was for Constable Stewart, being thrust into the cell beside a convicted murder.

On the ninth of May, Dr. King was able to muse that half of his time remaining on earth was now gone. He had one more month before his walk to the gallows. Stewart watched as Dr. King walked in the hall between the cells, obviously deep in thought and occasionally emitting deep, mournful sighs. He prayed, "Lord have mercy on him and heal his wounded spirit for Jesus sake."

Tuesday the tenth seemed to bring a sea change. On rising, Dr. King was in much better spirits, telling Stewart "he felt confident that God would forgive his sins, in praying last night he said he felt more liberty." Three prisoners were being let out of jail and Dr. King spoke to them through his door, bidding them farewell and giving them advice. "Farewell, Tom, I'll never see you any more, you will now taste the sweets of liberty denied to me…. Tom was like a brother, said he was greatly reformed since his confinement here, I have become a praying man."

A different visitor came on this day. Reverend William Bleasdell, an Anglican Minister from Trenton, sat with Dr. King for about two hours, after which Dr. King was "greatly cheered and encouraged … he had done him more good than any who had called to see him." Reverend

Bleasdell had a special knowledge of William Henry King and the King family because he was the minister who, in two sessions in 1852 and 1853, had baptized all of the King children. In hindsight, it seems a rather extravagant project. On June 30, 1852, George and Henrietta King had taken their five older children from Codrington all the way to St. John's Anglican Church in Carrying Place, which was part of the Trenton Anglican Diocese. Reverend Bleasdell baptized the five oldest children on that day. Then, on November 8, 1853, William Henry King and his sister Mary Louisa took the five smallest children on the same trip to have them baptized by Reverend Bleasdell as well. We might expect that the reverend, when he heard of the plight of one of his former flock, felt the need to participate, it seems to very good effect.

Stewart's evaluation of the prisoner at the end of this day was that he was not yet fully "restored to liberty, not yet adopted into God's family, but is I believe an earnest enquirer … Dr. a little more cheerful." which was comforting to the constable.

On Wednesday morning, mild, fresh air came flooding into the dank, stuffy cells when the jailer removed an outside window. This lightened the mood for a time but Stewart still describes the prisoner as being very sad, spending the day walking in the hall and praying as usual. There was much anticipation of Reverend Vanderburg's visit this day, seemingly because he valued Reverend Vanderburg's support and encouragement very highly.

It is at this point in the journal that Stewart further reflects on the days and weeks he had spent in such close quarters with the prisoner:

> Poor Dr., thy countenance indicates that deep sorrow and anguish have their lodgement in thy sad heart, yet what a noble mind thou hast, splendid talent far above mediocrity and a more generous heart never possessed a human breast. How unfortunate thou hast been "a brother born for adversity."

TWENTY-EIGHT

MY HEART, DEAR DOCTOR, BLEEDS FOR THEE

The next day Alexander Stewart continued to empathize with Dr. King:

> Poor Doctor; what anguish and sorrow inherits thy torn bosom; many, many a heavy sigh heaves thy tortured breast. How true, "the way of transgressors is hard"; yes, hard — it is hard work to repent and find forgiveness with an offended God. My heart, dear doctor, bleeds for thee. I may pity and pray for thee, but cannot effectually help thee. May God, whom thou hast offended by thy sin, when he has wounded thee by his Holy Spirit, heal thee by enabling thee to look to Jesus, by whose stripes we are healed.

The reader should be reminded by the lines of Alexander Stewart's journal that there were layers of intense activity engaged in this spiritual journey. Of course, Dr. King himself was struggling with his own salvation, and that was tough work. But the legal and religious communities were orchestrating the process, applying all the resources they could muster to have the maximum impact on the mind of the prisoner. For the legal authorities, a successful hanging would include a large crowd to witness the gruesome event, along with a docile and calm prisoner, who would not only make no fuss while going to the gallows, but would express high words that would impress on the minds of the public that justice was being done and that all was right with the world.

The religious community saw a hanging, as rare as it was, as an opportunity to demonstrate to the wider public that they could, with their methods of persuasion and teaching, move a sinful man to renounce his sins and make his peace with God before being hanged. This would be a great accomplishment, conducted in the broad public sphere, made even more satisfying by the nature of this man and his high level of intelligence and communication skills. In fact, they looked to Dr. King to do some of their job for them. The right words from the right man standing up on that platform would have a profound impact on the public.

On Friday, May 13, Stewart records that the jailer, Glover Bennett, returned to Cobourg after taking John Farreli, the robbery suspect and escapee, back to be tried in his home state. The authorities in Cobourg must have been very happy to be rid of that fellow!

Dr. King was in low spirits again this day, with many deep sighs and complaining of a headache. Reverend Vanderburg visited, as well as Mr. Salmon. Later in the day, Stewart records that "he told me he had more confidence in God's mercy now than ever."

The last words Alexander Stewart provides in his journal entry for this day are: "Jailor made some fuss about prisoner breaking jail." A week later, in the *Port Hope Weekly Guide* newspaper of May 19, we see a small item, which reads "Dr. King — A rumour that King had attempted to escape from the Jail has been current in Town for some days. The report has no foundation in fact."[1] For this to be in the newspaper a week or so later suggests that there was talk about a jail break around the thirteenth when Mr. Bennett, the jailer, is heard by Alexander Stewart to make a fuss about it. Despite the reporting, it seems that nothing significant happened.

Saturday the fourteenth brought the prisoner to contemplate and lament his fate in a somewhat more tangible way. "I will soon, said he, be in an eternity of misery or bliss, but the thought of the Gallows, oh! oh! oh! to be hanged by the neck, how dreadful the thought. If it was to die naturally I would give up at once into God's hands; but oh! the gallows! the gallows!" On a more positive note, Mr. Bennett brought the prisoner and his cellmate some meat and potatoes, certainly a treat inside the common jail. Reverend Vanderburg was there again and spent considerable time with Dr. King, praying, talking, and weeping. Dr. King made it clear that if his soul was saved it would be due largely to Reverend Vanderburg's efforts. Before retiring for the night, the doctor told Stewart, "It is a great mercy if God saves a sinner like me, and I believe he *will* save me."

The Lord's Day was filled with fasting and prayer, with the men "resolved to seek God till we find him." Stewart chides himself: "Satan busy with us, tempting me with sleepiness."

The next day, the sixteenth, we find Alexander Stewart expressing more sentiment regarding his assumed role as amateur clergyman in support of the prisoner's struggle toward salvation. He starts with: "During the past week the Dr. has passed through a painful ordeal, his convictions of sin very deep and pungent … oh! how terrible the upbraidings of a guilty conscience, terrible indeed, as he paced the hall, the very picture of remorse and despair." Later in the day, Dr. King said, "On the 9th June, I will bid farewell to Cobourg," and, more to the point for Mr. Stewart, "I hope Stewart you will represent my character in a true light after I am gone."

We don't know if Alexander Stewart expected to write an account of the King trial and hanging when he was assigned to live in a cell beside the convicted murderer for two months. However, we can see the development of his feelings for the prisoner and his situation as he records the events in his journal, day by day, evolving a greater sensitivity to the anguish and distress of his cellmate. It is easy to be cynical and say he merely wanted to cash in on his strategic position, but it seems it would be unfair to the man if we did not recognize his intense emotional journey with Dr. King over those weeks. Dr. King's direct entreaty on the point of representing him after he was gone must have hit home very deeply at that moment for Mr. Stewart.

On Wednesday, May 17, Dr. King received two letters. One was from his father and the other was from Rock, a man who had been charged with murder in Belleville and would be hanged on June 13. He very much appreciated both letters. On this day, Stewart finds the doctor writing most of the afternoon, until Reverend Vanderburg arrived around four o'clock.

Dr. King had a good night, and on the morning of the eighteenth Stewart records that "Dr. rose in good spirits this morning, when praying in his cell last night he felt more happy than ever he had yet done, felt now assured that God *would* save his soul." He spent part of the afternoon writing, Stewart believed to the judge. The prisoner said to his cellmate at one point, "How terrible that moment when the trap will give way under my feet on the scaffold."

The sheriff and some officers came in during the next day to announce that they were preparing to build the gallows and there was discussion about the procedures for that fateful day. Alexander Stewart noted that it was "only 3 weeks today till the fatal 9th of June — then my dear doctor must be led forth to the scene of execution, how painful the thought." For his part, the doctor was reaching back to see what he might have done differently. "Dr. walked the hall, sighing deeply, said 'Oh I wish I had never married … If I had never married how much better it would have been for me and for my parents.'" Reverend Vanderburg came up to see Dr. King and they spent two hours talking and praying. Stewart records: "We opened the Bible at 1 cor 2, 12, the Dr. read the passage, rejoiced, said 'now I know God will save me, will take me to heaven, the Sheriff may get the gallows ready.'"

TWENTY-NINE

SALVATION AND CONFESSION

It was beginning to look like a corner had been turned in the struggle for a sense of salvation. On May 20, Stewart records with obvious joy, "Dr. happy now in the love of God, he has cast all his sins behind his back into the depths of the sea, and blotted them out of the Book of remembrance. Bless be God! Praised be his holy name, now his arrow is turned into joy." Dr. Bethune came in this morning and engaged Dr. King in prayer, which seemed to make Dr. King very happy. In the afternoon Dr. King was writing again, this time to Mr. Cameron, his defence counsel. Reverend Vanderburg came in and "talked and prayed with us, we all engaged, Dr. more cheerful tonight, spoke of his confession being published in the *Star*." Stewart adds that last bit with no comment, although we might expect it caused some alarm and consternation around the doctor's cell. After all, he had been doing a lot of writing.

On May 21, Alexander Stewart begins his journal entry with an important revelation. "Learned last night that Dr. had made a full confession of his guilt to Mr. Vanderburg, he said he had embosomed all to God and man, Dr. had attained to more peace of mind since his confession than formerly, he in my opinion, ought to have done so weeks ago." No doubt most of the churchmen who had been visiting the prisoner would wholeheartedly agree with Stewart on this.

However, a different kind of confession was in the works on this day, which was a bit different from the personal one to Reverend Vanderburg. Stewart records, "Dr. writing his confession to the *Globe* for publication, sent off 13 pages full sheet by mail tonight, the remainder to be sent Monday." Apparently all of this confessing had a good effect on the prisoner as his cellmate reports at the end of the day, "Dr. in pretty good spirits today, at prayer to night expressed himself with confidence and hope in God's mercy."

At this time, Reverend Levi Vanderburg added his voice to the public excitement about Dr. King's case. On May 21, a letter by Reverend Vanderburg appeared in the *Port Hope Weekly Guide*, having been originally written to the *Cobourg Star*. He begins:

> Dear Sir, The *Sun* of last week contained a statement in relation to Dr. King and myself, which is so much at variance with facts, that I think it only due to the unfortunate convict publicly to contradict it, and, at the same time, afford some explanation of the real facts of the case.[1]

Reverend Vanderburg was concerned about the report that Dr. King had "doggedly maintained his innocence,"[2] which was not true. He also took exception to the wording used to describe how the doctor had "settled down into a complete melancholy"[3] after the final denial from the judge regarding commutation. All of this was "wholly unauthorized and destitute of any authentic foundation."[4] Having said this, Reverend Vanderburg states that Dr. King only recently made "a full confession of his guilt as a means of obtaining the pardon of his sins."[5] This event had not happened spontaneously, it seems, as Reverend Vanderburg says that they had "appointed the following day (Sunday) as a suitable one for the purpose."[6] One can comment as to the usefulness of this public airing of the prisoner's spiritual journey, but it was important enough to occupy a column in the newspaper and was obviously serious enough in the mind of Reverend Vanderburg to warrant a letter.

The Lord's Day opened with Dr. King bemoaning the fact that he had only two more Sabbath Days to enjoy on earth, but would have many more Sabbaths in Heaven. After prayers with Reverend Bethune, Dr. King was heard to say, "I feel I am going to heaven, I feel a dreadful load taken off my shoulders." Then, Stewart records, Reverend Bredin and Reverend Vanderburg "conversed with us, prayed, and administered the sacrament to Dr. and all of us, true it was a blessed season to our souls." Reverend Vanderburg was preaching upstairs in the jail in the evening and "Dr. sat by window and heard most of the sermon, said 'O what would I give to have my liberty again and go to hear sermons.'"

Monday the twenty-third was industrious, as Dr. King "continued writing his manuscript today, nearly all day, wrote altogether thirty-one pages large sheets, sent it off to the *Globe* by mail tonight." The prisoner's frame of mind continued on a positive trend, as Stewart records: "Dr. is in good spirits today, more cheerful than I have seen him yet." Reverends Hooper and Vanderburg were in to visit this day as well.

The manuscript that Dr. King was writing and sending off in the post turned out to be a seven thousand-word confession. Most would call it a verbose and crude attempt at self-justification. He employs seven thousand fine words trying to convince us that he is not really a bad fellow, that he murdered his wife because of the temptation of an attractive woman. A modern characterization of his message is *The Devil made me do it!* Somehow, the doctor does not fit the role of victim, but you wouldn't know it by reading his confession. We don't know what he said to Reverend Vanderburg as a confession, but it is unlikely the good reverend would have accepted, in a personal confession to his spiritual advisor, the kind of lies, half-truths, and shifting of blame that make up the written confession. Frankly, reading this document causes the blood pressure to rise! It would be almost comical if it was not so sad.

The queen's birthday was celebrated in Cobourg on this day, and a band marched past the jail, playing as they went. Dr. King was much affected by this, saying "O that I had my liberty again, I would like to give them a speech, I would tell them of the sweets of liberty, what an unfortunate man I have been. O that I had never sinned." Reverend Thompson of Napanee and a Mr. Lucas came to visit. Dr. King told them "he believed there was no hope of reprieve for him, not the least." The prisoner also walked the halls a good deal on this day, saying that the exercise was good for his health.

On Wednesday the twenty-fifth, Dr. King received a letter he had been expecting from his defence counsel, Mr. Cameron. The news was not good. Mr. Cameron said that he had been to see both the governor and the judge, but they insisted that there would be no alteration of the sentence. To enhance the gloom, carpenters began measuring the grounds outside the courthouse for the building of the gallows. When Alexander Stewart told Dr. King of this fact, "He seemed deeply sorrowful for some time, and sighed." As if he needed more bad news, he "saw in the *Globe* the cutting remarks regarding his manuscript, felt bad about it, said people would not believe him when he spoke the truth."

The "cutting remarks" were contained in a short item published in the *Globe* and also printed in the *Port Hope Weekly Guide* newspaper. The editor of the *Globe* was not amused.

Dr. King's Confession.

We have received by mail from Cobourg a long communication purporting to be the full confession of the unhappy man now under sentence of death for the murder of his wife by poison. Anything more abominable to be written by a person on the brink of the grave, and professing to be deeply repentant for his crime, we could not conceive. It is filled with base charges against his victim and her relations, and mawkish sentimentality in palliation of the fearful and cold blooded deed for which he is about to suffer. We can have no hand in giving such a document to the public, and earnestly hope, for the sake of humanity, that no publisher will be found to do so. If this reaches the eye of the unhappy man, we would urge him to cast aside the flimsy cobweb with which he seeks to cloak his crime, and to prepare seriously for appearing at that bar where no misconduct of others, real or imaginary, will justify any man's transgression.—*Globe.*

The editor of the *Globe* newspaper in Toronto wrote a scathing article in response to the confession Dr. King had sent, hoping it would be published. It appeared in the *Port Hope Weekly Guide* on May 25, 1859, and the attitude of the editor can be summed up in the phrase "anything more abominable." It was a very clear response that made clear that the confession would not be published.

We have received by mail from Cobourg a long communication purporting to be the full confession of the unhappy man now under sentence of death for the murder of his wife by poison. Anything more abominable to be written by a person on the brink of the grave, and professing to be deeply repentant for his crime, we could not conceive. It is filled with base charges against his victim and her relations, and mawkish sentimentality in palliation of the fearful and cold blooded deed for which he is about to suffer. We can have no hand in giving such a document to the public, and earnestly hope, for the sake of humanity, that no publisher will be found to do so. If this reaches the eyes of the unhappy man, we would urge him to cast aside the flimsy cobweb with which he seeks to cloak his crime, and to prepare seriously for appearing at that bar where no misconduct of others, real or imaginary, will justify any man's transgression. — *Globe*[7]

THIRTY

SHORT TIME ON EARTH

The bad mood continued the next day. Dr. King "said he had a very poor night of it, had shed many tears, thinking of his past life, the sins he had committed against God and their consequences." Reverends Corson and Vanderburg visited this day and found Dr. King "very solemn and serious … seemed more humble, penitent and prayerful than he had been for a few days past … The doctor now seems to feel his awful position keenly. How very short his time on earth now — two weeks today."

Friday the twenty-seventh of May opened with thunder, dark clouds, and rain, which made the dreary jail even more dark and foreboding. Stewart records that the prisoner "seemed very solemn today, said he was very sorry that ever he had sinned against God; prayed earnestly for forgiveness." Reverend Vanderburg came in and was probably not very happy to hear Dr. King try to explain his sin:

> On sitting down to eat, Dr. sighed and said, "I've been led astray by women; women have been my ruin; in trying to get out of a bad fix, I got into a worse one. O, my unfortunate marriage has been the cause of all my trouble, much better for me I had never been married."

The theme of women continued into the next day. Stewart records:

> Speaking of his late misfortunes, Dr. sighed and said, "Women
> are costly things. They have cost me much, they are dear crea-
> tures, doubly dear to me. I wish my wife was now alive, she
> was a good housekeeper, tho' not a person much educated. I
> was also an ardent admirer of the female sex, that will prove
> my ruin. The devil has got me in a snare and left me there."

After praying and visiting with Dr. Bethune and Reverends Vanderburg
and J.H. Poole, Stewart records: "Dr. very serious now, striving earnestly
to find acceptance with God."

No visitors appeared at the Cobourg jail to visit Dr. King on Sunday,
the twenty-ninth of May. Alexander Stewart and Dr. King had their
normal prayer and discussions through the day, including the obvious
fact that there was only one Sabbath left for Dr. King after this.

Early in the morning of Monday, May 30, Dr. King learned that his
father and sister would be at the jail to see him later in the day. In the
afternoon, the sheriff brought in George King and Mary Louisa King, the
oldest girl in the family, less than five years younger than William. Stewart
records: "In the course of the forenoon, the Sheriff, Dr. King's father and
sister came in to see him, stayed quite a while, talking with the Dr.; after
bidding him farewell and leaving us, Dr. wept profusely for a good while."
Reverend Vanderburg came in and the three men prayed and talked as
usual. Stewart tells us "after being locked up in cell Dr. said, 'I'll have a
weeping night of it tonight. My friends I may never see again.'"

On the last day of May, Alexander Stewart tries to put Dr. King's
situation in perspective. He lists several other men that are to be hung
around the same time. "Mitchel must suffer at Hamilton on the seventh,
the Dr. here on the ninth, Rock at Belleville on the thirteenth. Then
follow the Brantford murderers; what a number of executions, may it
be a warning to others that men may hear, and fear and do not more
wickedly." Dr. King continued weeping through the night, but during
morning prayers was intent on praying for others: "Dr. prayed very
earnestly, for himself, his parents, and friends, all prisoners, especially

those under the sentence of death, and all sorts and conditions of men."
Gradually, Stewart saw an improvement in the prisoner: "Dr. is now
much more composed and resigned to his fate. He has now after a
painful and severe struggle with the accusations of a guilty conscience
and powers of darkness, obtained that 'peace' promised in John 14, 27
and that 'rest' spoken of in Matt 11, 28."

The first day of June saw the prisoner in a much happier frame of
mind. "Dr. said 'I felt very happy last night in my cell, after prayers I
felt as if God had blessed me' ... 'This is the first of June, the ninth will
soon be at our heels.'" Stewart is as happy as his cellmate; "I do sincerely
believe the Dr. to be a true and sincere penitent." A new visitor, Reverend
Davy, city missionary of Toronto, came to pray a while and then Reverend
Vanderburg came by. All of these ministers and clergymen appear to have
had a positive impact on the prisoner. Stewart was convinced that "the Dr.
now seems to have no doubt he will go to Heaven."

There were no visitors on the second of June but the two men continued their prayer sessions and discussions of scripture. Dr. King wrote in
his notebook and marked passages in his Bible that his friends might read
when he was gone. Dr. King was now less than a week from death and this
was noted by a small piece in the *Port Hope Weekly Guide* on that day:

> Dr. King ... One week from to-day, the mortal existence of
> this wife poisoner, will terminate. His confession in detail,
> will probably never see the light of day; and the dear public
> will be cheated out of a rare dish of the "horrible." The public,
> however, will compensate themselves for the loss of the con-
> fession by going to see this unfortunate man hanged.

THIRTY-ONE

QUITE A SERMON

Upon rising Friday, June 3, Dr. King said to Stewart, "This will be the last Friday I see, before another week, I'll be in the spirit land." He spent most of this day in his cell, praying and reading his Bible — "Dr. very earnest to obtain a firm persuasion of his acceptance with God. Reading God's word a good deal today."

Saturday, June 4 proved to be an eventful day. The sheriff called on Dr. King early in the morning to tell him about some of the arrangements for the ninth and to let him know that there were some visitors from Brighton to see him later in the day. Archdeacon Bethune came in to discuss some of the arrangements for the ninth as well, since he was to be on the platform with the prisoner. Dr. King also wrote one last letter to his brother, Isaac, in California.

About four o'clock, the visitors arrived from Brighton. Jared O. Clarke was the constable who had taken charge of Dr. King in Brighton after Clinton Lawson had fetched him back from Cape Vincent. He brought with him his wife, Mary, as well as Hester Garratt, an aunt of Dorcas Garratt, who had been the first target of Dr. King's improper advances in the summer of 1858. Stewart records:

> After a time Hester Garratt, who I believe is a Quakeress, commenced and gave Dr. quite a sermon, urging him

earnestly to embrace Christ, not to deceive himself, or rest
in any false refuge, or trust anything else for salvation, but
the merits of Jesus and his righteousness alone, as time was
short, make sure work of salvation. It was the most earnest
appeal I ever heard. Dr. wept and I too wept; about 6 o'clock
she bade the Dr. farewell, to meet in Heaven.

In spite of this verbal battering, "Dr. pretty cheerful today, seems now
to look at death without fear, and as a conquered foe."

When Dr. King rose on Sunday, June 5, he was able to say that this was
going to be his last Sabbath on earth. In any case, the prisoner continued
on a positive note. Stewart records that "at breakfast he expressed himself
strongly in regard to his confidence in God's mercy. At morning prayers
he seemed to enjoy more liberty and access to the throne of grace than
formerly." Reverend Vanderburg came to visit and they could see that Dr.
King was in a place where "death is divested of its sting, and the fear of
dying taken away."

On Monday, June 6, the prisoner was seen to be "in pretty good spirits; his mind apparently composed and calm." Reverend Bleasdell came
in from Trenton and "stayed quite a while with him and gave him some
very wholesome advice." Alexander Stewart was counting the days as well:
"Two more days and the Dr. will be no more. He has now caught the
martyr spirit." Everyone was preparing for the final act of this long and
difficult story.

THIRTY-TWO

THE NOTEBOOK

A few days earlier, on June 2, Stewart mentioned that Dr. King was writing in a notebook. This is the first mention of the notebook but it will become a remarkable part of the story, largely because the notebook survives to this day. It was a leather-bound notebook with the title on the front *Smith's Homeopathic Directory, 1857*, which the doctor apparently acquired during his medical training in Philadelphia.

Dr. King used the blank pages in the book to write a prayer for his mother. On the first page inside

The notebook came from Dr. King's college days, and he used the remaining blank pages to write a prayer as his last parting gift for his mother. The cover of the smaller, leather-bound book shows the original title *Smith's Homeopathic Directory 1857*. This artifact was included in the King Collection, which now resides at Proctor House Museum in Brighton.

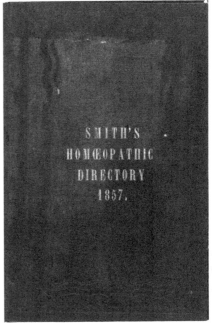

SMITH'S
HOMŒOPATHIC
DIRECTORY
1857.

Proctor House Museum, Brighton, Ontario

the front cover reads the title "A Last Prayer, Selected and Adapted for Dr. King, under sentence of death."[1] The prayer itself covers about ten pages, written with fine, large penmanship. The prayer closes with "To be kept Sacred to my memory By my Dear Mother ... Cobourg C.W., June 6th, 1859, Wm. H. King M.D. (Written by himself)."[2]

Considering the timing, we might expect that Dr. King knew about his father's last visit the next day and he wanted to have this final gift for his mother written and ready for his father to take home. The notebook was kept for many years in the King, Ames, and Jaques family collections, and recently came into the possession of a collector in Brighton. This precious article, along with other items related to these families, are now to be found in Proctor House Museum in Brighton.

Dr. King also had some visitors from the *Cobourg Star* on Monday, the sixth. A substantial article would appear on the eighth, the day before the hanging. The article said that it was good that the prisoner had confessed, "but it should not be forgotten that as the law would remain equally holy, so the sentence would be equally just and equally satisfactory without such an acknowledgement." In this case, the article insists, the confession is only useful "on account of its moral bearing in respect to the transgressor," and has no consideration for anyone else. In fact, guilt had been determined long before Dr. King made his confession and "throughout the length and breadth of the Province the public voice has echoed the verdict

Proctor House Museum, Brighton, Ontario

Dr. King completed his prayer in the notebook and signed it on June 6, 1859. He writes very clearly that this document is "To be kept Sacred to my memory By my Dear Mother," and he even emphasizes the fact that it is he, himself writing on these pages by adding in brackets under his name "Written by himself."

of the jury, without the recommendation to mercy." The *Star* reporter seems to have some skepticism about Dr. King's credibility, especially when they noticed "that he *smiled* as he stated to the Rev. L. Vanderburg, in our presence, his conviction that all was right between his Maker and himself." The word *smiled* is italicized in the text. There was little sympathy for the condemned prisoner.

Early in the morning of Tuesday, June 7, George King came to visit his son for one last time. Stewart records "a great deal of feeling, and shedding of tears on both sides." Dr. King handed his father the notebook that contained the prayer he had written for his mother, and we can expect there were more tears shed between the grieving father and his eldest child. Later there were practical matters for Dr. King to arrange and then Reverend Vanderburg arrived and stayed until dark, praying. They had another "season of devotion before parting. The Dr. seems remarkably calm today, so near his end."

Another, even more scathing article appeared in the *Port Hope Weekly Guide* on the seventh. The article was in response to the news that Dr. King had made a full confession. The article says, "his penitence is paraded before the public, and the due amount of clerical industry to effect a conversion. We are tired of these penitential exhibitions."[3] There had been several murders in the news and the gallows conversion of Dr. King was only the most recent example. "There is something repugnant in these conversions on compulsion, as if the hangman's rope were a more effective agency to reclaim the incorrigible, than the precepts of Christianity from the most eloquent preacher."[4] A little more delicately, the article comments that "these zealous clergymen ... hope to shine a little by reflexion."[5] We can see that the secular side of society had its own opinions on the matter.

THIRTY-THREE

LAST DAY

The first part of Alexander Stewart's journal entry for Wednesday, June 8 cannot be surpassed.

> To-morrow is the fatal 9th, then the unfortunate man must suffer the extreme penalty of the law for the awful crime of which he has been convicted. Poor man! How foolish, how unfortunate he has been! What trouble he has brought upon himself, his parents, and friends for nothing. What an expense to the county, all might have been prevented. Bartered life, liberty, character, everything earthly, and endangered the loss of his soul for what? For a mere shadow of the imagination, a mere nothing. O, how infatuated he has been! How insane! He has become the destroyer of his own happiness, and at the same time he was instrumental, as he has confessed in burying into eternity her, his bosom companion, whom he had chosen to be the partner of his hope, peace, joy and sorrow, until God seemed pleased to separate her from him by death. One can hardly tell what he deserves most, to be pitied or blamed. Let his late wife be what she may, no doubt she was imperfect, as all human beings are, still it was God's prerogative, not his, to take away

her life. However much I have done and still would do for his spiritual and eternal welfare, I cannot with the word of God before me but admit the justice of his sentence, and would uphold the majesty of the law in his execution.

Reverend McKenzie came to see Dr. King and spent a half hour encouraging him in his search of Jesus. Reverend Vanderburg came in around one o'clock and the men engaged in prayer and discussion. Stewart records Dr. King's words to them:

> There is a reality in religion that I could not have imagined weeks ago, that I could be so calm and composed so near my end.... The grand cause of all my difficulties was an unhappy marriage ... a year ago I was in Brighton a free man and had a good reputation, now a poor convict, in very humiliating circumstances.

Two other visitors came to see Dr. King on June 8, but are not mentioned in Alexander Stewart's journal. This information comes from a chapter in Reuben DeCourcey's account of the trial of Dr. King, which was published in July 1859. He called this chapter "Prison Scenes." It provides DeCourcey's impressions of Dr. King and his surroundings on that day before his death, taken from the point of view of someone who had known the prisoner since the two were children. DeCourcey explains, "I visited the Dr. in his cell in company with Geo. J. of Brighton; after passing through a hall we entered a dark ally, passed through a heavy door which opened into a hall which was used by the Dr. as a sort of reception room for visitors, and to exercise in." To DeCourcey, Dr. King was a former intimate who had enjoyed "wealth and kind friends, health, influence and everything that could render life happy," but now "O, fallen! Surrounded by gloomy walls, and instead of kind friends were the officers, and policemen, and outside the prison were workmen erecting the scaffold from which he was to be launched into eternity."

Dr. King and Reuben DeCourcey greeted each other as the friends they were and had some small talk about family and friends. The doctor wanted to make sure his friend received one of the portraits that had been produced a few days earlier. Then they discussed the publication of the prisoner's biography, which DeCourcey was working to complete:

> I showed him the first few pages of his life already published by myself, which contained an account of his early life, his elopement with Miss V., and the coroner's inquest, which he read and commented upon as each sentence came under his observation, which he deemed worthy of notice.

The doctor commented on many small points, most often wishing to correct an impression or change emphasis. He said that the report about his dislike or coldness for their first child was not true. He suggested that Dorcas Garratt had written the first letter to him and he had replied in turn. It was Melinda Vandervoort's talent for music that most charmed him. His wife was "a kind good hearted woman, a good house keeper and very economical but very illiterate, and would not try to improve her mind."

Toward the end of their meeting, Dr. King "spoke very earnestly about seeing Mr. and Mrs. Lawson, that night by 12 o'clock, not to talk over the past, but to have a mutual forgiveness passed between them." DeCourcey's travelling companion sent a telegraph to the Lawsons, but they replied that the notice was too short and they could not come to Cobourg. This was very disappointing for Dr. King. As a parting request, Dr. King asked his old friend if he would attend the funeral, which was to be held at the King home in Codrington on Sunday, with Reverend Levi Vanderburg officiating. DeCourcey said a tearful goodbye to Dr. King and writes, "I bade him farewell at 7:15 pm, again to mingle with the crowd who had come to see the scaffold."

Around six o'clock Archdeacon Bethune and Reverend Bleasdell came in and stayed for a while, making some arrangements for the morrow. Stewart records, "Rev. Vanderburg stayed up with us all the night, Dr. happy in his cell, slept a little, rose again about four o'clock." The day of reckoning was at hand.

The town of Cobourg and the surrounding communities were also preparing for this historic event. There had never been a hanging in Northumberland County and many folks were intent on seeing it for themselves. The local newspaper, the *Cobourg Star*, had avoided involvement in all the salaciousness of the trial and the public clamouring for a hanging. Reporters for the *Star* finally went to visit Dr. King in the Cobourg jail on Monday, June 6 (not recorded in Stewart's journal), and there was an article in the newspaper on June 8, the day before the hanging.

The tone of the piece is rather smug. It begins by commenting that it is fine to hear that Dr. King had made a confession, but it made no difference, really, since the evidence at the trial was so overwhelming and the opinion of everyone, from the judge, to the jurymen, and out to the wider public was that he was certainly guilty and deserved the death penalty. While the reporter is skeptical of Dr. King's repentance, he does give him credit for answering their pointed questions, in the presence of Reverend Vanderburg, regarding his guilt and the sentence. He seemed convinced of what he said.

The *Star* reporter makes a much stronger point, however, on the ugly nature of the coming spectacle. He commends Sheriff Fortune and the constables for arranging everything possible to minimize the possibility of disturbances as a result of crowds gathering to see the hanging. He comments that in the United States the practice of holding the execution of criminals inside an enclosure at the jail was much more civilized. The limit of fifty persons would be sensible, he suggests. In the end, he admits he cannot "dissuade our fellow townsmen from going up to the Court House tomorrow morning, for it would be blowing against the wind," but he did express the hope that attendance would be less than expected. A faint hope, as it turned out.

THIRTY-FOUR

THE MOURNFUL PROCESSION

The day of the hanging had finally arrived. Dr. King ate well at about six o'clock and joined the others in worship afterwards. They read Psalm 51 and Rev. 22, "then engaged in prayer, like the Saviour in the garden, he prayed 'more earnestly', he prayed for grace, special grace to sustain him in the last moments, for his friends, his spiritual advisers, the Sheriff, Jailer and Executioner, and all his enemies." Reverend Vanderburg, the old faithful friend during those long weeks, was present for the last step of the journey. Alexander Stewart was much impressed: "Rev. Mr. Vanderburg followed with much fervour and power. We all engaged for about 45 minutes; it was the most solemn prayer meeting ever I was at, or perhaps ever will be." After this solemn prayer meeting, "Dr. seemed very happy, a heavenly radiance seemed to be visible in his countenance, he walked arm in arm up and down the hall with Mr. Vanderburg, conversing about heavenly things."

The *Cobourg Star* reported that "about a quarter before seven, the Venerable Archdeacon Bethune and the Reverend William Bleasdell, M.A., the Incumbent of Trenton, entered the prisoner's cell and engaged in prayer with him. The Archdeacon afterwards administered the Holy Communion to the prisoner and those with him."[1] Reverend Bleasdell, Anglican minister in Trenton diocese, had visited Dr. King several times, and Venerable Archdeacon Bethune was archdeacon of York and an uncle of Dr. Norman Bethune, who had been a regular visitor at the Cobourg jail, over the last few weeks. The report continues with a touching incident that neither Stewart nor DeCourcey reported: "The portrait of his late wife being put into his hand, he was greatly moved, kissing it fervently and weeping profusely."[2]

At eight o'clock, the *Star* described the moment, "The hour of his execution having arrived the Sheriff entered the cell, and habited in his official costume, headed the mournful procession to the scaffold."[3] Alexander Stewart noted that "Dr. grasped Mr. Vanderburg's arm," and the *Star* reported that the prisoner "maintained his composure to the very last."[4]

A report from the *Port Hope Weekly Guide* sets the scene outside the courthouse:

> Last evening, persons living to the north, west, and east of the Court House, poured into Cobourg, and lodged in the Hotels in the neighborhood of the Jail, so that they might be on hand at an early hour. At half past three o'clock this morning those living in the neighborhood of Walton Street in this Town, were awakened by the rumbling of waggons over the pavement, and from that hour until half past six o'clock, there was almost a constant stream of waggons, gigs, carriages, horsemen, and pedestrians, from Hope, Cavan, Clark, and Darlington, rolling onward toward the Court House. Many of the occupants of the vehicles were women, young, middle aged, and old; and in some instances, good natured farmers had the younger branches of their families, both boys and girls, stowed away carefully among the straw in the bottom of their wagons.... At half-past eight o'clock the entire space from the temporary fence erected in front of the Court House, to Burke's Tavern on the west, to the opposite side of the street on the south, and to the tavern on the east, was occupied by a dense mass of human beings. It was estimated by persons accustomed to such calculations, that there were between six and seven thousand persons

on the ground in the vicinity of the gallows, which was erected close to and east of the steps leading to the Court House, there was considerable crowding, each man being anxious to get a position and keep it, but no confusion or disorder prevailed.[5]

One of the many thousands of souls at the Cobourg courthouse that day was twenty-one-year-old William Robison Losie, who had walked all the way from his family's homestead west of Warkworth in Percy Township. How many young men struck out on foot the previous day with a bundle of food, a bedroll, and a good pair of boots to mingle in the crowd around the scaffold that morning? Like many folks, William Losie may have attended the hanging out of morbid curiosity. However, William had a better reason. The Losie family lived near Warkworth, which is not far from the King farm at Codrington. William was five years younger, but could have known William Henry King personally. Certainly, he was familiar with the McKenzie family that lived just west of the King's, because in 1862 he married Sarah Jane McKenzie. A few months later, his sister, Abigail Losie, married Isaac Newton King, a brother of Dr. King. It could be that William Losie was not alone in his trek. We can easily picture parties of young men heading out to see a hanging. What an adventure!

THIRTY-FIVE

LAUNCHED INTO ETERNITY

The *Guide* report continues

> The Execution … About fifteen minutes before nine o'clock
> the Sheriff, followed by the prisoner, who was accompa-
> nied by the Venerable, the Archdeacon of York, the Rev. Mr.
> Vanderburg, another clerical gentleman, and his two brothers,
> issued from the front door of the Court House, and ascended
> the steps leading to the platform, passed out upon the gallows,
> one of the clergymen reading as they went, the Burial service
> of the Church of England. The condemned walked with a
> firm step to the front of the gallows, and in a voice clear and
> distinct, free from the slightest tremulousness, read the fol-
> lowing. "My fellow Christians, I stand before you today in the
> most awful position in which a human being can be placed
> — convicted of the most dreadful of crimes, and sentenced
> by the laws of my country to pay the penalty of my guilt by
> sacrificing my life."[1]

The crowd listened intently to every word, marvelling at the strong
voice and confident manner of a man about to meet his maker. He made
a point to "entreat my fellow Christians to take warning from my fate, and

to beware of the temptations of the evil one." He implored his audience to "live in the fear and love of God; honor his Sabbath; keep close to him in prayer and the reading of his word." It was his wish to be on good terms with all living beings, to thank all those who had supported him and to forgive those who had wronged him.

He said, "I beseech you, my dear Christians, pray with me now; join your prayer with mine, that my faith may not fail at this my last hour, — that no weakness of the flesh, no power of Satan, may separate me from God. Pray that I may experience his full pardon, and that believing as I do, heartily and sincerely in the Lord Jesus Christ, and deeply contrite for my sins, I shall be saved."

The *Guide* reports that the crowd was silent through Dr. King's address from the scaffold, except for a few muffled moans at the point where he asked people to pray with him. After his address, he "looked down upon the sea of upturned eyes; 'I bid you farewell — a *long* farewell!'"[2] He shook hands with those who had accompanied him to the platform, Archdeacon Bethune, Reverend Vanderburg, Reverend Bleasdell, and the sheriff. He then kissed his two brothers, who had come to claim his body after the hanging.

At this point:

> The hangman, whose face was covered with a mask, approached the prisoner, fastened his hands behind his back, placed the noose around his neck, and requesting him to kneel on the "drop," tied his feet together. The white cap was then drawn over his face, and with the voice of prayer ringing in his ears, the wretched man, at a signal from the Sheriff, was launched into eternity.[3]

Alexander Stewart records these last words in his journal:

> A crowd of some ten thousand people it is supposed witnessed the sad spectacle, who preserved the utmost good order during the whole time, for many of them were there by daybreak, all dispersed quietly and went to their respective homes, and the unfortunate Dr., I hope, went to home in heaven.

The *Star* reported the fateful moment in more graphic terms:

> A deep silence followed the sudden falling of the drop.
> The slightest possible struggle of the unhappy culprit was
> apparent for about half a minute, then a muscular twitch-
> ing of the extremities, and then — all was still. The body
> remained hanging for half an hour and was then cut down
> and placed in a coffin.[4]

In the end, the authorities had a *good* hanging. The prisoner had acted
honourably in the face of death and the crowd had behaved very well
in spite of all the excitement leading up to the event. The *Star* would go
on to comment:

> There were above ten thousand persons present, including
> from four to five hundred women. The arrangements of the
> Sheriff to preserve order appear to have been most excellent.
> A space of about thirty feet intervened between the scaffold
> and the fencing which kept off the crowd, and none but offi-
> cials were allowed within the enclosure.[5]

Everyone breathed a sigh of relief — "a respectful deportment befitting
the solemnity of the occasion being maintained throughout the whole of
the proceeding."[6]

On the other hand, it was reported that several members of the Lawson
family who were in attendance managed to gain possession of the rope
after the hanging. The rope was cut up into small pieces and the pieces
were sold as souvenirs. One might cringe at this indignity, but we can
understand the motivation to benefit from the misfortune of the murderer.
The scene is not hard to conjure, with a few young Lawson men pulling
in the cash until all the pieces of rope were sold. A local tavern may have
been the ultimate destination for their profits.

Even today, there are rumours that surface every now and then about
pieces of Dr. King's hanging rope that might be found in someone's attic
or basement. The reader is encouraged to pass on any information about

such a possibility they might come across. In the meantime, we will have to be satisfied with the idea that such a thing still exists.

The *Star* would also report on the uniqueness of the event: "So ended the first execution within the limits of the United Counties of Northumberland and Durham. May it be the last witnessed by any person now living."[7] Not only for those living in 1859, but to this day; no other execution has ever taken place in Northumberland County; Dr. William Henry King holds that ignominious crown.

The body of Dr. King was claimed by his two younger brothers, Charles Wellington King, age eighteen, and David Nelson King, age fourteen. The coffin was placed in the back of their wagon and they proceeded north up Burnham Street on the long and mournful journey to Codrington, where their parents were waiting. Imagine the trip! Two teenage boys with tears streaming down their cheeks and not a few sobs, dreading the moment when they would drive up to the farmhouse and present the body of their older brother to their grieving parents.

On Saturday evening, June 11, the body of William Henry King was buried in the yard of the King family home, near the southeast corner of the house. The *Star* reported this solemn event:

> We have only to add that the body of the unhappy criminal was interred on Saturday evening last in the family burying ground on his father's farm near Codrington, in the township of Brighton, Mr. Vanderburg reading the burial service used by the Wesleyan Methodist Church, an abridgement, in fact, of the sublime funeral liturgy of the Church of England. On the following Sunday morning Mr. Vanderburg preached in the village to an assembly of about fifteen hundred persons.[8]

The scene of 1,500 people gathered around the King family home in Codrington in June 1859 is rather difficult to fathom, especially for someone who grew up in that house one hundred years later and routinely looked out the upper-storey bedroom window at the trees and garden below. Where would all those people have come from? We have to imagine hundreds of buggies and wagons filled with families or couples, along with many folks riding one or two to a horse. Of course, many would have come on foot from the nearby farms and homes. People would have come up from Brighton and down from Warkworth, out from Colborne and Cobourg. The new Brighton and Seymour Gravel Road, which ran right through Codrington, would have been very busy that day.

And why did they come? It may be that Reverend Levi Vanderburg was the draw. He had been very close to Dr. King through his last weeks on earth and folks wanted to hear the gruesome details about the emotional journey of the notorious murderer. It might have been partly the desire to partake in what we might call simple entertainment. After all, this story had been the talk of the countryside for months and people could not get enough of it. More seriously, it could have been, for some, an opportunity to fortify the spirit with a story of sin and penitence. Or maybe it was just plain curiosity. Many people could not attend the hanging but wanted very much to learn what they could about this most fascinating, if sordid, episode in their local history. And many people just wanted to be where everyone else was meeting, to be part of the community, to participate.

THIRTY-SIX

PUBLISHING THE STORY

The Dr. King story made a lot of money for newspaper publishers for a few months in 1858 and 1859 as the public scrambled to catch every last detail. Reporters sat in the courtroom and scribbled down all the testimony and that text would occupy full pages in the newspapers over the next few days. Newspaper pages were nailed to taverns and hotels so folks could read all about it. We might characterize the Dr. King story as the O.J. Simpson trial of the 1850s. Of course, they lacked the technology and media in the 1850s that we had in the 1990s, but there were plenty of newspapers and they were all over the story; reporters swarmed around the courthouse, taverns, and likely the memorial service.

We can imagine that plans for publishing a full account of the entire episode were well underway before the hanging. As a result, several accounts were published in July 1859 to meet demand. At the Metropolitan Reference Library there are two accounts held on microfilm, both of which include the trial testimony but differ in additional material. The title pages for both of these accounts are not the originals but show us that Stewart and Vosper published the first and Wiman & Co. published the second.

The two published accounts differed in that the Stewart and Vosper account includes material written by Reuben DeCourcey, who was an old friend of Dr. King. He is the one who visited Dr. King the day before the hanging, and produced "Prison Scenes" as a result. He also appears to have

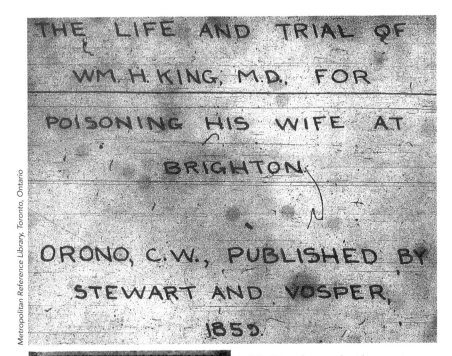

Metropolitan Reference Library, Toronto, Ontario

Toronto Metropolitan Reference Library, Toronto, Ontario

TOP: This rather crude title page is found in microfilm at the beginning of the account of the Dr. King story published by Stewart and Vosper, which we know to contain Reuben DeCourcey's material. We can speculate about why the original printed title page did not accompany these documents, but the second part of the microfilm, which contains the Wiman & Co. publication, does include the original title page for that document. *LEFT:* A second account of the Dr. King story was made available to the public in 1859, published by Wiman & Co. of Toronto. This account contains mainly the trial testimony, which had been transcribed by reporters and shared with the newspapers after the events of the trial and hanging.

made arrangements with those in possession of Dr. King's confession and Alexander Stewart's journal to include them in this account. One must wonder what kind of deal-making went on behind the scenes to assemble all of these documents. At the very least, we are indebted to Mr. DeCourcey for his efforts.

Aside from these two accounts on microfilm, there is a front page that appears in "Dr. Billy King" on the Cobourg History website. This must be the front page of another version of the story, in this case specifically published by Reuben DeCourcey and printed in Brighton.

This front page includes daguerreotype images of William and Sarah King; below the images we see "Daguerreotyped by Hawley Sanford, Brighton."[1] Hawley Sanford was a twenty-six-year-old dentist at the time and was likely doing daguerreotyping on the side. It was a common way to make portraits in the 1840s and 1850s, but was technically very difficult and would be replaced by developments in photography in the 1860s.

Down a bit lower on the cover we see "By R. DeCourcey,"[2] which clearly indicates that this account was the work of Reuben DeCourcey. The next line says "Brighton, July 1859,"[3] which indicates that this account of the story was published in Brighton.

Fast forward 155 years. During preparations for the Brighton History Open House of February 2014, Rose Ellery, a resident of Brighton, contacted me regarding papers she had in her family history collection. She said that she

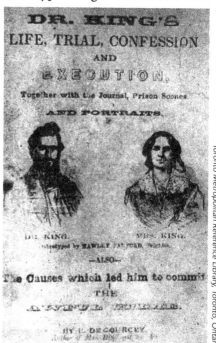

Toronto Metropolitan Reference Library, Toronto, Ontario

Reuben DeCourcey was an old friend of Dr. King and was writing a biography when he visited Dr. King the day before the hanging. He managed to gather the journal and the confession, along with all the trial testimony in a publication for the public in July 1859. The front cover included daguerreotype images of William and Sarah, produced by Hawley Sanford of Brighton.

had something related to the Dr. King story that I might be interested to see. Since the Dr. King story was going to be front and centre at HOH 2014, I was anxious to see what she had. Rose came to my home and carefully unfolded a book from a cloth covering and set it on the table. There were two heavy paper pages to pull back before the front page of the work was revealed. I gulped as I read the text; we were looking at an original copy of Reuben DeCourcey's account of the Dr. King story, published in July 1859, a month after the hanging. I could hardly believe my eyes!

The front pages are a bit worse for wear, but most of the front title page is still there, with all the critical information. This book is almost the same in content as the account found on microfilm that was published by Stewart and Vosper. The front page is slightly different, lacking the images of William and Sarah. However, the biggest difference is in the preface, which is extremely interesting. The author tells us that for the first edition, he did not have all the pieces of information available to him and did not know if he would be able to obtain them because they were in the hands

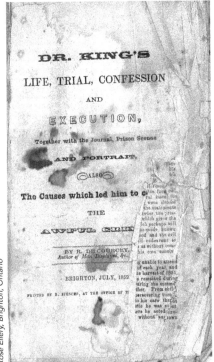

Rose Ellery, Brighton, Ontario

Rose Ellery, of Brighton, found this document in her family history collection and showed it to the author in January 2014. It is an amazing find because this is a slightly different version of the account of the Dr. King story that was published by Reuben DeCourcey in July 1859. The front cover of this version is in rough shape and does not have the daguerreotype images of William and Sarah, but the most important difference is the preface, in which he explains something about his efforts to collect all of the information about the story, namely the journal and the confession.

of others. The key phrase in the preface may be "by a great deal of persuasion,"[4] which may mean some kind of monetary compensation for
handing over the documents. It is speculation, but it is likely that Reuben
DeCourcey paid Alexander Stewart for the journal that appears in this
account. Obviously, Reuben DeCourcey worked hard to make sure the
whole story was told. Even though he was an old friend of Dr. King's, his
writing appears to be moderate and objective. He was quite a good writer
as well. The story is so much richer for us due to his efforts.

Rose Ellery, Brighton, Ontario

PREFACE.

When the first edition of the Life of Dr. King went to press, the
writer was not aware of the exact amount of matter he would receive.
The principal amount of information contained in the present volume
was then in the hands of different parties who had not decided positively to let the knowledge they possessed go before the public; since
then by a great deal of persuasion they have consented to do so.—
From the consideration that notwithstanding the many facts that
have been published, still rumor is not satisfied without fabricating the
most unwarrantable falsehoods on both sides that could possibly be
hoped to receive attention. In compiling the present edition we have
received our information from documents left by the Dr. himself and
from parties whose veracity cannot be doubted, viz: Rev Levi Van-
derburgh and Mr. Alexander Stewart, the Constable who was his
constant attendant in the prison during the last eight weeks of his
confinement. Other parties equally reliable, viz: Mr. J. B. Young,
Mr. and Mrs. Lawson have contributed their quota of information to
the stock received from the sources above mentioned. One fact ow
not be concealed from the reader which is that in several instances the
statements made by the friends of the late Mrs. King were denied
by the Dr. at the last hour of his life. Again some of the statements
which he made in that hour are denied by them and under the present circumstances we do not feel free to decide as to which gives the
most correct statements. Here then is a mystery which perhaps will
never be solved until the secrets of all hearts shall be made known
and every one receives the just retribution for the good and the evil
they have done in this present life. Hence we shall endeavour to
give to the public the narative as it has been given to us without comment or coloring, and leave the reader to arrive at his own conclu-
sions.

Reuben DeCourcey mentions in this preface the importance of documents
that were provided by Alexander Stewart (the journal) and Reverend Levi
Vanderburg, as well as members of the Lawson family. He states plainly that
there were disagreements between Dr. King and members of Sarah's family
but that he would try to provide all the information "without comment or
coloring" so that the reader could make up his own mind.

There are other copies of this document around Ontario. Happily, those copies do not have as much damage to the title page as Rose Ellery's copy, so we can make out the very bottom line, which provides an interesting detail. The last line says that the document was "Printed by R. Spencer, at the office of the 'British Flag.'[5] The *British Flag* was the local newspaper in Brighton at that time. A little research tells us that "R. Spencer" refers to Richard Spencer, who was the editor and publisher of the *British Flag* newspaper in Brighton from 1858 to 1864.

Rose and I speculated on how this book might have found its way into her family history collection. Rose's maiden name is Cheer and her great-grandfather was Henry Cheer, who lived in Brighton in the 1850s. In fact, the Cheer family lived very close to the Murdoff House at the corner of Sanford Street and Kingsley Avenue, where it is said Dr. King and his wife Sarah lived for those brief months from March to November 1858. If we look a little closer, we can see that Henry Cheer married Lucinda Victoria Davidson, a sister of Simon Davidson, who was the coroner responsible for the inquest into the death of Sarah Ann King. It was a small town!

THIRTY-SEVEN

DR. KING'S MEMORIAL: JOURNEY THROUGH TIME

Dr. King's memorial may have suffered an undignified death at the end of Lloyd Ames' favourite sledgehammer, but there is a lot more to the story than that. For instance, how did the stone get into the garden to be pulled up by the plough in 1965? Where was it during all those intervening years? And how do we happen to have pictures? The story is improbable and fascinating, and takes us back through several generations of my family history. Let's start with the most recent events and step back through time.

One Sunday afternoon in 2005 I visited my father, Reverend Charles Buchanan, and his wife, Shirley, at their home in Belleville. He was a retired minister but was still in demand for weddings and funerals, which kept him busy. I had asked him a while earlier to look through his cabinet full of family slides to see if there were any that I might use in the history of Codrington I was preparing to include in Florence Chatten's new book about the history of Brighton Township.

There were about thirty slides in the box and we started looking through them. Some were interesting and some not, but they were all fun to see and resulted in some delightful reminiscing. Then, the next slide he presented shocked me. It was the picture of a gravestone lying a few inches below the grass, as if it had just been uncovered. Before I could speak up, he changed to the next picture and I was even more amazed. It was a close-up of the gravestone of William Henry King! The inscription was very clear; there was no doubt what we were looking at.

I asked Dad if he knew what these two pictures were. Rather nonchalantly, he said they were Dr. King's gravestone. My shock continued and I asked him to tell me exactly how he managed to have two pictures of William Henry King's gravestone. He was not clear on the exact year, but the story goes like this: One summer in the middle of the 1950s, Dad and Grandfather (Lloyd Ames) were planning a major overhaul of the septic system, which was located at the south end of the house. In light of the potential for tractors and backhoes driving over the lawn at the southeast corner of the house, Grandfather told Dad that there was something in that area they should move. He said that the old gravestone of Dr. King was buried there.

The two men collected shovels and poked around in the grass until they heard a clang, indicating a stone just below the surface. Carefully, they removed the sod and some soil to uncover a long, rectangular memorial stone lying a few inches below the grass. While they dug, Grandfather told Dad the story of how the stone ended up in that position. In the early 1920s, his mother, Linnie (King) Ames, was increasingly agitated by the sight of the memorial of William Henry King standing proud-as-you-please at the southeast corner of the Ames farmhouse. It had been there since George and Henrietta King had erected it in memory of their son in 1860 and it was a constant reminder of the shame that the notorious murderer had imposed on his family. Linnie King was a niece of Dr. King, a daughter of David Nelson King, a younger brother of the murderer. She took it personally and had seen enough of Dr. King!

The family had to cope with gawkers who would often stop on the road and point up at the stone. Once they found a group of people standing around the stone when they came back from church. At some point, the presence of the stone became unbearable for Linnie, so she asked her two younger sons, Lloyd and Kenneth, to get rid of it. The boys did the expedient thing — they pulled the stone out of the ground, dug a shallow trench, lay the stone down in the trench, and covered it with sod. Mission accomplished! Out of sight, out of mind. In any case, their mother was happy. So that is how the memorial of William Henry King ended up in the ground at the southeast corner of the Buchanan house in the 1950s, when septic work motivated Lloyd Ames to move it.

Then, before they dug out the stone to move it again, Dad did his usual thing: he went to the house and got his camera. We often had fun teasing our father about his "Kodachrome Period." During the 1950s and 1960s he was an avid photographer. It was a popular habit in those days of growing baby-boom families, and the technology quickly developed to support the demand. As a result, our family enjoys a large collection of slides, including pictures of the kids, the cats, and the cows, along with some aesthetic renderings of bumble-bees, flowers, and snowflakes. It's an impressive collection that we cherish.

Dad took two pictures of the Dr. King memorial. One is a long view of the whole stone, showing where it had rested since the early 1920s. Then,

Author's photos

LEFT: The memorial of Dr. King contained the inscription: In Memory of William Henry King Who Departed This Life June 9, 1859 Aged 26 Y. 5 M 17 D.
RIGHT: Charles Buchanan, father of the author, took these two pictures of the memorial of Dr. William Henry King one day in 1955 when he and his father-in-law, Lloyd Ames, uncovered it with the intent of moving it out of the way for renovations. The stone was pulled out of this location and dragged a few yards to the middle of the garden, where it was buried once again, only to be pulled up by the plough a decade later.

he took a second picture up-close to provide a clear view of the inscription. It says clearly: "In Memory of William Henry King who departed this life June 9, 1859, Aged 26Y, 5M, 17D." Since the stone had been in the ground for so long it was in perfect condition, avoiding the acid rain and air pollution of the last century.

After the pictures were taken, the stone was lifted out of the ground and moved a few dozen feet to the middle of the garden. There, it was buried a couple of feet below the surface, hopefully never to be seen again. Unfortunately, about a decade later, this is where the plough point struck the stone, pulling it out of the ground and breaking it in half. This final act set the stage for the death of the memorial at the business end of Lloyd Ames's favourite sledgehammer.

THIRTY-EIGHT

SKELETON IN THE FRONT YARD

Many families have skeletons that stay well-hidden inside the proverbial family history closet. For the descendants of the George King family, the skeleton was, literally, right there in the front yard. It was hard to ignore. Dr. King's family had purchased and erected a very fine memorial for their eldest child soon after his death, in spite of his crime. George King was a prosperous farmer in a period of high wheat prices and it appears as if he did not scrimp on the memorial for his eldest son. The stone was impressive, beautifully inscribed, with the signature at the bottom that appears to say A. MOORE, BELLEVILLE.

In the 1870s, the King family would have a plot in the Warkworth Cemetery, but in 1859 it was too early for that. Besides, burial of a notorious murderer in a public cemetery would have been very much frowned upon. At that time it was still very common for each farm to have a family cemetery along a fence or out behind the buildings. We might consider it rather macabre that a very attractive memorial to their son, the murderer, would be placed in such an obvious and prominent position at the southeast corner of the large new two-storey brick home. However, for the grieving parents, it was the right thing to do.

We can only imagine the pain and suffering of the Lawson family after the tragic death of their daughter. It was a terrible, shocking loss that was felt through the entire extended Lawson family and into the community.

King/Ames/Buchanan Farm
Spring 1955

Highway
No. 30

Dr. King Buried Near South
East Corner of House

Codrington

Author's photo

This aerial photograph was taken around 1955 when Charles Buchanan took a ride in a small plane with a friend and took his camera. Number 30 Highway is on the right, and Codrington at the bottom. The author could be one of the folks standing in front of the house; he lived here from 1951 to 1971. The arrow shows where Dr. King was buried and the memorial was uncovered in 1955. The garden to the immediate southeast is where the memorial was reburied and then pulled up a decade later with the plough.

For the King family there was a painful loss as well — the loss of a son and sibling. But there was another kind of loss involved here. William Henry King had been the ideal son to his parents and the model brother to his siblings. With his degrees in teaching and medicine he had demonstrated his capacity for success and the consensus among family and friends pointed to bigger and better things in the future. And now this! Who could have imagined such a terrible deed from such an unlikely source? The parents, in particular, would have been baffled and almost unbelieving.

There are several tangible examples of the unconditional love of Dr. King's mother for her son, which we find in the very personal form of the creative arts. It turns out that Henrietta King was proficient in the art of needlepoint. We are extremely lucky to have a collection of King family artifacts and pictures, which was handed down through several generations. Henrietta handed it down to her son, David Nelson King, who passed it on to his daughter, Linnie (King) Ames. Linnie then passed it along to her daughter, Ollie, who married Harry Jaques. Finally, the collection rested in the estate of Russell Jaques, their son, who lived in Campbellford. When Russell's house was sold, the

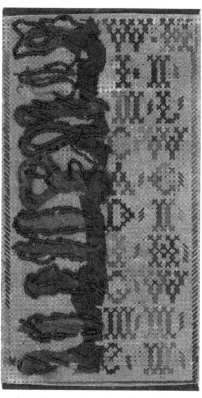

Proctor House Museum, Brighton, Ontario

LEFT: Henrietta King, Dr. King's mother, produced several works of needlepoint, which miraculously survived from the 1850s in the family collections of the King, Ames, and then-Jaques families. They are now included in the King Collection that resides at Proctor House Museum in Brighton. This piece is connected to the hair snips and initials and provides us with the message: THESE MEMORYES OF HENRIETTA KINGS DEAR AND AFFECTINATE FAMILY.

RIGHT: Henrietta King went to considerable effort to create this work of needlepoint. She collected snips of hair from all of her ten children and attached them with beads, locating them beside the appropriate initials of the children. We might recall that her oldest child, Dr. William Henry King, died in June 1859, so this work was created before that and kept in family collections all through the years, to end up at Proctor House Museum in 2014.

collection was sent to the auction house in Campbellford. One day at the Auction House, Roger McMurray, a collector from Brighton, purchased several of the boxes of this collection and took them home. Roger had recently seen *The Ghost Walk* at the Barn Theatre in Brighton, and this fun evening included a piece about Dr. King. Putting two and two together, Roger realized that these artifacts were an important part of local history. He then worked to obtain the other part of the collection, which he had not won at the auction. He paid a premium price but was able to bring the entire collection back together. In 2014, Roger generously donated the entire collection to the Proctor House Museum in Brighton.

Some of the most unique pieces in this collection are Henrietta King's work in needlepoint. One item shows a sentimental tribute to all of her children, with snips of their hair fastened beside their initials.

Another needlepoint shows an idealized version of the familiar scene at the southeast corner of the King farmhouse, where the grave-stone of William Henry King stood amongst the trees. Today, we may need to look at it rather closely to make out the message of this work. The top line clearly says M E M O, but just under the green leaves of the trees there is an "O" at the left side and an "F" on the right side. The word "MEMORIAL" is obviously intended here but Henrietta could not fit in all the letters, so we only see "M E M O." At the bottom we can make out W H KING, although we might have trouble arriving at the exact letters unless we know the history behind the scene that is depicted. Henrietta King was paying a touching tribute to her son in the best way she knew how.

One impact of the Dr. King tragedy for the King family was that most of the siblings moved far away from home. The next oldest son, Isaac Newton King, married Abigail Losie and stayed in the immediate Codrington area, but died at the young age of thirty-nine in 1875. His oldest daughter, Maud Evelyn King, married Frank Davidson and it is through their son D'Arcy M. Davidson that we have a good deal of the King family history. His daughter, Jean Hammond, donated Dr. King's violin to Proctor House Museum in the 1990s.

As we go down the list of siblings, the next oldest, Mary Louisa King, married David Hutchinson Ames from Mount Olivet, and in the late

1870s they move to Michigan. Charles Wellington King, the brother who visited Dr. King while he was in jail and brought his body back to Codrington after the hanging, was in South Dakota by 1870, and ended up in Oregon. Amelia Caroline King married John Dixon Garnett from Cavan Township and they moved to Manitoba. David Nelson King stayed around Codrington and was the father of Linnie King, who we have seen was the mother of Lloyd Ames. James Harrison King inherited the King farm at Codrington and then sold it to Walter Ames in 1890. The last of the King children were a pair of twins. Manly Manson King married Mary Eliza Bush in 1875, but she died soon after the birth of their daughter Emma, and later we find him in Barrie. The other twin, Melissa Emily King, married Daniel McKenzie from the family just to the west of the King farm, and they moved to Michigan.

The impact of the Dr. King story on the King and then Ames families was still very fresh in the mind of

Proctor House Museum, Brighton, Ontario

The most touching of Henrietta King's needlepoint works must be the scene of the memorial of her son, Dr. William Henry King. He was buried at the southeast corner of the King farmhouse in Codrington on June 11, 1859, and a substantial memorial was erected on the site sometime soon after. In this needlepoint, Henrietta has recreated the reverential scene of the overhanging trees and the dignified memorial with flowers and grass to complete the image. She did not have room for the full word "Memorial" so the inscription reads: MEMO OF W H KING.

Lloyd Ames, who had personally handled the gravestone when he was around eighteen years of age. He knew exactly where to find it in 1955. He loved his mother very much and was keenly aware of how much the story, and in particular the sight of the memorial, distressed her. In addition, Lloyd Ames

Author's photo

Picture of Walter Ames and Linnie (King) Ames c. 1900.
Linnie King was a niece of Dr. King. She married Walter Ames of Mount Olivet and they lived on the King/Ames farm at Codrington. Their son, Lloyd Ames, took over the farm and lived there until his daughter, Mary, married Charles Buchanan in 1949, when Lloyd and Louise moved to a house in Codrington and Charles and Mary began to raise a family on the farm.

Author's photo

Wedding picture, July 16, 1949, front of Ames/Buchanan farmhouse at Codrington. Charles Buchanan and Mary Ames were married at the Codrington United Church on July 16, 1949. The happy couple are in the centre with the groom's parents to his right, William and Bertha (Goodfellow) Buchanan. To Mary's left are her parents, Lloyd and Louise (Haggerty) Ames. The picture was taken at the front of the farmhouse where Dr. King's memorial still lay buried a few yards to the viewer's left.

told the story of a visit he and his father made to the House of Refuge in Cobourg sometime around 1915. The old building was still there, much as it had been in 1859, when Dr. King was incarcerated in the basement, awaiting the hangman. On the day of their visit, they were able to go down into the basement and see the corner cell where their notorious relative spent his last few weeks on earth. By the tone of the telling a lifetime later, it was clear that the young Lloyd Ames was mightily impressed by this experience.

My grandfather was always annoyed by reminders of the Dr. King story, even when speaking with his grandchildren. This was particularly evident during the discussions I had with him in his later years of life. There was an interesting dichotomy: he disliked the story because he found it directly insulting to his family honour, and yet his normal storytelling engine would kick into gear if prodded.

As the generations roll by, our family skeletons recede farther into the closet and are gratefully forgotten, most of the time. While some of my relatives and maybe some folks around Codrington may feel a bit uncomfortable with such a public airing of a sordid chapter in our history, my history instincts tell me it is a story that deserves to be told in a complete and accurate way. The fact that it is also a fascinating and entertaining story is a wonderful bonus.

I expect that if Lloyd Ames has been rolling over in his grave at the publishing of *Murder in the Family: The Dr. King Story*, it is only in preparation for getting up and going to the library to check out the book.

Grandpa, you'll love the story!

TRANSCRIPTION OF ORIGINAL DOCUMENTS

The Dr. King story is well documented. The documents that were used to write *Murder in the Family: The Dr. King Story* are available in archives and libraries, usually on microfilm that can be printed in PDF format. My trip to the Metropolitan Reference Library in Toronto netted a memory key full of files to work with. Several of the documents are of particular interest and have been selected for publishing with the story. Transcriptions are provided instead of the original documents because many of the pages of the original microfilmed documents are smudged, dark, and difficult to read.

CORONER'S REPORT

The coroner, Simon Davidson, who was assigned to conduct the inquest into the death of Sarah Ann King, presented this coroner's report to the coroner's jury at Delong's Railroad Hotel on Monck St., Brighton, on November 27, 1858. The report is transcribed from the original handwritten document, which was found in the Trent University Archives in Peterborough.

Province of Canada
County of Northumberland
One of the United Counties
Of Northumberland and Durham
To Wit.:

An inquisition under taken for our Sovereign Lady the Queen at the Township of Brighton, County of Northumberland, one of the United Counties of Northumberland and Durham, the twenty seventh day of November in the twenty second year of the reign of our Sovereign Lady Queen Victoria.

Before Simon Davidson, Esquire, one of the Coroners of our said Lady the Queen for the said United Counties of Northumberland and Durham at Richard Delong's Hotel in the township of Brighton in the county aforesaid.

On view of the body of Sarah Ann King then and there lying dead upon the oath of John Bowles, James M. Ferris, Abraham C. Singleton, Robert Barker, Robert Clark, Robert Wynn, William C. Proctor, Peter Davidson, E.J. Blood, Richard Kellogg, John McAlease, John Grems, William Simpson, James Taylor, Augustus Spencer, Richard Delong and John Abraham, Good and lawful men of said township duly chosen and who being then and there duly sworn and charged, to inquire for our said Lady the Queen when where how and after what manner the said Sarah Ann King came to her death do upon their oath say

That William Henry King of the township of Brighton in the County of Northumberland, Physician, not having the fear of God before his eyes but being moved and so decided by the instigation of the devil and of his malice aforethought wickedly containing and intending the said Sarah Ann King with [unclear] wilfully feloniously and of his malice aforethought to kill and murder on the third day of November in the year of our lord 1858 at the Township aforesaid in the County aforesaid a large quantity of a certain deadly poison called white arsenic did mix for and give to and administer unto …

The said Sarah Ann King and the same her the said Sarah Ann King did cause to take drink and swallow in the said William Henry King there and then well knowing the said white arsenic so mixed, as aforesaid, to be deadly poison and that the said Sarah Ann King to wit on the day and year last a foresaid did take drink and swallow down the said white arsenic so mixed for given to and administered unto her the said Sarah Ann King as aforesaid by the said William Henry King and which he the said William Henry King did cause her to take drink and swallow down as aforesaid the said Sarah Ann King not knowing that the same was white arsenic or any other poison. By means whereof, the said Sarah Ann King then and there became sick and

greatly distempered in her body and then Sarah Ann King
of the poison aforesaid [unclear text] her taken drink and
swallowed down as aforesaid did of the sickness occasioned
thereby from the said third day of November in the year
aforesaid until the fourth day of November in the same year
at the township aforesaid in the County aforesaid did lan-
guish and languished did live on which said last mentioned
day the said Sarah Ann King at the Township aforesaid in
the County aforesaid and the poison aforesaid and of the
sickness and distemper accessioned thereby did die and to
the Jurors aforesaid upon their oath aforesaid do say that
the said William Henry King her the said Sarah Ann King
in manner and form aforesaid feloniously wilfully and of his
malice aforethought did kill and murder against the peace
of our lady the Queen her Crown and dignity.

LETTER FROM PHILADELPHIA

This letter was part of the correspondence of Dr. King in the months leading up to his trial in Cobourg in April of 1859. Dr. King had attended the Homeopathic Medical College from the fall of 1856 and obtained his medical degree there in the spring of 1858. The college was intent on protecting one of their own, as well as promoting the methods of homeopathic medicine.

From C.F. Butler, President of the Hahnemannian
Medical Institute, Philadelphia, To Dr.
King, While in Cobourg Gaol
Philadelphia, Pennsylvania, U.S.A.
March 3rd, 1859.
To whom it may concern:
At a regular meeting of the Hahnemannian Medical Institute of the Homeopathy Medical College, of Pennsylvania, March 24, 1859, Thos. Geo, Edwards, M.D., of Texas, arose and laid before the Institute, the unfortunate position of our estimable acquaintance, and former President, William Henry King, M.D., of Brighton, Canada West. Where it was unanimously moved that this Institute do forward to the authorities concerned in the trial of Wm. H. King, a concise statement, of the

position, and unexceptional deportment of said King while a member of this Inst. Mr. King was elected president of this Institution at the commencement of the session of '57 and '58; and retained the chair during the entire session. In this capacity Mr. King displayed eminent talent in conducting the affairs of the Institution: winning from *all* their respect and esteem for his decision of character and superiority of intellect. As a student, Mr. King had no superiors in his class; as a man he was universally beloved for his affable manners, and kind and gentle disposition. Mr. King we looked upon as a man of unexceptional habits; his seat in the College was never vacant, and his marked attention during lectures stamping him as a student in every sense of the word. Judging from Mr. King's irreproachable conduct while a member of this institution, it would seem that he is more the victim to the force of circumstances rather than any intentional crime of his own. Hoping this testimonial of Mr. King's former unimpeachable character may receive some attention from your honorable body, I am your obedient servant,

Chas. F. Butler, Pres. Hahn. Med. Inst.
Edward Rawson, Sec. Han. Med. Inst.

LETTERS BETWEEN DR. KING AND MELINDA READ IN COURT

During Dr. King's trial Crown Counsel Thomas Galt became very annoyed with the testimony of Melinda Vandervoort because she was being coy and evasive. At one point he told her to go sit down and he proceeded to read the first two letters that were exchanged between herself and Dr. King. These two letters contained some of the most incriminating evidence of the trial because they demonstrated clearly that Dr. King was involved with another woman and was planning to get rid of his wife. The language is not necessarily direct but it is easy to read between the lines.

Melinda Freeland Vandervoort, examined — I know the prisoner at the bar; I received the letter produced from him; I sent him the likeness produced and the enclosed note.

Cross-examined — Mrs. King asked me to send the likeness to her; I never had any improper intercourse with Dr. King.

To Mr. Galt — I directed the likeness to Dr. King; I thought that when I got the letter it was written for amusement; I sent him this letter in answer, for amusement!

Mr. Galt (severely) — Go down; I must read these letters, but do not wish to do so in your presence!

The following letters were then read by the learned counsel:

Note: This is the first letter Dr. King sent to Melinda in response to the receipt of the "likeness":

W.H. KING, M.D.   Brighton, Oct. 10
Sweet little lump of good nature. — I long looked with pru-
dent anxiety for the arrival of the object of my thoughts,
but began to despair. Still, I had too much perseverance,
and alas! I walked to the P.O. this morning (Monday) and
found the most precious thing (except the original) on
earth; better to me than *all* California; I will not, however,
tell you what it was, but could I indulge in the hope that
those *winning* and *genial* smiles would ever be found in
my possession, all troubles would then cease. It is a perfect
infatuation to me. Can you keep from sacrificing yourself upon the hymeneal altar for the next year? I wish so.
Now, I am at a loss to know whether to take it as a token of
friendship or l--- . will you inform me which you mean if
for, and if the latter it will certainly soothe and refresh my
drooping spirits. All you say shall be *perfectly confidential.*
You need never have the least suspicion of this *token* being
seen or handled by any other than its present possessor.
Furthermore, if you correspond with me I will guarantee
upon my word and house that detection shall never happen;
you are, therefore, perfectly safe; but oh! could I but know
whether you could reciprocate my feelings or not. Much
would I give to be assured on this point: it might give me
the most exquisite joy, or it might cause me *bitter* pain. Yet
THIS TOKEN shall cheer me many a time while riding
through the lonely mile.

I must claim your indulgence that your sense of propri-
ety and good taste will adore me for thus punctually giving
expression to my feelings. Do not betray the confidence I
have reposed in you. O! I would like to say a thousand things
to you that flash through my imagination like a panoramic
display, but I must not venture for the present. May I hear

from that object so dear to my h---? Why is it so you might ask? Well, I would like to tell you that some other time.

Please accept ten thousand thanks for such a treasure as I received this morning; it shall always remain in my possession unless called for by its identity.

O! those lovely smiles, so plainly delineated; I must think you meant for something. I cannot possibly be deceptive. I have told you enough that you may judge where my h--- is, now could you be induced to tell me where yours is? O do!

You will observe that this letter is anonymous for fear somebody might get your keys, and read it; as it is, if they should, they would not be wiser but my name shall be ----. You know whom it is from just as well as if my name was appended. Do you remember ---, and cc. cc, and 'going to California.' Well, when you write sign Van. Do not judge of my literary attainments from the style of these hasty-thrown sentences, for I paid more attention to ideas than style. Come and visit whenever you can. --- is very sick — last night we thought she would die.

Your sincere l ---

Note: This is the letter Melinda sent to Dr. King in response to his first letter:

Sidney Oct. 18th, 1858
Dear Doctor. — The time has come to respond.
Yours of the 10th instant came to hand in good repair, and exceedingly pleased was I while perusing its contents. It is with much pleasure, but at the same time with a degree of embarrassment, that I embrace the opportunity to write you *one*. I feel an unusual warmth of friendship for you and not being in the habit of portraying my weakness by way of the pen, expect to find it no easy task — however, hope it will be accepted. I hardly know in what manner to address you,

as circumstances are with you, it appears almost in vain for me to think of you only as a friend. Yet something seems to whisper, 'still hope.'

Since I first had the pleasure of an introduction, my heart is constantly with you, and I'm not contented a moment. O! could I forever be with you; I think I should be happy, for indeed, I enjoyed myself to excess during my stay in your presence though I suppose now I must eradicate such thoughts from my mind; for *you* are married, and my destiny must be to love and not share your interesting society. We are some distance apart, yet trust our ties of friendship although of short production are such as not to allow time or distance to sever. Perhaps you'll pardon my familiarity when you come to realize that you have unlinked the tender cord of affection until you have an alarming influence over my girlish nature.

One smile only from *your* countenance can inspire a depth of veneration in my bosom never felt by me for any individual. Well now, Dr. don't you think it very wrong for me to correspond with you? I'm afraid if known it would destroy 'Annie's' happiness, and for instance, if I was in her position would much rather be in my grave than suffer the idea of your intimacy with another, though perhaps you merely express some of your ideas to me for pastime, so I hope you'll not continue them, for I am easily flattered and it may prove to be something very serious. I am very lonely. My 'sister' has not returned yet. I am pretty well, and hope you enjoy the same blessing. Please answer, if you deem me worthy. I hope you'll not criticise.

Your unwavering. L---- VAN

While the letters were being read, the prisoner showed no sense of shame; but rather seemed to share in the amusement which could not be repressed.

NEWS REPORT ON THE TRIAL

The Tri-Weekly Guide
Port Hope, April 7, 1859

Dr. King's Trial

We did not issue a paper yesterday, as we were anxious to give the full account of the exciting trial, recently concluded, in one number. To day we publish a sheet and a half, which contains the evidence, the speeches of the Counsel, and Judges charge complete. We are indebted to the *Globe* for the speeches and charge of the Judge. We took full notes of the evidence during the trial; but our Compositors availed themselves of the *Globe's* printed report of the evidence on the part of the prosecution, as it could be more rapidly set up than manuscript. The evidence on the part of the defence is as we took it down; and in some respects is slightly different from the *Globe's* report.

Too much praise cannot be given to Mr. Sheriff Fortune for the efficient manner on which he performed the difficult task of keeping the great crowd who could not gain access to the Court Room, in order and good nature. His arrangements were well and timely made, and thoroughly carried out by the staff of officers under him. It seemed perhaps hard to many who had travelled miles to be present at the trial to be shut out; but as the multitude would have filled a room five times as large as the one in which the Court was held, it is obvious that no blame can be attached to Mr. Sheriff Fortune.

Source: *Port Hope Weekly Guide* newspaper, April 7, 1859
Format: Microfilm
Item: Microfilm Reel #071.1357, Reel #3 1859
Location: Port Hope Public Library, History Room (upstairs)
Note: Took print copies as well as PDFs of pages re: Dr. King story.
Date: September 20, 2013

THE JOURNAL

Alexander Stewart was assigned the job of living with Dr. King for the two months between sentencing and hanging. He was to be his gatekeeper and close confidant while reporting all he learned to the sheriff and jailer. It is a wonderful bonus that Alexander Stewart was a sensible and literate man who decided to write a journal while he lived with Dr. King. It is some of the most important information available about Dr. King, as well as other people of this story. It is fascinating reading.

A Journal Of Dr. King While In Cobourg Jail
Under Sentence of Death
By a Constable

Thursday, April 14th. Very wet day, entered prison about 11 o'clock, Mr. Bennett the Jailer, took Dr. King from amongst the other prisoners and put him in an apartment alone, south side of the Jail, under ground, fixing our beds for a time. Dr. in very low spirit frequently saying — "O what an unfortunate man I have been." "O is it possible I must be executed;" after ten more composed. Jailer locked us up by 7 o'clock. I sleep in cell next to Dr., thought it was dreary place.

Friday, 15th. Cells opened by Jailer by 6 o'clock. Dr. rested badly last night. On rising morning first thing said, "O I wish I could see my mother; if I'm executed it will bring my mother to her grave." About 10 o'clock Sheriff entered, he told Dr. King distinctly, that there was no hope of a commutation of his sentence; Dr. wished to see his mother, Sheriff granted his request. About 11 o'clock Mr. Vanderburg, Wesleyan Minister came in to see him, stayed with him 3 or 4 hours, talked faithfully with him, and prayed with him. After he was gone Rev. Mr. Bredin also called and stayed a short time, said he would be up again on Tuesday, locked up by seven o'clock.

Saturday, 16th. Rose by 6 o'clock. Dr. rested a little better last night, on rising said first thing, "O I wish I could see my mother; could she stay with me all the time how I would like it"; had prayers and breakfast, shortly after Dr. Bethune came in to see him; talked and prayed with him. After dinner Mr. Levi Vanderburg came up again to see him, stayed with him till near dusk. Dr. Beaty up also. Mr. Vanderburg prayed before leaving, an excellent prayer, after prayer Dr. wept profusely, I talked with him in the evening on the promises of the Gospels. Dr. believed all I said, but complained of the want of genuine faith, read and prayed with him. Locked up by 7 o'clock.

Lords Day, 17th. Rose by 7 o'clock, had prayers shortly after, about 10 o'clock had prayers again. Dr. prayed first and I followed, seemed very penitent, read to him from the gospel in Ezekiel, he paid great attention, an excellent book. Had dinner, Dr. asked a blessing as he always does before eating, about 3 o'clock Mr. Vanderburg came up again stayed about 2 hours, talked and prayed with him, Dr. paid great attention, is fond of Vanderburg, speaks very highly of him, before going to bed we had prayers again, Dr. engaged very earnestly and devoutly. Locked up by 7 o'clock.

Monday, 18th. Jailer opened Dr.'s cell by 6 1/2 o'clock; Dr. asleep; rose about 7, rested middling well last night, washed, dressed, then had prayers. Read 2 Chron, 33; Dr. prayed very penitently, I followed. Had breakfast, Dr. eat hearty, then Dr. read Gospel in Ezekiel, walked the apartment awhile heaving many a heavy sigh, retiring to cell to pray, seemed anxiously seeking salvation. After dinner a schoolmaster, a relative to Dr. called to see him about 4 o'clock, Rev. Mr. Bredin and Mr. Vanderburg called to see him, conversed with Dr. King about an hour before leaving, Mr. Bredin engaged in prayer. Got a letter from J.R. Clarke. Evening took tea, conversed a short time. Locked up about 7 and went to bed.

Tuesday, 19th. Up by 6 o'clock, Dr. rose about 7, much noise and stamping in the cell opposite, disagreeable, read and prayed, Psa. 22. Dr. prayed earnestly and penitently for mercy and forgiveness, I followed; had breakfast, then wrote a little. Dr. wrote nearly all day intending to publish it, forenoon a Mr. Donnelly an itinerant lecturer came up to see Dr., stayed a short time. Afternoon Rev. Mr. Hooper into see Dr., conversed and prayed with him; shortly Dr. Bethune in he also talked and prayed with us. Dr. seems more composed and confident in God's mercy, a fine day. Locked up by 7 o'clock as usual.

Wednesday, 20th. Rose by 6 o'clock, Dr. rose about 7, washed and dressed, walked the apartment a short time, then we had morning prayers. I read Matt chap 27, Dr. prayed first very humbly, earnestly and penitently, I followed, had breakfast, Dr. read a little in the "Sinner's Friend," said it was a fine little book. In cell to-day, praying a good while. After noon Mr. Hughes called a short time. Mr. Vanderburg up also, stayed with us till dark. I was home 2 hours, Dr.'s uncle and cousin in to see him told him of the bad success of his petition in Percy and Seymour. Dr. went, had tea, read John 14, Dr. prayed very earnestly. Locked up about 7 as usual.

Thursday, 21st. Rose about 6, Dr. rose about 7, seemed to feel bad that all the world was against him, sighed deeply, said "seems nothing for me but execution," had breakfast about 8, read Psa. 146. Dr. prayed very earnestly for mercy and forgiveness, Dr. walked a while, then wrote a spell, Mr. Connelly up again to see him, stayed with him about 3 hours — told him plainly to put his trust in God and prepare for the worst. Dr. wrote two letters, talked with me a little on the case. Said his wife did not die from arsenic, Mr. Vanderburg called stayed, with him 2 hours, Dr. said he must look to God, as he expected little from man, Sheriff called this morning a few minutes. Locked up 7 o'clock. Dr. reading Caughey's in cell to night.

Good Friday, 22nd. Jailor opened our cell doors by 6 o'clock; brought in our usual quota of bread, being a 4 lb loaf each day. A prisoner on the other side released, time up; took out a petition with him for Dr. Dr. rose about 7, said "This is Good Friday, it will be the last I'll ever see," sighed deeply, said he felt worse last night than he had ever felt, used such expressions as these, "O, that it could be undone," "I believe that I did wrong, I have ruined my father for life," &c, at morning prayers. Dr. prayed very earnestly for himself, for his father and mother and friends, and for all under sentence of death. Forenoon J.R. Clarke called and saw him; gave him small hopes of a reprieve. Rev. Mr. Earl and Rev. A. Burpee called, talked and prayed with us, Dr. read in the "Sinner's Friend," said it was a beautiful little book. Talked on the promise. "The blood of Christ cleanseth from all sin," Mr. Salmen and Mr. Vanderburg called and stayed till dusk, read and prayed with us. Locked up by 7 o'clock.

Saturday, 23rd. Dr. bathed this morning, as he usually does on Saturday, Shortly after had breakfast, then had prayers, read Psa 45, Dr. prayed and I followed; had much liberty. Dr. expected his mother today; disappointed, Dr. reading

Caughey's Sermons to day. While it snowed he said "that will be the last snow I'll ever see." Dr. in cell several times to-day, praying. After tea had prayers. Afterwards Dr. wept profusely, said "O that my life could be spared, must be hanged, what disgrace it will bring on my parents, O will God hear my prayers, how awful if my soul be lost, &c." Locked up by 7 1/2 in the evening — stormy day.

Lord's Day, 24th. Ground covered with snow and frost; Dr. said "that will be the last snow I ever see." Said in prayer last night something struck him saying, "You shall be reprieved." Dr. seemed more cheerful a short time, had breakfast then prayers, read Matt 17, Dr. prayed very earnestly and penitently. Lord in thy mercy hear and answer my prayers! Dr. read a tract sent to him by a friend in Percy, then walked a while, I read to him from Meikle's Meditation sent to him by Mr. Allen, afterwards Dr. retired to cell for prayer, had dinner, read Acts 12. Dr. and I prayed; shortly after Mr. Vanderburg came up, stayed and conversed till dark. Dr. felt very sad, still clinging to hopes of a reprieve, Mr. Vanderburg talked ever plainly to him, then read and prayed with him; read Heb. 10. Locked up by dusk, Dr. reading in cell, Meikle's Meditations.

Monday, 25th. Rose by 6 o'clock, Dr. rose by 7 1/2, seemed more cheerful, took breakfast, had prayers, read Isa 6, prayed very earnestly and penitently, I followed. Dr. walked up and down awhile, talked a while, wrote a few receipts. Had dinner. Shortly, after Mr. Vanderburg came up, I went home three or four hours, came up to jail by 6 o'clock. Mr. Vanderburg left; asked Dr. how he felt, said "sad, sad." Mr. Bennet came in to lock up, talked with us a little, told Dr. to make up his peace with God and prepare for the worst and if he had peace with God he would have no fear of death. Dr. said that was his daily prayer. A crazy man came here to-day from Bowmanville; made great noise to-day.

Tuesday, April 26th. rose by 6 o'clock, Dr. rose half an hour after — had breakfast, then read Prov. 48. Dr. prayed. Shortly after Bishop Smith came in to see him, he talked very kindly and plain to him for about an hour; he told him that all manner of sin and blasphemy should be forgiven unto men, "so says Christ, Mat. 12, 12" he explained to him three last verses of 1 John 1, then prayed a most beautiful prayer for him, he told the Doctor to offer prayer, he did so, after which Mr. Smith bade us farewell — urging the Dr. to seek salvation as it was attainable even to him. After dinner Dr. Beatty and Dr. Powell came in near evening, talked and prayed with him and gave him a book, "Bishop Taylor's holy living and dying."

Wednesday, 27th. Dr. rose about 7 1/2, he had breakfast, then prayers, read Psa. 59, Dr. then prayed very earnestly, I followed in my weak way. The Dr. then walked a while then wrote a while, received 3 letters today, he felt sad, after dinner better. Mr. Vanderburg came up and stayed with him till dark, I went home three hours, which time the Dr. wrote three letters to the United States. He tries his best by God's help to prepare for death, he never looks at a newspaper or talks about the world, but seems deeply serious and concerned for his soul's salvation, but truly it is a bitter cup to drink, the cup of true penitence. Lord teach us to remember God in youth and health ere the evil day come.

Thursday, 28th. We rose early this morning, after being much disturbed by a crazy man in the opposite cell. This is not the place for crazy men they ought to be sent to the Asylum. The Dr. read and prayed, he can pray like a minister, I followed and enjoyed sweet peace, praise God. Doctor expected to see his mother today, and she did come. The Dr. then walked the floor, then read to his father. We heard that Sickles was acquitted, the Dr. felt bad, and said why can't I be freed also, bemoaning his sad condition greatly, we then had tea and then prayers. He then walked a while, then the turn-key came in with his bunch of keys and locked him up — the crazy man troubled us greatly during the night.

Friday, 29th. The jailor brought our bread and water and opened our cell doors, shortly after daybreak. Dr. King said he had a poor night of it fretting about the result of Sickle's trial contrasted with his own, we had breakfast, the Dr. ate heartily, then had prayers, he walked and talked a while, then read and sighed deeply, then took dinner, shortly Mr. Levi Vanderburg can in, talked and prayed with him. I went home a short time, when I came back I found the Dr. in middling good spirits. Locked up by 7 o'clock. Rev. Mr. Vanderburg takes great pains to instruct and comfort the Dr.'s mind, almost every day the Lord rewards him in these endeavours to save a soul from death, and thus hide a multitude of sins.

Saturday, 30th. Jailor brought our bread and water by 6 o'clock, unlocked cell door, Dr. asleep, sleeps best towards morning, rose by 7 o'clock, bathed himself, had breakfast and prayers, read Psa 51, and prayed very earnestly and I trust penitently, walked a while. Shortly after Dr. Bethune came in, talked very faithfully and affectionately to him, gave him good sound advice then prayed with him, left him a programme of daily exercises and prayers to be used by him. After dinner Mr. Vanderburg up again, talked and read and prayed with him. Three prisoners put in to day — one for peddling obscene books — one for stealing flour, and one named John Farreli, from Chicago, for robbery. Locked up at dusk as usual.

Lord's Day, May 1st, 1859. Now summer returns, after a long and tedious Canadian winter; but summer and winter are alike here — no vegetation here — no opening buds or blos-soms — no balmy zephyrs or odoriferous breezes, but on the contrary, gloomy walls — barred and grated windows, iron doors, and arched stone canopy over our head — surely this place was not made to entertain human beings but demons or the worst malefactor, then we must lie in iron beds and tho' lying alone are not alone; as bad as we are, we are not allowed on this hallowed day to get out to hear God's word preached nor enjoy the softening and civilizing influence of female society, no! the law sternly demands justice to be executed on the offender, but no mercy. Mr. Bennett with two letters, one from a brother in California who heard of his imprisonment and expected to hear of his verdict and sentence. "My poor Isaac," says he, "how it will wound your heart, you need to felt so proud of me, now how fallen!" We had breakfast, then prayers. Then Dr. commenced himself a programme of exercises laid down by Dr. Bethune, read Isa 27 and John 14 and the fifth Psalm then prayers of the English Church form, after dinner a short time our dear friend Mr. Vanderburg came in and stayed a short time, after tea Mr. V., the Dr. and myself all engaged alternatively in prayer trusting God was with us.

Monday, May 2nd. Dr. rose by 7 o'clock, read Isa. 64 and John 15, Pro. 9, 10, then engaged in prayer both of us, he walked and then read a while in his cell, he expected his father up today, he' did not come, the Dr. seemed to feel very sad, after tea we had prayers again, the Dr. read Psalms 46, 47, he and I then prayed, felt light and liberty, praise God — locked up at dark, no person in to-day. — Prisoner John Farrel escaped today.

Tuesday, 3rd. had breakfast and prayers as usual, Dr. read Isa. 61, Heb. 1, and prayed. Then the Rev. Mr. James, the English Church curate, came in, he talked and prayed with him, he told him he need not build himself up on any false hope of a commutation of his sentence as he believed there would be no change, urged him earnestly to prepare for death as time is on the wing, and the 9th of June was daily getting nearer, after his going away the Doctor felt very bad and wept bitterly, he was very sad and sorrowful a long time, we had dinner and prayer again, shortly after Mr. Vanderburg came up and stayed till near dusk. Mr. Hughes, and Mr. Bennett came in to see him a short time, the Dr. cheered up a little, he talked of the value of the Bible, repeated texts, and determined to seek the Lord till he found him, giving good evidence of unfeigned repentance — The Sheriff came in this morning a few minutes, he locked us up at dusk, the Dr. read Mrs. Palmer's works in his cell.

Wednesday, 4th. Dr. Rose at 7 o'clock, he seemed in very low spirits this morning, he used the English Church form, he sought the Lord earnestly, but has not found peace yet. Mr. Vanderburg, up in the afternoon as usual, conversed and prayed with him. His mother up to see him in the afternoon, in with him alone about two hours, she gave him some very good advice. After his mother went away Dr. wept and sobbed violently; said he would never see his mother but once again; spoke to his brother through the iron door; told him to be a good boy, obey his parents, keep the Sabbath, and never do anything wrong. Locked up at dark. Prisoner found who ran away.

Thursday, May 5th. Jailor brought in our accustomed quota of bread and water, unlocked Dr. cell, then had breakfast and prayers as usual, in the course of the afternoon Rev. T. Alexander from Percy, came in and talked with Dr. as short time, very appropriately; before leaving, read and explained to us the 51st Psalm; a favourite Psalm here with us; it seemed as if the Psalmist had just penned it to meet our case, then he prayed with us and left; Dr. much pleased with his visit; after dinner had prayers again, read Jonah first three chapters; Dr. then wrote a letter to his brother in California. Prisoners other side out in yard to-day, first time this spring, seemed glad to get out to breathe the fresh air; had tea and prayers. Locked up by dark.

Friday, May 6th. Dr. sent away a letter to his brother in California to-day, nothing of importance happened to-day; Dr. about as usual, earnestly seeking after Christ. Vanderburg gone to Toronto; Dr. Bethune came to see us this afternoon, talked a short time with Dr., then read and expounded 103rd Psalm, then put up a very appropriate prayer, left near dark, had tea, prayers, and bed about usual time.

Saturday, May 7th. Waiting still on Dr. King. He bathed again this morning shortly after had our breakfast and prayers. Read Isa 63, and Heb. 9, Dr. repeated the English Church form, concluded by prayers; Psalm 61st, he engaged with much feeling and earnestness, felt very sad forenoon evidently deep conviction of sin. Said the way of transgressors is hard said I am a great sinner, the chief of sinners, was almost despairing of God's mercy, said he was willing to give him to Christ, but could not feel that God had accepted him, about mid-afternoon we both joined in prayer again, after dinner I read Lam 3, had prayer again, after while Mr. Vanderburg came up, he back again from Toronto. He had seen the Governor, out of all hope of Dr. being reprieved. Dr. cried and wept sore. Said, I must see mercy from God, I see will get no mercy from men, towards evening Dr. more composed, me home two hours, locked up by 7. Dr. said, Sickles freed, me to be hanged.

Lords Day, May 8th. On rising this morning Dr. felt very poorly, said he had a poor night of it, slept very little, felt sad, very sad and dejected, Had breakfast and prayers, Dr. prayed most earnestly and penitently, surely such prayers will prevail with God. Read Isa. 49, and Heb. 13. Dr. said he had but a few more Sabbath's to live, very melancholy to-day. After dinner we read 107th Psalm, Dr. and I prayed alternatively, Dr. said he felt headache, went to bed a short time, after rising walked a while we then had tea. Dr. in great distress of mind. Satan

almost leading him to despair of God's mercy, said it would
be awful if he went to the scaffold unforgiven. He still looked
upon God as an angry judge, did not yet see him as a God
reconciled in Christ. I told him I thought any sinner who
sincerely repented of sin and earnestly sought forgiveness
could not be lost. Dr. said he wanted to make sure of his sins
forgiven before he went to the scaffold. We then had evening
prayers, Dr. read Isa 53. We then both engaged earnestly in
prayer. I trust God heard us and will answer these our prayers
in his own good time. Lord grant that this the time of our
extremity may be the time of thy opportunity. Lord save us
for thy name and for His mercies sake. Lord increase our faith.
Dr. a little more cheerful toward night. Locked up at dark.

Monday, 9th. Dr. and I rose to-day about 7 o'clock, washed
and dressed, then had breakfast, Dr. said this is the 9th of
May, one half of my time is gone, seemed very sad, after
breakfast had morning prayers, Dr. read Isa 51 and 1 Pt. 2,
also Psalms, then prayed very earnestly and most sincerely, I
prayed after, Dr. responding to every sentence after prayers,
Dr. walked awhile, apparently deep in thought, occasionally
a deep sigh. Lord have mercy on him and heal his wounded
spirit for Jesus sake. About 11 o'clock Mr. Vanderburg came
up, I was home he stayed with Dr. 3 or 4 hours, talked and
prayed with him, Dr. very sad, yet earnestly seeking salvation,
at evening prayers Dr. prayed for his father, that he might be
converted — Locked up by 7 o'clock.

Tuesday, 10th May. Dr. rose this morning a little past 6, and
he felt confident that God would forgive his sins, in praying
last night he said he felt more liberty. Three prisoners in the
cells opposite got their leave this morning, time up. Dr. talked
to them through the diamond hole, bid them farewell and
gave them good advice. Said "farewell Tom, I'll never see you
any more, you will now taste the sweets of liberty denied to

me," said Tom was to him as a brother, said he was greatly reformed since his confinement here, I have become a praying man. Had breakfast and prayers, about 10 o'clock. Rev. Mr. Bleasdal from Trenton came to see Dr.; was greatly cheered and encouraged by his visit, said he had done him more good than any who had called to see him, stayed about 2 hours with him, talked and prayed with him. Told Dr. to look to him whom the brazen serpent typed, viz, Christ on the Cross. Sympathized deeply with Dr. said he would come up again and see him if he wished, would be up at all events on the 9th June, on the day before Mr. Vanderburg up all afternoon endeavouring to comfort the Dr. and lead him to Christ, Dr. not yet restored to liberty, not yet adopted into God's family, but is I believe an earnest enquirer. Dr. a little more cheerful, evening locked up by dusk. Lord keep thy servants who put their trust in thee and save us for Jesus sake.

Wednesday, May 11th. Fine day, Mr. Bennett took out our window this morning to give us more air, this being a warm bad ventilated place, very unhealthy. Dr. seeming pleased to get the fresh air to breath. Dr. and I prayed as usual. Dr. felt still very sad, walked and read alternatively all forenoon praying all the time while walking the Hall, after dinner sometime our friend and Brother Vanderburg came up. Dr. thinking long for him to come, long before he did come. Poor Dr. thy countenance indicates that deep sorrow and anguish have their lodgement in thy sad heart, yet what a noble mind thou hast, splendid talent far above mediocrity and a more generous heart never possessed a human breast. How unfortunate thou hast been "a brother born for adversity" — John Farrel the prisoner shackled and off to Chicago to night.

Thursday, May 12th. Time rolls on; four weeks today is the fatal 9th of June; everything with us to-day went on the same as usual. Poor Doctor; what anguish and sorrow inherits thy

torn bosom; many, many a heavy sigh heaves thy tortured
breast. How true, "the way of transgressors is hard"; yes,
hard — it is hard work to repent and find forgiveness with
an offended God. My heart, dear doctor, bleeds for thee. I
may pity and pray for thee, but cannot effectually help thee.
May God, whom thou hast offended by thy sin, when he has
wounded thee by his Holy Spirit, heal thee by enabling thee
to look to Jesus, by whose stripes we are healed. — After
dinner Mr. Vanderburg came up; stayed near all afternoon;
me out a while. After coming in had tea, then prayed; locked
by half-past 7.

Friday, May 13th. Mr. Bennett returned again from Windsor,
where he took John Farrell, the prisoner, the Chicago robber.
Doctor rose early, in very low spirits this morning; said he
could not rest in bed; felt very disconsolate, took but little
breakfast, had prayers, to bed again, heaving many a heavy
sigh; surely his broken and contrite heart God will not despise.
Doctor's head ached to-day. After dinner and prayers Mr.
Vanderburg and Mr. Salmon came in to see doctor; talked
and prayed with him till near dark. Doctor a little cheered;
after retiring to cell prayed earnestly for half an hour; told
me he had more confidence in God's mercy now than ever.
Jailor made some fuss about prisoner breaking jail.

Saturday, May 14th. Dr. rose early this morning, said his
time was precious every moment of it. I will soon, said he,
be in an eternity of misery or bliss, but the thought of the
Gallows, oh! oh! oh! to be hanged by the neck, how dreadful the thought. If it was to die naturally I would give up
at once into God's hands; but oh! the gallows! the gallows!
Had breakfast and prayers. Dr. prayed earnestly, afterward
Dr. and I talked a little of the employments and enjoyments
of heaven; shortly after had dinner; Dr. read Isa. 53, and had
prayers. Mr. Bennett brought us in some meat and potatoes,

he was very kind, Dr. in cell a good while after about 3 o'clock. Mr. Vanderburg came up again, talked a good time with the Dr., had prayers; Dr. wept after, said he was glad, ever he saw Mr. Vanderburg, he believed he would be the means of saving his soul, said he could take him by the hand and feel he was like a brother, Mr. Vanderburg speaks kind and faithful to him, and does his very best to comfort him with the promises of God's word. Locked up as usual at dark, Dr. said: it is a great mercy if God saves a sinner like me, and I believe he *will* save me. Lord save us, and bless us for thy name and mercies sake.

Lord's Day, May 15. Spent this day the fore part of it in fasting and prayer, resolved to seek God till we find him. Satan busy with us, tempting me to sleepiness, Dr. think of worldly things, prayed earnestly for light and grace, found help, praise the Lord. Mr. Vanderburg up a while, Dr. went to bed rejoicing in a sin pardoning God.

Monday, May 17th. During the past week the Dr. has passed through a painful ordeal, his convictions of sin very deep and pungent. He has been led past the thunder of Sinai, and heard Jehovah from Mount Horeb, proclaiming his fiery law. He has been led to the very verge of hell, and thought himself almost engulphed in its dark abyss. He has felt indeed the arrows of the Almighty drinking up his spirit, and has experimentally found that "sin is exceeding sinful" — His is no superficial religion, as alas! we have too much of it in our day, but a deep, a real work of Grace. He has felt the pangs of the new birth, and tasted somewhat of the miseries of the last; oh! how terrible the upbraidings of a guilty conscience, terrible indeed, as he paced the hall, the very picture of remorse and despair; surely his most inveterate enemies could they see him would be moved with pity and the hardest heart would melt, but alas, there are too many who are always savoring too much

of Moses, and too little of Christ, who magnify the faults
of others and forget their own, who are pulling a mote out
of their brother's eye, and forgetting the beam in their own.
To-day we spent the time much the same as usual. Reading
and praying writing, talking, &c. Dr. in a little better spirits,
said he would soon be where his enemies can't reach him.
"On the 9th of June," said he, "I will bid farewell to Cobourg"
— said "I hope Stewart you will represent my character in a
true light after I am gone."
Note: The original has May 17 for both Monday and Tuesday.

Tuesday, May 17th. Dr. received two letters last night from
Mr. Bennett, one from his father, another from Rock, the
prisoner in Belleville, declaring God's goodness to him, in
that he had found pardon, and urging the Dr. earnestly to
seek the Lord. Dr. took it very kind of him; did not rise very
early this morning; disturbed again by the crazy man, last
night screaming; had breakfast and prayers; Dr. writing
most all forenoon, had dinner and prayers. Dr. writing till
Mr. Vanderburg called 4 o'clock. Mr. Vanderburg talked very
earnestly to him, and prayed with him; Dr. in pretty good
spirits, only his faith in God's mercy not so strong to-day,
mind wavering. The devil doing all he can to shake his faith
in God's word and promise. O! what an adversary we have to
contend with. Lord dethrone Satan from his usurped domin-
ion in our souls, and save us for thy name sake.

Wednesday, May 18th. Last night female prisoner brought
here from Port Hope for larceny; always some one breaking
the law. It is impossible in this sinful state but that offences
will come; Dr. rose in good spirits this morning, said "when
praying in his cell last night he felt more happy than every
he had yet done," felt now assured that God *would* save his
soul, had breakfast and prayers, Dr. read Jer. 1, Rom 9, Psa.
90, 91 and 92, Prayed earnestly. Repeating the words of

the ?1st Psalm, said while walking, "O, how short is time, a day is past and gone, and it seems only a few minutes." "How terrible that moment when the trap will give way under my feet on the scaffold," oh! oh! Dr. writing to the Judge forenoon and part afternoon. Sheriff in a short time in the evening, had prayers, went to bed at usual time. Dr. Bethune's son buried to-day.

Thursday, May 19th. How quick time flies? Only 3 weeks to day till the fatal 9th of June — then my dear doctor must be led forth to the scene of execution, how painful the thought, the Sheriff and officers coming in and telling us to get ready, the last farewell to this dismal place, then the scaffold, the ascent to it, the fatal drop, the gazing multitude. Dear Doctor, the Lord strengthen thee in that solemn hour and be with thee on entering the dark valley, may thy last struggle be short, and may angels be commissioned to convey thy ransomed spirit to the realms of bliss. Dr. rose about half past eight this morning, washed and dressed, had breakfast and prayers, Dr. walked the hall sighing deeply, said "O I wished I had never married, how many offer themselves for the hymeneal altar, they are nothing but vanity, how many blacks to one prize. If I had never married how much better it would have been for me and for my parents." Talking on the 8th chap of Romans, now a favorite chapter with the Dr., said "I wish to make an entire surrender of myself to God, if I knew anything more I could do, I would do it I find I can do nothing of myself." Dr. wrote a letter to-day to Rock the prisoner in Belleville, in answer to his. About 2 o'clock Rev. Mr. V — up to see Dr. stayed about two hours, talked and prayed to God to direct us to some passage to suit our ease. We opened the Bible at 1 cor, 2, 12, the Dr. read the passage, rejoiced, said, "now I know God will save me, will take me to heaven, the Sheriff may get the gallows ready."

Friday, May 20th. Dr. happy now in the love of God, he has cast all his sins behind his back into the depths of the sea, and blotted them out of the Book of his remembrance. Bless be God! Praised by his holy name, now his arrow is turned into joy, his language now is that of the ancient church, recorded Isa 12, 1. "I will praise thee O Lord, tho' thou wait angry with me they anger is turned away and thou comfortest me." About half-past ten Dr. Bethune came and talked with Dr. and left with him a beautiful form of prayer, had dinner and prayers, Dr. wrote a letter to J.H. Cameron, Toronto, by three o'clock Mr. V. up to see us, talked and prayed with us, we all engaged, Dr. more cheerful to night, spoke of his confession being published in the Star, had tea, locked up for the night, a very fine day, warm.

Saturday, May 21st. Learned last night that Dr. had made a full confession of his guilt to Mr. Vanderburg, he said he had embosomed all to God and man, Dr. had attained to more peace of mind since his confession than formerly, he in my opinion ought to have done so weeks ago. This morning Dr. bathed himself as usual on Saturdays, had breakfast and prayers, writing all day nearly, what he intends publishing in the *Globe*, Rev. Mr. Salmon came up to see us to-day, stayed quite a while, conversed and prayed with us, Dr. writing his confession to the *Globe* for publication, sent off 13 pages full sheet by mail to-night, the remainder to be sent on Monday. Dr. in pretty good spirits to day, at prayer to night expressed himself with confidence and hope in God's mercy. Mr. V. up again 2 hours near evening.

Lord's Day, May 22nd. Dr. rose this morning a little past 8 o'clock, washed and dressed, shortly after said "only two Sabbaths more to spend on earth and then a continuous Sabbath in Heaven," had breakfast and prayers, Dr. read over the form of prayer left by Dr. Bethune, a very excellent prayer, afterwards said, "I feel I am going to heaven, I feel a dreadful load taken off my shoulders." Blessed be God. Had dinner and prayers, afterwards Rev. Mr. Bredin and Mr. V. came up, conversed with us, prayed, and administered the sacrament to Dr. and all of us, true it was a blessed season to our souls, the Sheriff up a short time with the Dr. Mr. V. preaching up stairs this evening, Dr. sat by window and heard most of the sermon, said "O what would I give to have my liberty again and go to hear sermons." Went to bed by 8 o'clock.

Monday, 23rd. Last night Dr. and I sat by our window, the night being calm, we heard Rev. Mr. Vanderburg preaching up stairs, Dr. said "this may be the last sermon I'll ever hear, O how I could wish to have my liberty again, and go to church, how I would prize it, but no, law is inexorable, here I am, I for seven long months shut up within bars and gates, not permitted to breathe the pure air of heaven, admire the beauties of Creation, nor behold the glories of the noon-day Sun, liberty gone, reputation gone, once I was counted a credit to my friends and an honour to my profession, but now I am set up as a mark for the shafts of calumny to shoot at. Oh me! How fallen, nothing for me now but imprisonment, ignominy and the gallows! Lord have mercy on my soul." Dr. continued writing his manuscript to-day, nearly all day, wrote altogether 31 pages large sheets, sent it off to the *Globe* by mail to-night. Dr. is in good spirits to-day, more cheerful than I have seen him yet. Rev. Mr. Hooper and Rev. Mr. Vanderburg up after a short time, a fine day, a little frost this morning.

Tuesday, May 24th. Dr. on retiring to bed last night said "I feel very tired writing all day, wrote 10 pages to-day, large sheets," 14 days more after to-day till the fatal 9th of June. Dr. rose this morning about half-past 7 washed, dressed, walking the hall said, now if I were in heaven enjoying that eternal rest, it would be much better for me than to be in prison here. After breakfast Rev. Mr. Thompson from Napanee and Mr. Lucas called to see Dr. conversed exhorted and prayed with us, told Dr. he believed there was no hope of a reprieve for him, not the least, bade him farewell, Dr. wept profusely, he walked the hall a good deal to-day for exercise finds it necessary for health, we talked a little on the greatness of Christ's love in dying for us. Queen's Birth Day, Band came past jail playing Music, Dr. said "O that I had my liberty again, I would like to give them a speech, I would tell them of the sweets of liberty, what an unfortunate man I have been, O that I had never sinned."

Wednesday, May 25th. Dr. received a letter from J.H. Cameron, Toronto, informing him that he had seen the Governor and Judge and that there would be no alteration of his sentence. Carpenters here this morning measuring the ground to build the gallows, I told Dr. of this fact. He seemed deeply sorrowful for some time, and sighed, saw in the *Globe* the cutting remarks regarding his manuscript, felt bad about it, said people would not believe him when he spoke the truth, about 1 o'clock Mr. V. came up and talked and exhorted him very plainly and affectionately, and prayed with us, left near dark, Dr. determined now to divest his mind of everything earthly, and prepare to meet his god, as time is short.

Thursday, May 26th. On rising this morning I asked the doctor how he felt; he said he had a very poor night of it, had shed many tears, thinking on his past life, the sins he had committed against God and their consequences. At breakfast Dr. said "If I could be sure of Christ being with me in my last moment, I would not fear death."; I quoted a passage Isa. xliii. 2, "When thou passest through the waters I will be with thee"; Dr. said that was a great promise. He quoted Prov. xxviii. 13, "He that confesseth and forsaketh his sins shall have mercy." I said there was a condition on our part "to confess and forsake sin," and a promise on God's part, "shall have mercy."

After breakfast and prayers Rev. Mr. Corson in a few minutes, talked and prayed with us. Doctor very solemn and serious to-day, seemed more humble, penitent and prayerful than he had been for a few days past; Mr. V. up again. The doctor now seems to feel his awful position keenly. How very short his time on earth now — two weeks to-day, then his ransomed spirit must take its everlasting flight, we trust washed in the blood of Christ, to mansions in the skies, "where the wicked cease from troubling, and the weary are at rest."

Friday, May 27th. This morning it thunders, dark clouds hover around and over us, which makes this place dark; now it rains, Doctor rose this morning about 8 o'clock, seemed very solemn to-day, said he was very sorry that ever he had sinned against God; prayed earnestly for forgiveness. — Mr. V. was up a short time afterwards. On sitting down to eat, Dr. sighed and said, "I've been led astray by women; women have been my ruin; in trying to get out of a bad fix, I got into a worse one. O, my unfortunate marriage has been the cause of all my trouble, much better for me I had never married; said I ought to write an essay on marriage to be a warning to others; Dr. said I'm not the first nor only one led astray by women, the strongest and wisest of men have been led astray by them. My unfortunate marriage has resulted in bringing me to the scaffold. O woman! Thou art my ruin in time. O women, they have cost me my life." Dr. in pretty good spirits to night, locked up by half-past 7.

Saturday, May 28th. Dr. rose this morning about half-past 7, does not generally rise early, cannot sleep after going to bed, sleeps best towards morning, bathed again as usual on Saturdays. Speaking of his late misfortunes, Dr. sighed and said, "Women are costly things. They have cost me much, they are dear creatures, doubly *dear* to me. I wish my wife was now alive, she was a good housekeeper, tho' not a person much educated." "I was also an ardent admirer of the female sex, that will prove my ruin. The devil has got me in a snare and left me there." In course of the forenoon Dr. writing a little, he shook his head and said, "this is a serious time." In the course of the forenoon Dr. Bethune called to see Dr., conversed, prayed with him, immediately Mr. Vanderburg came in, stayed about an hour with us; in the course of the afternoon Rev. J H Poole came in to see Dr., conversed quite a while with him, and prayed before leaving. Dr. very serious now, striving earnestly to find acceptance with God.

Lord's Day, 29th. Often have I heard the Dr. say, "how short time is, how gladly would I take hold of the wheel of time and hold it back and impeded his progress." In rising this morning Dr. said, "only one Sabbath more on earth for me, this is the Holy Sabbath, what a display of the wisdom of God in giving us the Sabbath." Had breakfast and prayers, reading in Caughey the tokens of evidence of true repentance. "Not to attempt to palliate or excuse our sin, nor blame any one but ourselves, admit the justice of our God in condemning and punishing us; and never to forgive ourselves for having sinned against and offended God. These are the signs of real repentance that cannot be mistaken."

Monday, May 30th. Dr. rose this morning earlier than usual, having heard that his father and sister had come up to see him, had breakfast and prayers. In the course of the forenoon, the Sheriff, Dr. King's father and sister came in to see him, stayed quite a while, talking with the Dr.; after bidding him farewell and leaving us, Dr. wept profusely for a good while; Dr. spoke about his latter end very composedly and confidently, after his friends leaving Mr. Vanderburg came in to see us, conversed religiously with us a while and joined very earnestly with us in prayer before leaving; after being locked up in cell Dr. said, "I'll have a weeping night of it to night. My friends I may never see again."

Tuesday, May 31st. Dr. said he had wept a good deal that night. He had many things to think of, both retrospectively and prospectively. Mitchel must suffer at Hamilton, on the 7th, the Dr. here on the 9th, Rock at Belleville on the 13th. Then follow the Brantford murderers; what a number of executions, may it be a warning to others that men may hear, and fear and do no more wickedly. 9 a.m., had prayers, Dr. prayed very earnestly, for himself, his parents, and friends, all prisoners, especially those under the sentence of death, and all sorts and conditions of men. Dr. is now much more composed and resigned to his fate. He has now after a painful and severe struggle with the accusations of a guilty conscience and the powers of darkness, obtained that "peace" promised John 14 27, and that "rest" spoken of, Matt 11 28. Rev. Mr. Jones in to day a short time conversed and prayed with us, Dr. writing a good deal to-day.

Wednesday, June 1st. On rising this morning, Dr. said "I felt very happy last night in my cell, after prayers I felt as if God had blessed me," said again, "This is the first of June, the 9th will soon be at our heels." I exhorted him to look to Calvary, and I doubt not but he will yet be enabled to shout "Victory thro' the blood of the Lamb." We are very short sighted mortals. I may be mistaken, as God alone can judge the heart. I do sincerely believe the Dr. to be a true and sincere penitent. I believe he has been brought thro' Bunyan's Slough of Despond, entered by the wicked gate, and had a view of the cross by faith, the burden of his sin has fallen off into Christ's sepulchre. He has experienced the pangs of the new birth, and is now an adopted child of God. Praise to the glory of his sovereign grace! Hosanna be to the son of David! In course of forenoon, Dr.'s wife's uncle in to see him, had dinner and prayer; after Rev. Mr. Vanderburg came in to see us; about 3 p.m. Rev. Mr. Davy, City Missionary, Toronto, came in and talked and prayed with us a good while, a most excellent man;

did the Dr. much good; trust in answer to his most earnest prayers has got a fresh baptism of the Holy Spirit. The Dr. now seems to have no doubt but he will go to Heaven.

Thursday, June 2nd. Spent a good part of the day in marking passages in his Bible for his friends to read when he is gone, a short time in writing in his Note Book. We had prayers 3 times as usual, hopes he may be as well prepared as Fleming was when he went to the scaffold. Mr. Davy told us, he was singing for joy, and had bright evidences of his acceptance with God. In reading Luke Chap 23; these words "Father into thy hands I commend my spirit", Dr. said "these will be the words I'll use when I'm about to drop into eternity." No person in to day.

Friday, June 3rd. Dr. rising this morning said "This will be the last Friday I'll see, before another week I'll be in the spirit land." I wish I could die as triumphantly as Fleming did. I'm afraid I can't. Spent the whole of this day in fasting and prayer; near noon I asked the Dr. if I would make ready the dinner for him. He said no, he would fast all day, he was willing to do anything to save his soul. In cell a good while to-day praying, while walking the Hall praying. Had Worship 3 times to day, as usual. Dr. very earnest to obtain a firm persuasion of his acceptance with God. Reading God's word a good deal to-day. Dr. trying to improve every moment of his time for the best, determined to secure if possible the salvation of his soul. 5 days more and the Dr. is no more.

Saturday, June 4th. Sheriff called this morning early. Dr. not up till 8 o'clock. Dr. rose, washed, dressed, had breakfast and prayers. Dr. prayed earnestly, for pardon, and purity, for grace to sustain him in the last conflict, and for everlasting life in Heaven above. Afterwards he and I looked over a number of the scripture promises in the Old and New Testament. Dr.

repeated one in Isa 41 10, repeatedly; about 10 o'clock Dr. Bethune came in to see Dr., stayed with him about an hour, told me about the arrangements for the 9th June, after dinner had prayers again; surely if ever a man was in earnest for salvation Dr. King is, writing a last letter to his brother Isaac in California. Afternoon about 4 o'clock, J.R. Clark, his wife and Hester Garrett came in to see the Dr.; after a short time Hester Garret, who I believe is a Quakeress, commenced and gave the Dr. quite a sermon, urging him earnestly to embrace Christ, not to deceive himself, or rest in any false refuge, or trust to anything else for salvation, but the merits of Jesus and his righteousness alone, as time was short, make sure work of salvation. It was the most earnest appeal I ever heard. Dr. wept and I too wept; about 6 o'clock she bade the Dr. farewell, to meet in Heaven. Surely we are well privileged with good instructors and godly ministers, beyond the lot of many. May god bless them all, and make them a blessing to us. Dr. pretty cheerful to-day, seems now to look at death without fear, and as a conquered foe. O! death where is thy sting! O, grave where is thy victory! Thanks be to God who giveth us the victory, through our Lord Jesus Christ.

Sunday, June 5th. Dr. on rising this morning said "this will be my last Sabbath on earth!" At breakfast he expressed himself strongly in regard to his confidence in God's mercy. At morning prayers he seemed to enjoy more liberty and access to the throne of grace than formerly. About 10 o'clock Rev. Mr. Vanderburg came up, we had a season of prayer, Dr. seemed very happy afterwards and was rejoicing in God as a reconciled God in Christ. Had prayers again after dinner, Dr. rejoicing now with joy unspeakable and full of glory. Now the love of God is shed abroad in his heart, now death is divested of its sting, and the fear of dying taken away. The Dr. felt as now placed upon a rock, the rock Christ Jesus, and his anchor surely fixed within the vail.

Monday, June 6th. The Dr. seems in pretty good spirits; his mind apparently composed and calm, seemed to be willing to submit to his fate with a Christian resignation, seemed more spiritually minded to-day. The Rev Mr Bleasdal of Trenton in to see him to day, stayed quite a while with him and gave him some very wholesome advice. Near evening he got his portrait taken — Sheriff in a few minutes near dark. Locked up by 8 o'clock. Two more days and the Dr. will be no more. He has now caught a martyr spirit. He is now with Moses on mount Pisgah, viewing the promised land, and tasting of the grapes of Eshcol, and earnest of the Heavenly inheritance.

Tuesday, June 7th. Shortly after eight in the morning, the Dr.'s father came up to see him, a great deal of feeling, and shedding of tears on both sides; the Dr. arranged some secular matters to-day, part of the time he felt tired, at night complaining of head-ache. Dr. Burns of Toronto in to see him to-day, also the Rev. Mr. V., after stayed with us till dark, had a season of devotion before parting. The Dr. seems remarkably calm to-day, so near his end. "What hath God wrought." Surely nothing but divine grace could make a man so cheerfully composed — calm so near his end.

Wednesday, June 8th. To-morrow is the fatal 9th, then the unfortunate man must suffer the extreme penalty of the law for the awful crime of which he has been convicted. Poor man! How foolish, how unfortunate he has been! What trouble he has brought upon himself, his parents, and friends for nothing. What an expense to the county, all might have been prevented. Bartered life, liberty, character, everything earthly, and endangered the loss of his soul for what? For a mere shadow of the imagination, a mere nothing. O, how infatuated he has been! How insane! He has become the destroyer of his own happiness, and at the same time he was instrumental, as he has confessed in burying into eternity her, his bosom companion, whom he had chosen to be the partner of his hope, peace, joy and sorrow, until God seemed pleased to separate her from him by death. One can hardly tell what he deserves most, to be pitied or blamed. Let his late wife be what she may, no doubt she was imperfect, as all human beings are, still it was God's prerogative, not his, to take away her life. However much I have done and still would do for his spiritual and eternal welfare, I cannot with the word of God before me but admit the justice of his sentence, and would uphold the majesty of the law in his execution.

Other criminals may be punished with greater or less severity, according to the nature of the crime. But according to the law of God and the law of our land, to which we are subject, the murderer forfeits his life. Rev. Mr. McKenzie, of Baltimore, in to see Dr. about half an hour this afternoon, exhorted him to look to Jesus and to trust to him alone for salvation; Dr. thanked him very kindly for his advice, and expressed his firm confidence in the mercy and grace of God through Christ. Rev Mr Vanderburg came up to see us about 1 o'clock, had a season of prayer, arranged a little business, Dr. gave us good advice, said, "I have learned that the way of transgressors is hard, and the wages of sin is death. There is a reality in religion I could not have imagined weeks ago, that I could be so calm and composed so near my end, had I avoided the appearance of evil I should not have been here. Had I read my Bible more, I should not have been here; but one step led me to another, and another, until it landed me where I now am. The grand cause of all my difficulties was an unhappy marriage, had I loved my wife, all the women in the world could not have led me astray. I thank the Lord he has taken away the fear of death from me; I have no fear of hell, a little fear of the pain of death, how much better for me that I had not yielded to temptation, a year ago I was in Brighton a free man and had a good reputation, now a poor convict, in very humiliating circumstances." About 6 o'clock Dr. Bethune and Rev Dr Bleasdale came up, stayed and conversed a short time with Dr., made some arrangements for the morrow, we sat up till near eleven o'clock the Rev Mr Vanderburg stayed up with us all the night, Dr. happy in his cell, slept a little, rose again about four o'clock.

Thursday, June 9th. Now the fatal 9th of June has come at last, we rose about 4, had breakfast near 6, Dr. ate well, as usual, had worship afterwards, Dr. read Ps 51, and Rev. 22, then engaged in prayer, like the Saviour in the garden, he prayed "more earnestly," he prayed for grace, special grace to sustain him in the last moments, for his friends, his spiritual advisers, the Sheriff, Jailer and Executioner, and all his enemies; Rev Mr Vanderburg followed with much fervour and power. We all engaged for about 45 minutes; it was the most solemn prayer meeting ever I was at, or perhaps ever will be; after prayer Dr. seemed very happy, a heavenly radiance seemed to be visible in his countenance, he walked arm in arm up and down the hall with Mr. Vanderburg, conversing about heavenly things. About half-past six, Dr. Bethune, and Rev. Mr. Bleasdell entered, and stayed with him to the last. About eight o'clock the Sheriff came in, all was then ready. Dr. grasped Mr. Vanderburg's arm. They followed the Sheriff and the aforesaid clergyman up the scaffold on to the fatal drop. The Dr. read his speech in a firm clear and distinct manner. Rev. Mr. Bleasdell read part of the fourteenth chapter of Job. Dr. Bethune engaged in prayer; while pronouncing the benediction the drop fell, and the Dr. was soon no more. A crowd of some ten thousand people it is supposed witnessed the sad spectacle, who preserved the utmost good order during the whole time, for many of them were there by day-break, all dispersed quietly and went to their respective homes, and the unfortunate Dr., I hope, went home to heaven.

THE CONFESSION

Dr. King gave a confession to Rev. Vanderburg on May 20, 1859, but he was not satisfied with a personal confession to his clergyman. He then wrote a seven-thousand-word confession, which he sent by mail to the editor of the *Globe* newspaper in Toronto, expecting it to be published. Instead of publishing it, the editor of the *Globe* wrote a short article, which was distributed to all the newspapers, utterly destroying the document. The reader may find this document disturbing or just plain infuriating to read. The content is very telling if we wish to understand the pathology of the murderer.

> I beg to claim your indulgence for space in the columns of your valuable journal, as a medium or channel through which I can communicate to the external world the influences brought to bear on me, and motives by which I was actuated in the committal of a crime, the penalty for which I am shortly to endure.
>
> The Press have me down as being a cold black-hearted murderer without cause or provocation. Well, I will lay open the facts and allow the world to sit in judgement and then pass its sentence. To begin with, I must confess that I have done wrong, and for what I am guilty no man could feel more sorrow, or repent more deeply both before God and man than I do.

My present unfortunate position is the result of an unhappy marriage.

In my former life I had made it a rule never to speak disparagingly of, or say ought against the dead, but justice to myself, and an imperative duty to God compel me to unmask the whole tragedy, to lay open to and before the world in as clear, lucid and concise a manner as possible, the chain of events and circumstances which have led to such an unhappy result, however painful the task may be.

Indeed, I approach the subject with the same degree of solemnity that I should feel were I standing on the scaffold — I feel that I have now no end to attain, by making misstatements, while on the other hand, I would only deceive myself were I to do so, and therefore seal my everlasting doom.

I am one of those persons who cannot hold a "grudge" against any person for any length of time, but on the contrary if a person abuses me however much, I can forgive them the next moment. Indeed, it affords me much pleasure to feel this moment that I have no hard feeling against any person living or dead. I forgive all who have trespassed against me, freely.

After I had reached the goal of my ambition, I next had to choose some field to practice my profession. My own parents as well as the parents of my wife would not consent for me to locate far away and the consequence was that on 17th March 1858 I commenced practice in Brighton, and alas! to my sorrow as it has turned out. There seemed to be no difficulty in getting into a practice. My success was eminent and in a short time I had overcome all the prejudices of my youth, had inspired the most refined and intelligent in the community with confidence in my integrity and professional skill, and found myself in a fair way to acquire both fame and wealth. But a man's prosperity often proves to be the very instrument of his ruin. It was all very flattering to

have a good reputation and to see one's self surrounded with
the most brilliant prospects in the external world, but while
everything appeared calm and serene without there was a
deep chasm or vacuum in my heart unseen by strangers. I
tried to cultivate a Christian spirit, and live a Christian life
amid all my difficulties.

I made up my mind that I was an unfortunate being in
this respect, and concluded to bear it patiently as one of the
trials of this life.

It had never entered my cranium to use any means to
shorten, or put an end to her life. I was too conscientious to
entertain such a thought, for one moment, neither did she
ever suspect such a thing. The fact is, the organ of destruc-
tiveness, the Phrenologists say in me, is entirely minus, and
it is a notorious fact, that I could never kill a hen or any
other domestic animal. The very thought of taking the life
of a fellow being would excite a perfect horror in my mind.
I could never, for one moment, think of doing such a thing
even in self defence. All went on as usual; we kept house
on Sandford Street, and Mrs. K. became pregnant about
the 8th of June, and after three weeks *"morning sickness"*
came on and was very troublesome to her. At the same time
a state of ulceration of the *osuteri* developed itself which
had a tendency to increase the irritability of the Stomach;
arising from an impregnated *Uteriu*. This state of affairs
continued more or less till her death on the 4th of Nov,
the symptoms varying according to the different stages of
development of the *foetus*.

On the 28th Sept she fell, while attempting to descend
from the buggy, the hem of her dress and petticoats having
caught on the button or knob on the arm of the seat and literally hung herself, she fell on her head, and when extricated
could not stand on her feet for some time. This catastrophe
was followed by symptoms of *concussion* of the brain and
partial rupture of the ligaments of the womb on the left side.

She never saw a well day after this accident, but continued to be ill until the evening of the 14th Oct, when at 1 o'clock in the night, she was attacked with all the symptoms of *Cholera Morbus*, purging and vomiting, &c, and continued to get worse until the next day about noon, when the symptoms began to rally, reaction was established, and she came out of the stage of collapse in which she had been for some little time. Her prostration was very great.

It has been suggested that I gave her poisonous doses of arsenic to cause this sickness. Now I must solemnly declare and will do so the moment before I expect to meet my God (and I hope to meet Him in peace) that I never gave her one particle of arsenic until after this *Cholera Morbus* was fully developed. Here I may observe that the whole scientific world are deceived in reference to the cause of death. If this goes on record as a case of arsenic poisoning it will be a most lamentable mistake; for I assert most emphatically that arsenic had nothing to do whatever in causing death. There have been a great many suggestions thrown out as to the real cause of death.

But with all the speculations of our scientific men, none have yet arrived at the truth, some have suggested that she did not die from *arsenic*, but from *morphine*; now what I said in reference to arsenic I would repeat in reference to morphine — morphine had nothing to do in causing death. Here is an important fact to toxicologists viz, that arsenic is a *Cumulative* poison.

If all the Toxicologists in the world were to array themselves on one side, and agree in asserting that this is not a cumulative poison, I should not believe them; because I know myself or have seen with my own eyes I cannot be deceived in. I therefore assert most positively (*and I know I am correct*) that the 10 grs. of arsenic found in the stomach of the late Mrs. King, accumulated there from a repetition of small doses, not larger than those laid down in the parmacopias. It is not at all necessary for me to assert that it was *not* given in poisonous doses, for it was clearly proven on the trial, that if it had been administered in poisonous doses then there would inevitably have been unmistakeable signs of inflammation, but there was no trace of it to be found.

I do not mean to say that it does always accumulate, but in this case, it most certainly did. There are doubtless, certain conditions of the system which favor its elemenation but this case ought for ever to settle the long mooted question among Toxicologists as to the *cumulative doctrine* of arsenic.

If there are any scientific men who yet think that death resulted from *arsenic or morphine*, I would take this opportunity of undeceiving them. Those *only*, who have laid it down as being an *obscure* case, have had an approximation to the truth. Alas! how easy it is to be mistaken. However my own opinion is, that no scientific man, now believes that she came to her death by arsenic. No doubt, by this time, the reader is curious to know what *did* cause death. That has always been a secret with me, but now I will make it public. She died from the anaesthetic effects of chloroform and *not from opium or morphine* as many have supposed. Let us put aside all controversy on the *real* cause of death. The next question arises, how did she come to take it? Who gave it? And the result.

It becomes necessary for me here to make a digression from the subject and introduce the third actor of the scene, which is the unfortunate Miss Vandervoort, with this sad and lamentable affair; but since she has acted a prominent part in the "drama," it is quite impossible, in order to trace from cause to effect, to leave her off the stage. It is with much diffidence and delicacy, and with due regard for her feelings and character that I introduce her name here, but it is inseparably connected with my present and humiliating condition.

I conceive her to be as fine a young lady as can be found in the Township of Sidney, but poor girl she has immortalized her name in a very undesirable way. Had I never seen her, I should not be where I am; she has cost me my life, which is all any man *could* pay for a woman. Oh! What a jewel. What a *dear* (in a double sense) creature.

I will now proceed to give a short history of our acquaintance. Miss V. came to my house on the 23rd day of September last, (I had not seen her before) on a visit to see my late wife, with whom she had been acquainted for two or three years, I believe. I happened to be home, and after having received an introduction to her, we soon engaged in conversation, and finding her a very intelligent young lady, we soon became quite intimate. She remained about four hours until near evening, when I got my horse up and drove her and my wife down to my Father-in-law's, we stayed there about an hour, left her (Miss V) to stay all night, and I drove home. My wife said to me, "Miss V. says she has fallen in love with you." I said that was very singular indeed, when Mrs. K. went on to say that Miss V. had seen my likeness while on a visit to my Father-in-law's, during the winter I was in Philadelphia attending medical lectures and had fallen in love with me from the picture. This ended the conversation. The next day Miss V. came back with my wife's brother to our place and remained the night with us. By this time I found out that she was a professed vocalist; she could sing "Old Dog Tracy," "Hazel Dell," "Kitty Clyde," &c., &c., &c., splendidly. I had heard many young ladies sing in concerts in Philadelphia, and other places, but thought Miss V. could surpass them all, and I passed some very flattering remarks on her musical taste and attainments.

In fact, her beautiful voice completely intoxicated me, besides, she could play on the piano, melodeon, &c.; what a desirable accomplishment in a companion, thought I to myself.

Mrs. K. had no time at all and I never knew her to sing a word; she had no taste for music, the very thing I was particularly fond of — I had urged her very strongly to try to cultivate a taste for and learn music, but it was quite impossible. Here was a great contrast between Mrs. K. and Miss V. Miss V. and myself were greatly enamored of each other. Actions speak louder than words, and I knew that she loved me, and that I could not help loving her in return. (It may be considered weakness in me to acknowledge it, but my object is to tell the truth, and under these conditions, I feel impressed to state the facts as they are.) She was both lovely and loving. I looked upon her with all her personal charms, and attracting graces and virtues, her attainments, and literary acquirements, her mild and affectionate disposition, her genial smiles, and affable manners, her good character, and winning ways, and while she perfectly reciprocated all my affections, it was as impossible for me not to love her as it would be to fly to the moon. Oh! how I wish she had not fired the fatal dart into my heart. She knew long before this I did not love my wife, and no doubt on this account she felt more liberty or less restraint in giving expression to her feelings. Oh! that fatal moment when our hearts met. When I first viewed her as above described, I thought I could just see in her the counter-part of my heart, as it were. The picture is not yet complete. My imagination became vivid; I thought what a little heaven on earth it would be to have such a help-meet, (I think here my insanity commenced, for I can call it nothing else, because reason was entirely dethroned, and judgement not called into requisition or exercise at all, and by the bye if the jury had acquitted me on the grounds of insanity they would only have done me justice.) The public may call it what they choose, but now in my candid moments, while reflecting on the past, present and future, and viewing every thing I did with all the influences brought to bear on me, I can call it nothing else but an *insane* act; but this is a digression from my subject. To return then: I thought she was a most precious of the earth's pearls, the star of my existence. Something suggested to my mind what a contrast there would be between the state of bliss I should enjoy with Miss V. and the miserable existence I felt I had for nearly five years dragged out. My doctrine of the philosophy of human nature had always been this; that every heart has the object of its affections some where in the opposite sex, and that when ever we meet that object it will be made known to us by intuition.

Here, then, I had found the object of my affections, and the next thing was to get possession of that precious gem I had found; but there presented one obstacle in my way — my wife. It was only now that I allowed the thoughts to enter my mind of doing anything to shorten her life.

If I had loved my wife (as every man ought or else not live with her) all the young ladies in Christendom could never have led me astray by all the artifices they could devise; but here I was completely thrown off my balance — in other words, I was operated upon by two forces; viz: a positive and a negative. The negative fore was the absence of love for my wife (which I could hot help if I were to be hanged) thus repelling me from her; and Miss V. a positive force, (and so powerful that I could not resist) drawing me away in the direction of the negative force.

The law may compel man and wife to live together, but I defy it to compel them to love each other. Oh! How lamentable beyond description that so much misery and unhappiness should arise from unhappy marriages. Oh woman! Oh wine! Oh money! Three roots of evil in the world; all useful when properly used, but dangerous when abused. Well, when Miss V. returned home she was to send me her likeness, which she did in a few days, with a short note. I answered according to request (my letter was published with the trial) and her letter (published) in reply came to me on the 24th October. I will here take my departure of Miss V. for the present and returned to Mrs. K. I will now proceed to narrate the chain of events and circumstances which seemed to conspire to lead me into this fatal snare, but before doing so, I think it may be appropriate to introduce the symptomology of the 3rd and 4th of November.

Symptomology of the 3rd and 4th November
Nov. 3rd. — Gave patient this morning a small dose of opium; was quite easy afterwards. Dr. Fife called at 10 1/2 A.M. Complained of sore throat, [unclear text] congested, difficult deglutition, some hoarseness, tongue coated yellow and dry, pulse quick and frequent. Dr. F. recommended a formulation of hops to the throat, and inhalation for the vapors of hops and vinegar; ordered me to continue treatment and left, promising to bring Dr. Clark from Cobourg in at half past 12, but as Dr. C. did not come to Brighton, Dr. F. called at 7 in the evening and pronounced the patient better; she took a little nourishment, but did not vomit today as formerly; felt almost free from pain, was quite hoarse. When Dr. F. left he went to the bed and bade Mrs. K. good night, but while we had been in the office a few minutes, she had fallen into a doze and did not recognize him when he spoke to her. She soon woke and insisted on her father, mother and myself all going to bed, as she said we were all dogged out, having been up for nearly three weeks. She said she was quite easy and felt as if she would get a good night's rest, so we all went to bed (the old folks slept up-stairs) about 9 o'clock. About 12 a rap came to the door for the "Dr." Her father got up, went to the door and told the man "The Dr.'s wife is very sick and he could not go." Mrs. K. heard the conversation at the hall door and urged me to go as it was an urgent case, telling me to be quick. The man went for Dr. F. as I requested him. Her father came in the room, to the bed, and did not get up till after

daylight. We were awake a little before daylight. Mrs. K. said to me I did not love her; I said "why?". She then asked me "if I was engaged to be married to that girl in Sidney." I said "no." She said "our folks are almost crazy about it." "About what?" said I. She said "You *are* engaged to her." I said "*you* are crazy." She vociferated, "Oh! That b----ch! That b---ch!" and then "Oh Lord; take me out of this world; I don't want to live. Can't you give me something?" Now, here was a temptation that I could not resist. It seemed to me as if the very thing which I had desired had allowed thoughts for the past three weeks to pass through my mind to try to shorten her life, yet I would never have killed her by violent means, if the temptations had been a thousand times as powerful as they were; but here was something (something whispered to me) just what you want, and you will not be guilty yourself. I said "Will you take any-thing yourself?" "O, yes," responded she. The devil said, "*try chloroform.*" The thought of shooting or stabbing, or using any violent means to cause death would excite a perfect horror in my mind; nay more, I, with all my insanity, would *never* have committed such a deed in the world; neither could I muster courage enough to administer a single dose of poison that I knew would kill. But the evil one said to me "here is just what you want; you can get the means and then your conscience will be clear; you can say you did not kill her, &c., &c., &c. He went into a very elaborate argument on the subject, and finally (he all the time pictured Miss V. before my mental vision in the most glowing style) I yielded to his suggestion, got a 1/2 oz. vial containing about 1 drachm of chloroform, which I gave her just at daylight. She seemed to be rather uncon-scious; I watched the pulse, saw no change in its frequency or volume, and thought that in a very few minutes the effect would pass off. I would here remark (and I will say the same thing on the 9th of June) that I did not believe that it would be fatal; I thought it would be an experiment, but I did not feel impressed that it would be fatal. My impression was that before the old folks got up, its effects would all have passed away, but I found my-self deceived, and after a reasonable time had elapsed I became very much alarmed. To continue the symptomology: we all got up after daylight; Mrs. K. was only partially unconscious at this time; her mother and myself got her up by a little assistance, and she sat in an easy chair while I washed her hands and face, bathed her neck, &c., as we had been accustomed to do before, and her ma made her bed; she had taken no medicine from the evening before. While sitting in the chair she began to get quite dull and drowsy. We laid her down again, and when asked a question she would seem to awake out of a sleep and answer, and fall immediately into the same state again, with eyes closed; she continued to be this way until about 10 o'clock a.m. on the 4th, when I became seriously alarmed. I now would have given the world, had it been in my possession, to undo what had been done. Coma came on, the respirations labored and rather sterterous, and from 6 to 8 in the minute could be heard all over the house; did not appear to suffer the least pain; pulse soft and easily compressed. She soon got so that we could only wake her by shaking her or by pinching the skin. I applied cold water affusions to the surface and caused her to inhale ammonia. She asked for nothing to eat or drink this day, nor took any medicine; cold water, camphor water, and alcohol were applied to the surface; but soon profound coma came on and she did not speak for several hours before death, except once about 2 hours before dissolution, when she raised up in the bed and said the house was on fire. Now I would have given worlds to have brought her to. I tried everything but could not succeed. O! what an awful feeling I then felt. How I repented; but, alas, it was too late! I just began to realize what had been done. Oh! The bitter pangs that I experienced cannot be imagined. The devil had led me headlong into difficulty, but now came the remorse of conscience. Oh! How sharp, how pungent! I felt like death, and thought I would die.

Dr. Fife called in at 3 o'clock p.m., and Dr. Gross at 4 p.m., but did nothing except feel the pulse. She lay perfectly quiet, eyes closed — pupils contracted and turned up — respirations 6 in the minute — no signs of subultus tendinum or convulsions of any kind — the extremities were not cold until a few minutes before death. She expired at half-past 7 p.m. without a struggle. My feelings at this time cannot be described by words. Were I to attempt it, language would entirely fail. I would have given ten thousand worlds, if I had possessed that much, to have done what was then impossible to do — but I must here drop the curtain and proceed to notice one point which has done me very great injustice by fixing a prejudice in the minds of the public against me.

I refer to the testimony given by the father and mother of my late wife. Before I get any further, I would say that I cherish no malice or ill-feeling towards them in any way, but that for all the injustice they did me by their misstatements, I freely forgive them, I love their souls, could extend to them the right hand of fellowship and hope to meet them in heaven. I shall be obliged to say on the scaffold that their testimony was a complete tissue of falsehood. I will mention a few of the most prominent points. 1st, the statement that "I held my wife down and would not allow her to vomit." God is my judge, and I can with a clear conscience in the moment of my death declare that I did not lay the weight of my finger on or touch her to prevent her from rising up and vomiting. 2d, that "I ordered the linens (chemise) burned because they had stains on them which were poison and might poison some one." Now then let it be understood that these stains or discolorations were produced by the nitrate of silver (causative) which every physician would be apt to employ as a local application in treatment of the *osuteri*. These stains were in the linen for more than two months before the 14th Oct. My wife had shown them to me, I told her they were indelible stains of nitrate of silver, but did not mention "poison." This was the last I ever heard or thought about them till I was told they would be brought against me on the trial. I believe it has been said that I even cut out the stains. The fact is I never saw them at all after my wife asked me what caused these stains (nearly three months before her death) till they were produced in court. Is it not simply absurd to believe such stuff, for they have never been in my reach, because as soon as my wife died my father-in-law immediately after she was buried on Sunday, sent for his boys and came with teams and insisted on taking every thing I had right away to his own place, but for shame's sake he was persuaded to wait till dark and then commenced packing and had his teams going all night, and by 9 o'clock on Monday morning he had every article of furniture I had in my house, all my office fixtures, and in fact every movable thing, so that all I had was the clothes on my back.

If there had been anything about the clothes, I did not wish seen, most certainly I would have destroyed them, ere they were removed. I regret to learn that the jurymen on view-ing the clothes which were exhibited were heard to remark that "here is the poison that passed through her," (meaning through her bowels) and because there happened to be a place torn (caused I suppose by the rottenness of the cloth and much handling, though no portion was gone) they said he has tried to tear it out! OH! Oh! Oh! Fatal mistake! Sad indeed!

Gentlemen of the jury, did you not observe that the stains were on the front of the chemise, and, therefore, did not come from the bowels at all, but from the *vagina*? You ought not to have fallen into such a fatal delusion, besides arsenic could not cause such stains. If any one chooses to doubt my state-ment all they have to do is to send those stained clothes to Prof. Croft, Toronto, and he will soon by chemical test show that it is just what I say it is. If I tell a lie it is an easy matter to prove me a liar.

I should be sending my soul to hell by telling lies now, therefore what I say may be taken for granted. 3rd, that "I sent my wife home to inform her parents that she had a disease of the womb, that she was liable to die very suddenly, &c., &c." I deny in total ever having had such a thought in my mind, much less expressing it; 4th, that I predicted my wife's death in her presence. I did give an unfavorable prognosis of the case, but never said she *must* die, in the contrary I told Dr. Fife the night or two before she died, I think in the presence of her parents, that I thought she would get well. 5th, that "I refused to have any other physician called in except Dr. Fife." I never refused to have any one sent for except Dr. Gross, and I said if "Annie" was willing I would not object. I told them they could send and get any Dr. they wanted, and on the Sunday before she died my wife's eldest brother got the horse at the door to go to Colborne for Dr. Pugh, and Mrs. Lawson went to the hall and deterred him from getting on her own responsibility. I should remark that Mrs. K. would not consent, she said while she had her senses, to have Gross called. There are many other statements made by the old man, and expressions coined by the original with himself; time is too precious to me to note them here.

They swore that the last dose of medicine was whitish and that she never spoke after taking it, which they know themselves is entirely false. The fact is the powder referred to was a darkish colored substance (mer-gol) and produced no change whatever in the appearance or feelings of the patient. Oh! It chills the blood in my veins almost to think of such false oaths. My earnest prayer to Almighty God is that he may give them true repentance, and pardon all their sins as He has mine, and that I may meet them in Heaven. Their statements in reference to the vomiting &c, &c, are entirely incorrect. (If my days were not now numbered and so few I would write a pamphlet of 13 or 16 pages on the symptoms, course and termination of her sickness, showing every remedy that was prescribed, how often repeated and its effects &c.)

With every grain of truth, they incorporated a mountain of falsehood and the credulity of the 19th century being almost infinite, their statements have left the impression on the mind of the masses that I am a man devoid of human feelings altogether. But here I must bid the old folks *farewell*.

I will recapitulate and lay before the reader a bird's eye view, as it were, of the circumstances over which I had no control and which seemed to conspire to render me an easy pray to the tempter of all men. 1st, then my ardent passion of love for the opposite sex, (and of all the violent passions of the human heart, love is the strongest and most difficult to restrain) which nature has implanted in me. 2nd, that I was too young when I married and consequently easily flattered and deceived by one older than myself. 3rd, the development of facts some three months subsequent to my marriage, which broke my heart and rendered that which I once loved, now an object of hatred. I thought I had a virtuous wife, but had not, my peace gone — happiness ended for life. 4th, the unfortunate moment that I was introduced to Miss Vandervoort, which resulted in a union of our hearts nearly as instantaneously as two chemical affinities and resulting in a compound.

5th, the absence of love for my wife or the negative force of which I spoke before, repelling me away from her (for we are so constructed that we only love that which is beautiful or lovely in our eyes and we cannot love anything that appears hateful). 6th, my love for Miss V. who, I must confess led my heart captive — this a positive force tending to draw me still farther off my proper balance and driving me to the borders of the insanity for here began my first insane notions. And the way I account for all this giving away to my afflictions is this: as I stated before, if I could have loved my wife after finding out that she was not the virgin I married her for, all the young ladies in Christendom could not have infatuated me in the least; but as it was otherwise, it seemed as if all the affection I should have lavished upon my wife during the last four years, had remained dormant till this object presented itself and then completely overwhelmed me and from this dates my *insanity*. 7th, With all these facts, I don't think I would ever have indulged in the thought of doing anything to get rid of my wife, if she had been perfectly well, but the fact is she had not seen a well day after the 8th June before her death, (this can be proved by good witnesses;) so that when Miss V. was there on the 23rd, 24th and 25th Sept., she was all the time complaining as she said of being "half dead," and from that she told of her feelings, I think left the impression in Miss V.'s mind that she (Mrs. K.) had some fatal complaint about her. 8th, On the 28th of Sept. she fell from the buggy, striking her head, as I detailed before, producing *concussion* of the brain, partial rupture of the ligaments of the womb, and a whole train of other symptoms which I need not enumerate here, and after this she was not able to be about the house scarcely at all. The device would say to me after this "everything is prospering finely, you will get your wish." On the 14th Oct. she had the attack of "*cholera morbus*," which caused very great prostration, the moving sickness which had been very troublesome long before this now became more aggravated, the irritability of the stomach continued to within about two days of her death and then ceased. In reference to the treatment pursued I would just say, that I gave remedies according as indicated by the symptoms. 9th, the fact that she desired to die, prayed to God to take her out of the world, and asked for something to do it with the morning before she died, on the 4th Nov. The reader will remember what controversy took place between the devil and myself on that occasion, that he went into such an elaborate and powerful argument with me that I complied with her wishes but at the same time did not *feel* that it would terminate fatally.

Here you have briefly narrated the different successive steps that have led a young man just entering the threshold of life into the most unfortunate position a human being can occupy. Oh! Most fearful! What a false snare I have got into! What could be worse? Alas! how frail and weak is man. Oh! That the grace of God had restrained me from yielding to the suggestions of the evil one. I never drank a glass of spirituous liquor in my life. I never went to a house of ill-fame in my life. I never went to a theatre but once in my life, and the thought to swear did not come into my mind, from one year's end to another. I was perfectly honest in my intentions, could not bear to cheat anybody out of one cent. The golden rule of my life was "to do unto to others as I would they should do unto me." But with all these things I had my weak points in common with all men; I was not without my besetting sins and my temptations were of such a character as to overcome me, and when I glance upon my past short life, I am forced to believe that we are the creatures of circumstance in this world to a very great extent. I feel this moment and shall while I have a being here that I am *the victim of circumstances*. It seems to me and I cannot believe otherwise, that I have been unfortunate and almost unconsciously as it were driven to commit a deed which to satisfy the ends of justice demands my life. Oh! It is hard, it is *terrible*. To contemplate an ignominious end! How lamentable beyond description. But what is my loss, I hope will be other's gain; and I cannot close without offering a solemn warning to the countless millions who now throng the busy pathway of life. To every young man who contemplates marriage at some future time, I would say take a glance over that last five years of my life and see where my misfortune began — in marriage. Remember it is the most important event or epoch in a man's existence because the most important things result from the marriage contract — upon it will depend your weal or woe — it may not only ruin you in time, but also in eternity. Oh! Think if it in all its relations and bearings and don't marry as young as I did. Let no man sacrifice himself on the hymeneial altar before he is 21 at least.

It is no trifling matter. You can never know its importance until perhaps you find yourself in a miserable fix for life, and then you may try to extricate yourself from a miserable pit or prison, (for I used to feel as though I were in prison) and get yourself into a worse one or on the gallows.

I mean what I say and I say it for your own good. May you profit by my experience, may you exercise judgement and discretion in a matter of so much moment. The way to avoid trouble is not to get in. Better far not to marry at all than to do so to your trouble. To those who are married my parting advice is to pray to God for grace to guard you against all manner of temptation. Love your wives if you can possibly do so, and use them kindly (for good women are dear creatures, in fact angels, I was always an ardent admirer of all the grace and virtue that adorn the female character, and without them would be no refinement, no good society), and affectionately if you can; but both men and women have their proper spheres in this life and sometimes they get united and there is no harmony in the family circle; if you cannot love your wives my advice to you is to separate, for you will either do one of two things; viz: be tempted to commit a crime that was perhaps the most foreign to your mind before, and that may force you first into gaol, then into the witness box to be put on trial for your life and have the sentence of death passed on you, and thence face the halter and die a violent ignominious death amid a congregated multitude, and go to a premature grave; or, you will be compelled to live a life of torture and drag out a miserable existence. If I had my life to live over again

I should do neither of these things; if I could not love my companion, as I did not, I should go to some foreign clime and spend my days in solitude.

Oh! Take warning I earnestly entreat you. It is very important for you to know the rock on which I split. Here I am deprived of my liberty and civil rights, (and, oh! How sweet would liberty taste to me now) my motives impugned; my character gone; my reputation which I had labored long and toiled hard (many a midnight) to acquire, blasted; my name an opprobrium, and myself put up as a public target at which the world directs its shafts of scorn, contempt and ignominy; my parents and brothers and sisters grieved, heart-broken and disgraced; nay more, my body confined within the walls of the dark, dreary and lonely prison, kept there by bars and iron gates, with an arched stone canopy over my head, deprived of the pure vital air of heaven to inhale into my lungs, nor allowed to behold the beauties of the noon day sun, nor to see the very grass laugh at the radiance of the noon day rays, nor to view the pleasures of the social circle, nor to taste the sweets of liberty, nor even allowed to attend public worship to hear the gospel preached, but on the contrary have to look forward to nothing else but that ignominious and violent death on the 9th of June, when I must go hence to be no more; when I must sever all those ties that bind me to my kindred relations, take a short glance at perhaps thousands who will out of morbid curiosity assemble on the melancholy occasion, and bid farewell to earth, and then drop into eternity.

Now my dear friends, strangers or whoever, you are, take warning, take a warning and avoid the very appearance of evil, you have above a daguerreotype of just what you might come to, or in other words you might look into this mirror and see yourselves, only for the goodness of God. Oh! May God bless all who are similarly situated to what I was and give you his retaining grace to keep you from following in my tracks. I have confined myself to a statement of facts without endeavoring to make any display. My time is very short and Oh! How precious, therefore, I must take my departure of and bid a long farewell to all those who will not hear the sound of my voice. *Farewell! Farewell!*

No. of Words: 7,006
Source: Toronto Metropolitan Reference Library, Yonge St., north of Bloor
Location: 2nd floor, microfilm collection, Human Social Sciences
Microfilm: Film B6275, Reel 3, No. 5
Note: Document printed from microfilm to PDF Sep. 12, 2013; transcribed by Dan Buchanan Friday, September 13, 2013.

THE APPROACHING EXECUTION OF DR. KING

This article appeared in the *Cobourg Star*, June 8, 1859, the day before the hanging. The reporter had visited with Dr. King a few days before and we see some of their discussions reflected here although the reporter is not convinced anything the doctor might say is of much significance. In the end, he smugly suggests that the public avoid going to the hanging, an idea few heeded.

The Approaching Execution of Dr. King

To-morrow's sun is the last that will rise upon the unhappy convict who has for the last two months been lying under sentence of death in our jail. We need not reiterate our own conviction of the justice of that sentence, since he himself acknowledges that the extreme penalty of the law is a righteous reward for his transgression. It is well that we have this acknowledgement from the prisoner's lips; but it should not be forgotten that as the law would remain equally holy, so the sentence would be equally just and equally satisfactory without such an acknowledgement. The admission of the justice of any sentence is valuable chiefly on account of its moral bearing in respect to the transgressor, and in the case before us it derives *all* its value from this consideration; for so overwhelmingly clear was the evidence of Dr. King's guilt *before* his own confession of it, that throughout the length and breadth of the Province the public voice has echoed the verdict of the jury, *without* the recommendation to mercy. No withholding of the full confession on the part of the prisoner would change this deeply settled conviction of the public mind. The admission of his guilt and of the justice of his sentence on the part of Dr. King is therefore only valuable as affording an indication of a change of mind in the part of the prisoner. We earnestly hope that a radical change of mind — "repentance to salvation" — has already taken place. It is not for us to say whether this has or has not taken place — and we shall not, though we paid him a visit for the first and last time on Monday last, give the slightest index to our own opinion in relation to his spiritual condition. We deem it, however, no more than right to say that the prisoner expressed himself as being quite happy in his mind in the prospect of his great change, and though he shrank (how could it be otherwise) from the manner of death, he had no fear as to the future. We particularly noticed that he *smiled* as he stated to the Rev. L. Vanderburg, in our presence, his conviction that all was right between his Maker and himself. We hope that the "reconciliation" of which he spoke has really and truly taken place. Of this, however, as we said before it is not our, it is not any man's, place to judge.

We ought to add, perhaps, in fairness to the prisoner, that he expressed a conviction that the public would judge him more favourable after his death, when all the particulars of the case were known. We asked him, in reference to this statement, whether he thought that any circumstance did or could justify his own crime? He at once frankly owned that it did not — that he was guilty and without excuse for his crime. He also afterwards admitted, in answer to a direct question from us, that his sentence was "just." But this admission was given after a short pause, and, apparently with some reluctance.

Of to-morrow's execution we shall only say that all due preparations have been made by the Sheriff and his subordinates for the due execution of the sentence passed upon Dr. King, and all due precautions taken for the repression of tumult or disorder. We deeply regret that any such should be necessary. We sincerely deplore the existence of that morbid curiosity which leads thousands forth to witness (frequently at no small degree of trouble, fatigue and expense) the last dying struggles of a fellow creature; and we are inclined to wonder that the boasted civilization of the nineteenth century has not taken away the opportunity of indulging in such an unhealthy, such a prurient curiosity. There is scarcely another particular in which the administration and execution of the law in the United States differs from our own that we at all admire or covet; but we do think that in the avoidance of the execution of criminals in public we should do well to follow the wholesome example of our neighbors in the neighboring republic. It is the practice there to have the execution of a criminal within the enclosed court of their prisons, admitting only a select number of respectable citizens, varying from twenty-five to one or two hundred as witnesses. There is not the slightest occasion for more than the smallest of these numbers as witnesses that all was fairly done, but at most *fifty* should, in our estimation, be the limit, and these chosen in such a way that there should be no opportunity of finding fault with anybody for the omission or selection of any particular person or persons.

We will not insult the understandings of our readers by any formal attempt to combat the antique notion that the making the execution of a criminal a spectacle to the world is attended with any moral effect. The experience of ages has abundantly proved that the very reverse is the case. The hideous spectacle so far from deterring men from crime affords the opportunity for the vicious and depraved to take one step more towards the same miserable end, which is by no means neglected; and, in the eyes of the unthinking populace, invests the wretched criminal himself with a sort of heroism, which transforms the so called "*moral* spectacle" into a hot-bed for the worst of crimes.

We will not waste words in attempting to dissuade our fellow townsmen from going up to the Court House tomorrow morning, for it would be like blowing against the wind. We shall therefore simply express a hope that the students of tomorrow's "great moral lesson" will be much fewer in number than we have any reason to anticipate."

Taken from microfilm at the Cobourg Public Library, the *Cobourg Star*, June 8, 1859.

ADDRESS FROM THE SCAFFOLD

Address from the Scaffold is the speech that Dr. King gave from the scaffold before he was hanged June 9, 1849. Those in attendance marvelled at his strong, steady voice in delivering the speech, considering he would meet his maker in a matter of minutes.

> My fellow Christians. — I stand before you to-day in the most awful position in which a human being can be placed — convicted of the most dreadful of all crimes, and sentenced by the laws of my country to pay the penalty of my guilt by sacrificing my life. It is very hard to be deprived of my life in comparative youth; but I do not dispute the justice of an all-wise Providence. I have had time to think over the evil of my ways; to bewail my grievous sins and great wickedness with a deep contrition; and to go to the fountain of healing for pardon. I have besought Almighty God night and day for forgiveness. I look to the cross of Christ — to the merits of His precious sacrifice — as my only stay, my only hope. Unworthy as I feel myself to be of God's compassion, I have a firm reliance upon His gracious redemption, that He willeth not the death of a sinner. I humbly and devoutly believe that he has pardoned me — chief of sinners though I be — for the merits of Jesus Christ, our blessed Redeemer.

I fully and entirely confide in the all sufficiency of His atonement, and I humbly trust that through the efficacy of His precious blood, my Heavenly Father will accept me, a broken-hearted penitent, into His Kingdom of peace and blessedness.

I entreat my fellow Christians to take warning from my fate, and to beware of the temptations of the evil one. I have been blinded by the evil passions of our corrupt nature, and seduced into the greatest of crimes through the instigations of the corrupt flesh and the snares of the devil. I affectionately exhort you to guard against this, and to seek steadfastly the grace of God as your only sufficient protection and safeguard. Acknowledge Him in all your ways; live in the fear and love of God; honor his Sabbaths; keep close to him in prayer and the reading of his word, and maintain communion with Him in the blessed ordinances of religion.

My Christian friends, I leave this world in charity with all men, and with a heartfelt prayer that God would bless the souls of all my brethren of the human race. I pray that His kingdom of peace and truth may spread everywhere, and that his will may be done in earth as purely and universally as it is in heaven.

In those my last moments, I heartily thank all those who have shown me any kindness, especially those who have aided me during my recent trials with their council and their prayers, and from my soul I forgive all those who have done me any wrong or injustice.

I beseech you, my dear Christian friends, pray with me now; join your prayers with mine, that my faith may not fail at this my last hour, — that no weakness of the flesh, no power of Satan, may separate me from God. Pray that I may experience his full pardon, and that believing as I do, heartily and sincerely in the Lord Jesus Christ, and deeply contrite for my sins, I shall be saved.

W.H. KING
Cobourg Jail, June 9, 1859
Included with "Prison Scenes" in *Life and Trial of Wm. H. King*

PRISON SCENES

Prison Scenes was written by Reuben DeCourcey, an old friend of Dr. King's who visited him on June 8, 1859, the day before the hanging. DeCourcey was writing a biography of Dr. King at the time, and took pages for him to comment on. DeCourcey would also publish an account of the Dr. King story, which includes wonderful personal insights into the man and his situations.

> The object the writer has in view in compiling this chapter is to present the public with facts and sayings of the Dr. which will be found particularly interesting as they show the state of his mind during the last few days of his life.
>
> On Wednesday pm the 8th June, I visited the Dr. in his cell in company with Geo. J. of Brighton; after passing through a hall we entered a dark ally, passed through a heavy door which opened into a hall which was used by the Dr. as a sort of reception room for visitors, and to exercise in. When I entered the cell it was under the most distressing circumstances mentally, that could be imagined. I was about to be brought into the presence of one whom I had known under the most promising circumstances in which a young man could be placed, surrounded by wealth

and kind friends, health, influence and everything that could render life happy, but now, O, fallen! Surrounded by gloomy walls, and instead of kind friends were the officers, and policemen, and outside of the prison were workmen erecting the scaffold from which he was to be launched into eternity. Reader imagine yourself entering the prison house of a former intimate and highly esteemed friend now under sentence of death acknowledging the justice of the sentence, and his guilt in the committal of one of the blackest of crimes, and if you possess a very sensitive mind you can form some idea of my feelings while passing through those gloomy halls. But when I met the Dr. his remarkable composure in a great measure relieved my feelings from the embarrassment I had experienced. He seemed perfectly composed if not happy. He talked about his execution and funeral with as much ease and freedom as any person outside the prison. He even spoke of some outstanding accounts with earnestness.

When I first entered the prison he very cordially enquired after my health, bid me be seated and commenced conversation upon some general matters respecting my receiving his likeness and the publication of his biography.

I showed him the first few pages of his life already published by myself, which contained an account of his early life, his elopement with Miss V., and the coroner's inquest, which he read and commented upon as each sentence came under his observation, which he deemed worthy of notice. I reminded him of his present situation and the object of my visit, requesting him to correct any statements which were incorrect and make others he wished to go before the public, stating that I would have them published as he gave them.

His first remarks were upon the love which he bore to his wife for the first three months after their marriage, which was very ardent on both sides.

He said that Mr. Lawson never gave him any money to defray the expenses of his education in Philadelphia, except a fifty dollar gold piece, which he (Dr. King) had repaid, and unless Mr. Lawson would give up to the Dr.'s father some furniture which belonged to the Dr. the debt would be paid four times over. Mr. Lawson's version of the case is that he (Mr. L.) gave him $50 and at another time the late Mrs. King sold a cow which had been given her, and sent the money to the Dr. while he was in Philadelphia, and if I mistake not borrowed of her friends, making in all a sum of $100, which had never been repaid, and that the furniture in the house belonged to Mrs. K, as a part of her marriage portion.

He said that the report which was circulated about his disliking his child was false, that no parent ever liked his child better than he did. He said that the child was unnatural in its formation about the abdomen, which caused its death. This statement was corroborated by a Mrs. Alison of Codrington. He denied having held down his wife when she had taken his medicine — Said that he might have touched her, but thought not. He denied having family prayer during Mrs. King's illness — said that he never done so after he received Miss Garrett's letter on the 5th of June; but previous to that time he did so. When Mr. Hunt called upon Mrs. K, he merely responded to certain petitions which the Rev. Gentlemen offered up for the salvation of her soul. He said that Miss Garrett wrote the first letter to him, asking him if he considered her health to be good enough to warrant her in getting married. He replied he did, and asked her if he was not too bold or inquisitive, why she referred the question to him, she replied again, she had an offer of marriage, but yet the gent was not the man of her choice; and if she was to choose for herself the Dr. would be the man above all others to whom she should like to give her hand; this was the first idea of marrying some other woman. He said that her offer was fascinating, but yet he never had any idea of marrying her, that he had never had his mind fixed upon any person until he saw Miss Vandervoort, and in her he saw the very counterpart of himself. Her talent for music was what first charmed him.

He said that his wife was a kind good hearted woman, a good house keeper, and very economical but very illiterate, and would not try to improve her mind. But that was no excuse for him, he had done the deed and his punishment was just; he said that he was the sole perpetrator of the crime, no other person had any knowledge of his guilt but himself. But, the girls had a wonderful influence upon his conduct, but he would not criminate them. During the time of my stay in prison the Dr. spoke very earnestly about seeing Mr. and Mrs. Lawson, that night by 12 o'clock, not to talk over the past, but to have a mutual forgiveness passed between them. He solicited Mr. J. to telegraph them, which he did; they did not get the telegram until dark, and the reply was that the notice was too short, at which the Dr. seemed much disappointed. When about to part he held me some time by the hand, said that before another evening his soul would be in heaven; then Oh what an unfortunate man! and several much like expressions — said that he loved all men and wished all to forgive him, as he wished to die in charity with all, said he felt no fear of death as his sins were all forgiven, said it was extremely painful for him to speak anything against his late wife, but what he had written was true; after which he said that Rev. Mr. V. was to preach his funeral sermon, on the 12th, at Codrington, and wished me to be present; after which I bade him farewell, at 7:15, p.m., again to mingle with the crowd who had come to see the scaffold.

ADDITIONAL INFORMATION

BRIGHTON IN 1858

Dr. King tells us in his confession that he began his medical practice in Brighton on March 17, 1858. At that time, Brighton was a prosperous place that had enjoyed a period of significant growth and development. It was no surprise that the new doctor began generating good income immediately.

The growth and development of Brighton was inevitable simply because of the strong need for people to find good farm land in the first half of the 1800s. The land around Presqu'ile Bay and up into the concessions to the north contained rich loam clay, which turned out to be perfect for growing wheat, a product much in demand. Farmers in those early years were amazed at the yields and scrambled to clear more of their land to grow more wheat. At the same time, lumber was in high demand both in the growing towns of Upper Canada and across the border in New York State. Tariffs were reduced by English reforms, and lumber merchants in Brighton realized major profits by sending schooners full of lumber across the lake. This trade escalated during the 1840s and hit a peak in 1853, when almost six million linear feet of lumber was handled through the wharfs at Presqu'ile Bay. It was big business.

To facilitate that trade, the government in Toronto undertook improvements to the inland waterways, which resulted in the building of the Presqu'ile Point Lighthouse in 1840. The modern lighthouse served sailors piloting schooners in and out of Presqu'ile Bay much more effectively, and traffic grew apace. The next year John Nix built his wharf at the east end of Price Street in Gosport. Actually, the village was still called Newcastle, a carry-over from the original village that was across the Bay on the Point. In 1797 it had been surveyed, named Newcastle, and given the status of County Town for Newcastle District. Then, HMS *Speedy* sank in 1804 and the status of County Town was revoked, leaving Cobourg as the county seat of Northumberland County. In the 1820s the village of Newcastle was moved across to the north shore of the bay because there was no road access to Presqu'ile Point at that time. During the 1840s the name of the village was changed to Gosport, to avoid conflicts with the larger Newcastle to the west on the lakeshore.

Major change happened in the provinces of Canada West (later Ontario) and Canada East (later Quebec) in 1849, when Robert Baldwin's reformers won a landslide victory at the polls, finally defeating the traditional powerhouse Family Compact. Within the next two years, massive amounts of legislation came out of this victory, with the result that governance of the province was modernized. One very key piece of legislation was *The Corporations Act*, which gave the status of corporation to every municipal entity, including cities, towns, counties, and townships. Corporate status provided financial tools that smaller organizations had never enjoyed, and it also imposed responsibilities for effective administration of public resources that were badly needed.

Very soon after these changes, on January 1, 1852, Brighton Township was created. It was an unusual step but in the end proved to be a masterstroke. The eastern lots of Cramahe Township and the western lots of Murray Township were combined to form the new Brighton Township. The result was a municipal entity with the important transportation hub of Presqu'ile Bay and the burgeoning town of Brighton anchoring a rich and productive hinterland.

Before the citizens could begin to understand this change, disaster struck. On April 21, 1852, a small lake northwest of Hilton burst through its gravel bank and sent a tsunami of water, rocks, and trees cascading down the creek bed to the northeast. One sawmill was destroyed and another damaged. Worse yet, two men were washed to their deaths.

Later coined "The Breakaway," the event was a major blow to the community. Two families had to cope with the tragedy of losing their bread-winner and two sawmills were out of commission at a time when the traffic in lumber was at a peak.

For the broader community there was another serious impact. The Old Percy Road was severely damaged because it had run on top of the gravel bank that disappeared during the deluge. This had been the primary north-south route from Presqu'ile Bay to Percy and Seymour Townships since the early 1800s, and its age was demonstrated by its familiar name, "The *Old* Percy Road." Detours would be needed for all those teamster wagons running down to Brighton and Presqu'ile Bay. It was a crisis of significant proportions for the fledgling Brighton Township Council. However, the new council set to work and in the spring of the next year construction began on the Brighton and Seymour Gravel Road. The road would start at Presqu'ile Bay, at the large new wharf near the bottom of Centre Street, and by 1856 it would run all the way to Mallory's Corners, now County Road 29.

Two separate consortiums of investors were formed to make contractual arrangements with Brighton Township Council, one to build the road and one to construct the wharf, which would later be taken over by William Quick and thus known as Quick's Wharf. It was a timely and effective response to a dire situation and the community would prosper as a result of the new facilities. Wagons would rumble quickly over the new and much better road, and products would flow out through the Bay onto all those schooners. Prosperity was the result.

The King family would have experienced significant change, as the new road ran between the two lots they had purchased. The new road also put a new village on the map — George King would name the village Codrington and a post office would be set up in the King house when the road came that far north. The new road would have been a boon to the Kings and other inhabitants in the north concessions of Brighton Township because it provided much faster access to the business and social centre at Brighton, and resulted in much less wear and tear on horses, people, wagons, and buggies as human and material cargo made its way south.

In 1858 most folks in Brighton Township may have thought that prosperity would go on forever. To some degree that is what happened as people built new homes and businesses grew. However, trouble was just around the corner. The American Civil War in the early 1860s would disrupt trade systems, which had a negative effect on the economy of Canada West, impacting the pocketbooks of many people, including the residents of Brighton. Confederation in 1867 would provide a more secure national umbrella for all the small communities of Canada but the growth and prosperity of the previous two decades would not be seen again until well into the 1900s.

TREES BY DAN

Since 2000 my primary activity, outside of computer consulting, has been research into family trees. I started with my own family names and extended out into the community. Starting in 2004 my research details have been published on my website www.treesbydan.com. In 2009 some of my history stories were added as downloadable PDF files, including a brief story about the memorial of Dr. King.

As my genealogy database grew, I began to see it as something more than just my own family tree. Now it is what I like to call "Community Genealogy," not just a bunch of family lines but a complex web of interconnected family trees. At one point I looked at it and realized that it was starting to look like local history but seen through the prism of family histories.

During my research on the Dr. King story I had lots of opportunity to investigate specific family names connected to people who were involved in the story. For example, I was able to find most of the members of the coroner's jury in my data or to add them with some further research; same for the jury for Dr. King's trial. Most of the people who gave depositions for the inquest are also included in family trees on www.treesbydan.com.

Besides this, I have added many "tags" to the personal records for William Henry King and others of his family with details related to the events around the story. I have done this as much for my own understanding of the events as to provide it to others. I use my genealogy database as a research tool in a lot of ways.

I know most folks can't keep their eyes from rolling over in their heads after thirty seconds of this kind of arcane stuff, but for anyone who is interested, feel free to visit www.treesbydan.com and maybe drop me an email from the site if you have questions or information that might be useful. The information is there to be shared so help yourself. Or course, I would appreciate attribution if you use information from my website in publications of your own.

THE KING FAMILY

William Henry King was the first child of George King and Henrietta Jenkins and would eventually be one of ten kids. George King had come to Prince Edward County from Kingston in the early 1830s, soon before marrying Henrietta, the daughter of William Jenkins, a shoemaker in the small village of Northport, Sophiasburgh Township, Prince Edward County. At this time the small towns around Prince Edward County were booming centres of trade and transportation with wharfs and boat-building facilities, which created lots of work for young men who moved to Upper Canada. Family history shows that George King was born near Syracuse, New York, but it has not been possible to determine who his parents were, at least not yet. There is a very strong possibility that he changed his surname when he came to Upper Canada in the 1820s. Marriage registers show that he was recorded as George King or Leroy, or as George Leroy King. While this is not proven, more evidence has been provided by research into the Dr. King story because of the likelihood that several Leroy men were in Cobourg during Dr. King's incarceration and could have been planning to break him out of jail. See "The Leroy Theory" later in this book.

THE KING-AMES CONNECTION

George King (1811–1873)
Henrietta Jenkins (1812–1884)

William Henry King (1833–1859)
Sarah Ann Lawson (1833–1858)

David Nelson King (1845–1913)
Martha Pickle (1844–1925)

Linnie King (1871–1928)
Walter Ames (1866–1935)

Lloyd Ames (1902–1993)
Louise Haggerty (1897–1987)

Mary Alberta Ames (1929–1967)
Charles Buchanan (1925–2012)

Dan Buchanan (1951–)

Family connections are often easier to explain with a picture, especially if they go back several generations. The link between the author and Dr. King is illustrated here with a simple box descendants chart.

Start with me at the bottom and go up. My mother was Mary Ames and her father was Lloyd Ames. His mother was Linnie King, a niece of Dr. King; Linnie's father was David Nelson King, a younger brother.

The family link is even stronger because the King farm passed down this same line. That explains why the author, as a kid, looked out of his bedroom window to the spot where Dr. King was buried.

THE KING COLLECTION

On February 20, 2014, the King Collection was unveiled to the public at the opening event of the Second Annual Brighton History Open House. At this event, Roger McMurray of Brighton declared that he would donate the King Collection to Proctor House Museum in order to make it available to the people of the Municipality of Brighton.

Here are Roger's words explaining how he gained possession of the King Collection and why he decided to donate it to Proctor House Museum:

> It was an uneventful day at the Campbellford Auction Hall in 2003. My eye was drawn to a cardboard box with a number of photos, newspaper clippings, and needlepoint work relating to a local family. The albums looked interesting, so when they were auctioned off I bid on them, but was unsuccessful. I did bid on the box of clippings, loose photos, and needlepoint, which I did win.
>
> A few days later I went through the box of loose papers and discovered a 1931 copy of *Maclean's* magazine with a story in it about the murderer, William Henry King, who was executed in Cobourg in 1859. Having been on a Ghost Walk in Brighton, I recognized the name and knew that this guy was one of Brighton's most infamous residents. The light

bulb finally went on. What I had was a very rare segment of Brighton's history. In addition, my wife's family grew up in the Codrington and Orland area. In order to reassemble the whole collection I tracked down the two buyers of the albums and purchased them as well.

I did think about selling the collection at one time but considering its historical value I was loathe to. This material was a valuable link to the past and was irreplaceable. I then decided to donate the material to Proctor House Museum so all residents and visitors could see the interesting items in the collection and get a feel for life in the Victorian era.

There are eighty-eight examples of photography from the late 1800s and early 1900s in the collection, as well as a number of needlepoint works. Notable among these is a needlepoint with snips of hair from each of the ten King children woven beside their initials. A similar work shows the memorial to Wm. H. King. The most poignant item in the lot was a small book entitled "Smith's Homeopathic Directory 1857." It contains a number of pages upon which Dr. King penned "A Last Prayer" as a gift to his mother. Dr. King signed it on June 6, 1859, three days before he was executed.

I decided to do my part to make our little piece of Canada a more interesting place. The story of Dr. William Henry King has the potential to spawn books and plays. It has all the elements of a good morality play, with retribution, pride, greed, love, lust, betrayal, vanity, murder most foul, and just reward.

—Roger McMurray

THE LAWSON FAMILY

John M. Lawson was a prosperous farmer in the neighbourhood called "Lawson Settlement," which is south of Smithfield and east of Brighton. He was born in Poughkeepsie, Dutchess County, New York State, in 1796, the son of Matthew and Margaret Lawson. The Lawson's were United Empire Loyalists who had been forced to flee their well-established homes and farms in the 1790s as it became evident that they would find no safety at home. They were settled at Concession B, Lot 29 and 30 in Murray Township as early as 1800 according to the census and land records.

THE LEROY THEORY

While we don't know for sure who the parents of George King were, there are some very strong hints, enhanced by research into the Dr. King story, that he may have changed his surname from Leroy to King when he came to Upper Canada in the 1820s. The name "Leroy" is a simple French translation of the name "King," and we see evidence of this change in several other families around that time.

What we do know is that George King was thought to be a Huguenot, which means he was descended from French Protestants who came from the north of France in the late 1600s due to religious persecution. Many of these families settled in New York State and in particular up the Hudson Valley. Many of their later generations became United Empire Loyalists (UEL) who came to Upper Canada during and after the War of Independence. George King was not a UEL since he came much later, but his link to the Huguenot heritage adds credence to the name-change theory.

Other evidence of this name change is found in a marriage record in the Anglican Church archives in Kingston. George King and Henrietta Jenkins were married October 16, 1832, at the Presbyterian Church in Sophiasburgh Township by Reverend Robert James McDowall. George King's name in this record is actually recorded as "George Leroy King."

Then we have the Dr. King story — a fascinating piece of evidence of the heritage of William Henry King comes from the "Calendar of Prisoners," which is found in the Northumberland County Archives. It shows the people who had been committed to the Cobourg Jail and includes the name, age, country of birth, and crime. As expected, we see a record for Dr. King's arrest in November 1858, but even more interesting is the page dated June 14, 1859. The last name on the list is "Frank Leroy." He is recorded as being twenty-eight years old and born in the United States. His crime is "Larceny" and he was committed on the 14th, just a few days after Dr. King's hanging.

Even better, just below his name a sentence reads as follows: "*The man that stole the lines gave information of the proposition to rescue Dr. King from Gaol.*" Right there on the page we see evidence that this man, Frank Leroy, was somehow involved in a plot to break Dr. King out of jail. Earlier we had seen that an uncle and a cousin had visited Dr. King, according to Alexander Stewart's journal. This is on top of the knowledge around the jail that Dr. King had written many letters to New York State during the long winter of incarceration. It is not definitive, of course, but the preponderance of circumstantial evidence leads us to feel that some of Dr. King's Leroy family members from New York State were trying to break him out of jail. That clearly suggests that his father, George King, was somehow related to the Leroy family.

THE MURDOFF HOUSE

This spooky old house does not exist today, but is said to be the house where William and Sarah King lived from March to November 1858, until Sarah died and Dr. King went to jail. The address is 28 Kingsley Avenue and it was located at the northwest corner of the intersection of Sanford Street and Kingsley Avenue. The Anglican Church parking lot occupies that land today.

In the mid-1900s this house was known in town as "the Murdoff House" because the last occupants of the house were Gerald Murdoff and his wife, Edith Onderdonk. Gerald Murdoff was a shoe merchant in Brighton during the 1940s and 1950s. His widow lived in this house for some time after he died.

This picture comes from Memory Junction in Brighton, courtesy of Ralph and Eugenia Bangay. During the Brighton History Open House in February 2014, Richard Ibbotson noticed this picture in Ralph's extensive collections at Memory Junction while looking for something else. He recognized what it was and, with the kind approval of Ralph and Eugenia, brought it to the HOH displays, where many interesting discussions ensued.

Rose Ellery says she recalls as a kid sleigh-riding down the hill in front of the house and asking the old widow lady who lived there to use the bathroom. Tom Plue recalls the spooky nature of the old house and

Memory Junction Museum, Brighton

This spooky old house is said to have been the home of Doctor and Sarah King when they lived in Brighton in 1858. It was located at the northwest corner of Sanford Street and Kingsley Avenue until it was torn down in the 1980s and the property became a parking lot for the local Anglican church. It is known as *The Murdoff House* because of the last residents, Gerald and Edith Murdoff. This photo comes from Memory Junction Museum, courtesy of Ralph and Eugenia Bangay.

grounds, which were in decline and not well cared for in the last few decades before the property was sold to the Anglican Church and the house torn down.

GRAND TRUNK RAILWAY STATION — MEMORY JUNCTION

Memory Junction Museum is a fascinating place where you can step back in time to the age of railways. Operated by Ralph and Eugenia Bangay and a dedicated band of volunteers, Memory Junction presents many railway artifacts, as well as items from the broad scope of Brighton history. One boxcar contains the history of the apple business and another is chock full of a small portion of Ralph's extensive collection of school class photos. You can spend hours there!

The centrepiece of Memory Junction is the Grand Trunk Railway station, which was built in 1857, just a year after the railway first ran through Brighton and a year before Dr. King and his crime generated a good deal of traffic on the train. We know that Dr. King ran to his sweetheart's home in Sidney in his horse and buggy, but we can expect that Clinton Lawson, who was issued the warrant for Dr. King's arrest, went to Kingston by train and, after arresting Dr. King, brought him back by train. The train was critical as well in transporting the pickle bottle containing Sarah Ann King's stomach to be examined by Professor Croft in Toronto. Another pickle bottle was sent on the train to Professor Croft with Sarah's liver inside. Later, in June of 1859, we can only imagine how many people took the train to Cobourg to attend the trial or make up part of the crowd of 10,000 people who watched Dr. King hanged for his crime.

Memory Junction Museum, Brighton, Ontario

The Grand Trunk Railway started running through Brighton in 1856, and the railway station was built in 1857. It was a new phenomenon for the people of the area and it was used to good effect during the Dr. King episode. The original railway station still stands today and is the centrepiece of Memory Junction Museum.

DELONG'S RAILROAD HOUSE HOTEL

This establishment was built soon after the Grand Trunk Railway started running through Brighton in 1856. It was strategically located right across the street from the railway station at the corner of Monck and Railroad (Maplewood today) Streets. It would later become the Occidental Hotel and in the 1890s the property would be acquired by William C. Butler and would become a fruit storage facility. We can still see the old storage building on that corner looking out over Memory Junction and the old railway station.

THE COBOURG COURTHOUSE AND JAIL

The courthouse and jail that hosted Dr. King from November 1858 to June 1859 was located at the northwest corner of Burnham and Elgin Streets in Cobourg. It was a two-storey building with majestic round pillars holding up a portico on the top level in the middle of the structure. Porches with railings extended all along the front of both levels and a stone staircase provided access to the public in the centre, between two pillars.

This building was built in 1830 and was the second courthouse and jail (then-spelled "gaol") in Cobourg. The first one had been on the east side of Burnham Street, a bit north of Elgin and had been built in 1807 on land donated by Asa Burnham. There was a need at that time for a jail and courthouse for Newcastle district because the legislature had revoked the County Town status of the town of Newcastle that was located on Presqu'ile Bay, shortly after the sinking of HMS *Speedy*. The area around the intersection of Burnham and Elgin Streets was called Amherst in those days, but it would eventually become part of the city of Cobourg.

In the spring of 1859, when the trial of Dr. King was proceeding at the old courthouse at Burnham and Elgin, the new and marvellous Victoria Hall was being built on King Street down near the lakeshore. In 1860 the court and jail would move from the old courthouse to Victoria Hall.

The original building would remain, and in the 1890s the House of Refuge would occupy it. In 1934 there was a devastating fire that destroyed the building. However, a new building was built on the same spot and would continue as the House of Refuge. This is why there appears to be two different buildings on that location. The newer building looks very different from the old one, as it has square pillars all along the front and the peaked portico is gone.

In the 1980s the Golden Plough Seniors Residence would develop on this site, named in honour of an international ploughing match that was held nearby. Today a Golden Plough monument stands at the northwest corner of Burnham and Elgin Street, near the site of the old courthouse building.

DOCTORS IN BRIGHTON, 1858

The most respected doctor in the Brighton area at the time of Sarah King's death was Dr. Pitkin Gross, who had been practising for many years. He had initially gained a reputation as a regimental surgeon during the War of 1812. After the war he lived in Murray Township near Carrying Place, and was very active in medical roles with various militias around Upper Canada. In the 1850s he was sixty-six years old, nearing the end of his career, and lived in Brighton Village. Another younger, but well-respected, doctor in Brighton was Dr. Amos Edward Fife, who was always referred to as Dr. A.E. Fife. Also, Dr. Pellatiah R. Proctor of the local and prosperous Proctor family had recently obtained his medical degree, but would tragically die at age thirty-four in 1860. Homeopathic medicine would have been new and mysterious to the people of Brighton and area and we can expect that the established doctors may have looked askance at the aggressive young doctor who not only set up a new practice in Brighton in the spring of 1858, but also started practising this new-fangled thing called homeopathic medicine.

PROFESSOR HENRY CROFT

Born in England in 1820, Professor Henry Croft was offered the chair of chemistry at King's College in Toronto at the age of twenty-two. He survived the conflict regarding control of King's College by the Anglican Church and in 1853 became vice-chancellor of the University of Toronto. Professor Croft had developed a high level of expertise in the detection of arsenic in the body. He is often called the first forensic chemist in Canada.

After his involvement in the Dr. King episode, Professor Croft would experience extreme highs and lows related to the Fenian raids, and in particular the Battle of Ridgeway near Fort Erie in 1866. He was a major promoter of raising militia from the enthusiastic young men in the colleges of Toronto. He sponsored the "University College Rifles," who would participate in the debacle at Ridgeway to the horror of many green and untrained youths. Professor Croft would never live down the failure to equip and train the militia effectively, though he shared responsibility with many others at the time. The hot emotions of patriot-ism and martial glory coloured the practical realities of preparing for war, and young men died as a result.

NOTES

CHAPTER 6

1. Clinton Lawson, in "Trial," *The Life and Trial of Wm. H. King, M.D., for Poisoning His Wife at Brighton* (Orono: Stewart and Vosper, 1859), film B6275, reel 3, no. 5, 20.
2. Dr. A.E. Fife, ibid.
3. John H. Lawson, ibid.

CHAPTER 7

1. Reuben DeCourcey, "Trial," *The Life and Trial of Wm. H. King, M.D., for Poisoning His Wife at Brighton* (Orono: Stewart and Vosper, 1859), film B6275, reel 3, no. 5, 20.

CHAPTER 8

1–2. Dr. P.R. Proctor, "Trial," *The Life and Trial of Wm. H. King, M.D., for Poisoning His Wife at Brighton* (Orono: Stewart and Vosper, 1859), film B6275, reel 3, no. 5, 20.

CHAPTER 9

1. Simon Davidson, "Trial," *The Life and Trial of Wm. H. King, M.D., for Poisoning His Wife at Brighton* (Orono: Stewart and Vosper, 1859), film B6275, reel 3, no. 5, 20.

2. Robert Barker, ibid.

CHAPTER 10

1–2. Miss M.F. Vandervoort, "Trial," *The Life and Trial of Wm. H. King, M.D., for Poisoning His Wife at Brighton* (Orono: Stewart and Vosper, 1859), film B6275, reel 3, no. 5, 29–30.

3. George King, *Inquisition Records, Death of Sarah Ann King, November 4, 1858*, Trent University Archives, Special Collections and Rare Books (Peterborough: Trent University), 84-020, Box 49.

4–7. Clinton Lawson "Trial," *The Life and Trial of Wm. H. King, M.D., for Poisoning His Wife at Brighton* (Orono: Stewart and Vosper, 1859), film B6275, reel 3, no. 5, 29–30.

CHAPTER 11

1. Simon Davidson "Trial," *The Life and Trial of Wm. H. King, M.D., for Poisoning His Wife at Brighton* (Orono: Stewart and Vosper, 1859), film B6275, reel 3, no. 5, 20.

2. James Keeble, ibid.

3. Prof. Henry Croft, ibid.

4–5. E.D. Moore, ibid.

6–8. Prof. Henry Croft, ibid.

CHAPTER 12

1–5. Sarah R. Young, *Inquisition Records, Death of Sarah Ann King, November 4, 1858*, Trent University Archives, Special Collections and Rare Books (Peterborough: Trent University), 84-020, Box 49.

6–7. Hester Garratt, ibid.

8. Joseph Ellison Lockwood, ibid.

9–10. George King, ibid.

CHAPTER 13

1. "Coroner's Report," *Inquisition Records, Death of Sarah Ann King, November 4, 1858*, Trent University Archives, Special Collections and Rare Books (Peterborough: Trent University), 84-020, Box 49.

CHAPTER 14

1. "Trial," *The Life and Trial of Wm. H. King, M.D., for Poisoning His Wife at Brighton* (Orono: Stewart and Vosper, 1859), film B6275, reel 3, no. 5, 17.

2. Isaac Newton King, *Isaac King Letter*, King Collection, Proctor House Museum (Brighton).

3–8. *Port Hope Weekly Guide* (March 29, 1859).

9. *Trial of Dr. W. H. King for The Murder of His Wife at the Cobourg Assizes April 4th 1859* (Toronto: Wiman & Co., 1859), film B6275, reel 3, no. 6, 4.

CHAPTER 15

1–5. Reuben DeCourcey, "Trial," *The Life and Trial of Wm. H. King, M.D., for Poisoning His Wife at Brighton* (Orono: Stewart and Vosper, 1859), film B6275, reel 3, no. 5, 17.

6–10. Hon. Thomas Galt, ibid., 18.

11–14. Judge Robert Burns, ibid., 19.

CHAPTER 16

1–3. Simon Davidson, "Trial," *The Life and Trial of Wm. H. King, M.D., for Poisoning His Wife at Brighton* (Orono: Stewart and Vosper, 1859), film B6275, reel 3, no. 5, 19.

4–7. Prof. Henry Croft, ibid., 20.

8. Dr. E.A, Fife, ibid., 21.

CHAPTER 17

1–4. Mrs. Elizabeth Lawson, "Trial," *The Life and Trial of Wm. H. King, M.D., for Poisoning His Wife at Brighton* (Orono: Stewart and Vosper, 1859), film B6275, reel 3, no. 5, 24.

5. Rueben DeCourcey, ibid., 25.

6–8. Dr. Norman Bethune, ibid., 25.

9. Dr. E.M. Hodder, ibid., 26.

10. John M. Lawson, ibid., 27.

11. Sarah Rachel Lawson, ibid.

CHAPTER 19

1–5. John H. Vandervoort, "Trial," *The Life and Trial of Wm. H. King, M.D., for Poisoning His Wife at Brighton* (Orono: Stewart and Vosper, 1859), film B6275, reel 3, no. 5, 29.

6–10. Clinton Lawson, ibid., 30.

11.   Jared O. Clarke, ibid.

12.   Hon. Thomas Galt, ibid.

CHAPTER 20

1.   Reuben DeCourcey, "Trial," *The Life and Trial of Wm. H. King, M.D., for Poisoning His Wife at Brighton* (Orono: Stewart and Vosper, 1859), film B6275, reel 3, no. 5, 30.

2–13. Dr. Hempel, ibid., 31.

14–15. Dr. A.H. Flanders, ibid., 32.

16.   Reuben DeCourcey, ibid.

17.   Hon. Thomas Galt, ibid.

18.   Dr. A.H. Flanders, ibid.

19–20. Hon. Thomas Galt, ibid., 33.

21.   Dr. Thomas Nichol, ibid.

22.   Henry Belford, ibid.

CHAPTER 21

1.   Reuben DeCourcey, "Trial," *The Life and Trial of Wm. H. King, M.D., for Poisoning His Wife at Brighton* (Orono: Stewart and Vosper, 1859), film B6275, reel 3, no. 5, 33.

2–10. Judge Robert Burns, ibid., 34.

CHAPTER 22

1.   Clerk of Court, "Trial," *The Life and Trial of Wm. H. King, M.D., for Poisoning His Wife at Brighton* (Orono: Stewart and Vosper, 1859), film B6275, reel 3, no. 5, 35.

2.   Reuben DeCourcey, ibid.

3–4. *Port Hope Weekly Guide* (April 9, 1859).

5–6. Reuben DeCourcey, "Trial," *The Life and Trial of Wm. H. King, M.D., for Poisoning His Wife at Brighton* (Orono: Stewart and Vosper,

1859), film B6275, reel 3, no. 5, 35.

7. Hon. Thomas Galt, ibid., 36.

8. Judge Robert Burns, ibid.

9. Dr. Wm. H. King, ibid.

10–15. Judge Robert Burns, ibid.

16–17. Reuben DeCourcey, ibid., 37.

CHAPTER 28

1. *Port Hope Weekly Guide* (May 19, 1859).

CHAPTER 29

1–6. Reverend Levi Vanderburg, *Port Hope Weekly Guide* (May 21, 1859).

7. Editor of the *Globe*, *Port Hope Weekly Guide* (May 25, 1859).

CHAPTER 30

1. *Port Hope Weekly Guide* (June 2, 1859).

CHAPTER 32

1–2. Dr. William Henry King, *Notebook*, King Collection, Proctor House Museum (Brighton).

3–5. *Port Hope Weekly Guide* (June 7, 1859).

CHAPTER 34

1–4. *Cobourg Star* (June 9, 1859).

5. *Port Hope Weekly Guide* (June 9, 1859).

CHAPTER 35

1–3. *Port Hope Weekly Guide* (June 9, 1859).

4–8. *Cobourg Star* (June 9, 1859).

CHAPTER 36

1–3. *Dr. King's Life, Trial, Confession and Execution, Together with the Journal, Prison Scenes and Portraits* (Brighton: July 1859), R. DeCourcey, Cobourg History, www.cobourghistory.ca/stories/dr-billy-king.

4–5. *Dr. King's Life, Trial, Confession and Execution, Together with the Journal, Prison Scenes and Portraits* (Brighton: July 1959), R. DeCourcey, Rose Ellery's Family History Collection, 2014.

SOURCES

The materials used to create *Murder in the Family: The Dr. King Story* are mostly archived documents from several archives and libraries.

TORONTO REFERENCE LIBRARY

The Life and Trial of Wm. H,. King, M.D., for Poisoning His Wife at Brighton, Orono, C.W. Published by Stewart and Vosper, 1859. Film B6275. Reel 3 No. 5. (The first part of this series of documents is Reuben DeCourcey's description of Dr. King's life, trial, and hanging. It also includes the "Journal" by Alexander Stewart, the "Confession" and "Address on the Scaffold" by William Henry King, and "Prison Scenes" by Reuben DeCourcey. This series of documents falls under one page-numbering scheme and references to quotes from subsections, such as the "Journal," are given the global page number found in the original microfilm bundle.)

Trial of Dr. W.H. King For The Murder of His Wife at the Cobourg Assizes April 4th 1859. Toronto: Wiman & Co., News Agents, 1859. Film B6275. Reel 3 No. 6. (The Wiman account is shorter than the Stewart and Vosper account because it does not contain the secondary documents such as the Journal and the Confession. This document is on the same microfilm reel as the Stewart and Vosper documents but in a separate section, No. 6., and there is a separate page numbering scheme.)

TRENT UNIVERSITY ARCHIVES, PETERBOROUGH

Calendar of Prisoners. Trent University Archives. Special Collections and Rare Books, Trent University, Peterborough. 84-020. Box 26.

Inquisition Records, Death of Sarah Ann King, November 4, 1858. Trent University Archives. Special Collections and Rare Books, Trent University, Peterborough. 84-020. Box 49. (The Inquest Records are loose-leaf pages with no page numbering. References to quotes in these pages include the name of the deponent only.)

NORTHUMBERLAND COUNTY ARCHIVES, COBOURG

Cobourg Daily Star (also called *Cobourg Star*). Northumberland County Archives, Cobourg. (Articles from the *Cobourg Daily Star* were printed from microfilm to PDF format.)

Port Hope Weekly Guide. Book for 1859. Northumberland County Archives, Cobourg. (Digital images were taken of articles in the *Port Hope Weekly Guide* book from 1859 at the Northumberland County Archives in Cobourg.)

PORT HOPE PUBLIC LIBRARY

Port Hope Weekly Guide. Articles on Microfilm. Port Hope Public Library, Port Hope. (Articles in the *Port Hope Weekly Guide* from 1859 were printed from microfilm to PDF format at the Port Hope Public Library.)

PROCTOR HOUSE MUSEUM, BRIGHTON

A Last Prayer. Dr. William Henry King. Written in the notebook on June 6, 1859. King Collection, Proctor House Museum, Brighton.

COBOURG HISTORY (WWW.COBOURGHISTORY.CA/STORIES/DR-BILLY-KING)

Dr. King's Life, Trial, Confession and Execution, Together with the Journal, Prison Scenes And Portraits. R. DeCourcey. Brighton. July 1859. (This single-page image is the title page of one of three accounts of the Dr. King story that were published in July 1859. It is not certain which document it headed but it is obvious that Reuben DeCourcey published this account in Brighton.)

Dr. King's Life, Trial, Confession and Execution, Together with the Journal, Prison Scenes And Portraits. R. DeCourcey. Brighton. July 1859. Rose Ellery's Family History Collection, Brighton, 2014. (This is a full original copy of the account of the Dr. King story published by Reuben DeCourcey in Brighton in July 1859, printed at the local newspaper office.)

www.treesbydan.com. Dan Buchanan. Genealogy and history website containing family tree information for most of the people involved in *Murder in the Family: The Dr. King Story.*

INDEX

ALSO FROM DUNDURN

The Last to Die
Ronald Turpin, Arthur Lucas,
and the End of Capital Punishment in Canada
Robert J. Hoshowsky

Short-listed for the 2008 Arthur Ellis Award for Best Crime Non-Fiction

Although they committed separate crimes, Arthur Lucas and Ronald Turpin met their deaths on the same scaffold at Toronto's Don Jail on December 11, 1962. They were the last two people executed in Canada, but surprisingly little was known about them until now. This is the first book to uncover the lives and deaths of Turpin, a Canadian criminal, and Lucas, a Detroit gangster. The result of more than five years of research, *The Last to Die* is based on original interviews, hidden documents, trial transcripts, and newspaper accounts.

Featuring crime scene photos and never-before-published documents, this riveting book also reveals the heroic efforts of lawyer Ross MacKay, who defended both men, and Chaplain Cyril Everitt, who remained with them to the end. What actually happened the night of the hangings is shrouded by myth and rumour. This book finally confirms the truth and reveals the gruesome mistake that cost Arthur Lucas not only his life but also his head.